Developing SAP® Applications with Adobe Flex

 **PRESS**

SAP PRESS is a joint initiative of SAP and Galileo Press. The know-how offered by SAP specialists combined with the expertise of the publishing house Galileo Press offers the reader expert books in the field. SAP PRESS features first-hand information and expert advice, and provides useful skills for professional decision-making.

SAP PRESS offers a variety of books on technical and business related topics for the SAP user. For further information, please visit our website: *www.sap-press.com.*

Carsten Bönnen, Mario Herger
SAP NetWeaver Visual Composer
2007, 524 pp.
ISBN 978-1-59229-099-4

Ryan Leask, Mathias Pöhling
SAP xApp Analytics
2007, 408 pp.
ISBN 978-1-59229-102-1

Norbert Egger et al.
SAP Business Intelligence
2007, 656 pp.
ISBN 978-1-59229-082-6

Bertram Ganz, Jochen Gürtler, Timo Lakner
Maximizing Web Dynpro for Java
2006, 497 pp.
ISBN 978-1-59229-077-2

Armin Lorenz, Dr. Gunther Schöppe, Felix Consbruch,
Daniel Knapp, Frank Sonnenberg

Developing SAP® Applications
with Adobe Flex

Galileo Press

Bonn • Boston

ISBN   978-1-59229-119-9

1st edition 2007

Translation Lemoine International, Inc., Salt Lake City, UT
Editor Stefan Proksch
Technical Review Dirk Wodtke, Aptos/USA (SAP); Sven Doelle, München (Adobe Systems)
Copy Editor John Parker, UCG, Inc., Boston, MA
Cover Design Silke Braun
Layout Design Vera Brauner
Production Bernadette Blümel
Typesetting SatzPro, Krefeld
Printed and bound in Germany

Contents at a Glance

Contents

5 ActionScript 85

1 Introduction

Adobe Flex[1] is a programming model for the presentation layers (front ends) of applications and enables the creation and operation of *Rich Internet Applications* (RIA). Adobe Flex is an integral part of SAP NetWeaver 2004s.

Adobe Flex and Rich Internet Applications

The RIA concept was introduced by Macromedia to describe applications that used *Macromedia Flash Player* for the presentation of their user interfaces. Flash Player enables you to develop Web applications that go beyond the boundaries of HTML-based Web applications to become fully functional for use on the Internet and all platforms that run Flash Player. Flash applications can act as self-contained objects in this context.

In its early days with Flash applications, the concept of RIAs was generalized. Today, RIAs describe Web applications that replace traditional Web sites with functional applications that contain their own client-side logic. In this context, the term RIA classifies applications that combine the global prevalence of Web applications with the capabilities of the multimedia GUIs of client applications. Thus, RIAs merge the simple ways of using Web applications with improved response times and attractive design.

For this reason, RIAs seem predestined to be used in the SAP environment. Flex applications make it possible to provide the numerous functions and the information pool of the various SAP systems in an appealing and stable design to a heterogeneous audience of users. Using Flex, you can equip SAP systems with the functions of a multimedia user interface and complement these functions with the option to distribute data via the Internet. SAP-based Flex applications provide a wide range of users with the degree of usability that is necessary for the challenging contents of SAP systems. This

---

1 Macromedia was acquired by Adobe in 2005. After this acquisition, the former *Macromedia Flex* product was renamed *Adobe Flex*. We'll use this new name in this book.

includes both the option to design the application and the response time of the application on the client PC.

Adobe Flex and the associated Flex architecture are based on the idea that users should be able to render and compile the presentation and contents of the front end at runtime. Not only does the tag-based language enable you to dynamically provide server-side content for the client, but also to address the different display requirements. For example, you can provide different display variants at runtime for different clients and screen sizes. The actual application is not stored in an encoded file. Instead, the tag-based source text is processed with every request.

To develop dynpros, particularly with regard to Web Dynpro in the SAP environment, it makes sense to use the dynamic Flex variant. This facilitates the portal integration significantly, especially from the point of view of maintenance and development. In contrast, the Flash file, which is compiled only once, provides dynamic content at runtime but without giving you the opportunity to change the layout and the interface definitions at runtime.

Contents of this book
This book describes how you can use Adobe's Flex Application Framework to develop intuitive, SAP-based user interfaces in Flex.

Chapter 2 introduces you to the basic principles of using RIAs in general and of using Adobe Flex applications in particular. Here, you'll learn about the basic structure of Flex applications and the components of the development environment.

The development environment for Flex applications—Adobe Flex Builder—is described in great detail in **Chapter 3**. Various screenshots are used here to illustrate all the important tools and their functions in order to enable you to quickly start using this tool.

Chapter 4 contains an introduction to the options provided by Multimedia Extensible Markup Language (MXML), the page-description language of Flex applications. Here you can find basic concepts and elements that you can also use in your own applications.

Chapters 5 and 6 focus on the ActionScript language, which is used to implement the application logic of Flex applications. We'll particularly consider the use of ActionScript in the SAP environment. While **Chapter 5** describes the basic principles, **Chapter 6** introduces you to the object-oriented aspects of this language. Furthermore, the chapter describes the multimedia elements supported by Action-Script.

In **Chapter 7** we'll develop a sample application to be used for planning and time-recording purposes. The individual steps to be carried out in the Flex Framework and in the SAP system are described in great detail here.

The book concludes in **Chapter 8** with an overview of the possible options for using Adobe Flex in the SAP environment. Of particular interest are SAP Analytics and the SAP NetWeaver Visual Composer.

Appendix A contains the ActionScript files of the sample application developed in Chapter 7.

This book is primarily intended for developers who want to use RIAs in the SAP environment. In addition, the book also addresses readers who have a profound interest in the subject of SAP-based Flex applications. | Target audience

In order to keep communication transparent and to clarify the functionality of Flex, we used a function module for the back-end connection to the SAP system described in this book. Naturally, this function module could be replaced with a Web service. | Presentation

Consequently, the variant described in this book would only represent the first stage in a live environment. In a second step, you could provide the application dynamically as a server-based application. After all, this would be the only way to fully utilize the potential benefits of a server-based RIA, namely:

▶ A user interface compiled in real time

▶ Easy maintenance

▶ Implementation in distributed developer teams

▶ Flexible and dynamic creation of layout and content

▶ Use of dynamic interfaces via Web services

▶ Flexible use of SAP and non-SAP back-end systems

If you want to re-develop the sample application described in Chapter 7, you need an SAP Web Application Server Release 6.10 or higher (ABAP engine) and the Adobe Flex development environment. You can, for instance, obtain a "mini" SAP system with the | Prerequisites books *The Official ABAP Reference* (SAP PRESS 2005) and *Web Programming in ABAP with the SAP Web Application Server* (SAP PRESS 2005), or directly from the SAP Knowledge Shop. You can find it by navigating from *http://www.sap.com* to **Our Company • SAP Shop • SAP Knowledge Shop**. You can download a test version of the Flex development environment from the Adobe Web site at the following address: *http://www.adobe.com/downloads*. Basic ABAP and BSP programming knowledge are also required.

The example presented in this book works with the static Flash variant. If Flex server architecture is available, you can provide the application as server-based at any time without having to implement significant changes.

As it would go beyond the scope of this book to describe all components of Flex, we have limited ourselves to the most important and necessary ones with regard to developing in the SAP environment. You can find the original Adobe Flex documentation at *http://livedocs.macromedia.com/flex*.

In addition, the *SAP Developer Network* (SDN) represents another useful source of information regarding Adobe Flex. You can access the SDN at *http://sdn.sap.com*.

Acknow-
ledgements
The authors had to spend many interesting, tough, and exhausting hours to carry the initial idea of writing this book through to its completion. Several families, many friends and colleagues, and Stefan Proksch of Galileo Press had to suffer from this. We would therefore like to thank all these people for their understanding and great support.

And last but not least, we should acknowledge our customers, who had asked us to find new solutions to their problems and still gave us the necessary freedom to write this book at the same time. Many requirements, ideas, and inspirations emerged during discussions with customers, so we should say "thank you."

And finally, a big thank you goes to Bernd Will, who is the author of the SAP PRESS Essentials guide, *Rich Internet Applications on the SAP Web AS*.

This chapter introduces you to the underlying principles of using Adobe Flex applications. It describes the basic structure of Flex applications and the components of the development environment. In addition, you'll learn why Adobe Flex is an excellent complement to the familiar application development technologies in the SAP environment.

2 Adobe Flex in the SAP Environment

The primary goals of any business application are to provide a stable functionality, user-friendliness, and fast response times. This holds true for SAP applications as well. To reach these goals, SAP applications are supported by the SAP NetWeaver framework, which integrates smoothly with the Flex technology. Until now, SAP GUI, Business Server Pages (BSPs), and Web Dynpro have been the core components of SAP's graphical user interface (GUI) These components are now complemented by the Adobe Flex technology, which enables users to easily create complex business applications, particularly on the basis of and in combination with Web Dynpro technology. One of the great advantages of Adobe Flex is that it provides client-based communication services.

Business applications

2.1 Developing Business Applications

Up to now, SAP-based business applications have communicated with the user via the traditional SAP GUI. In order to support more flexible GUI concepts that involved browser-based user interfaces, SAP managed to implement different techniques that enabled the development of HTML-based business applications. Adobe Flex continues to follow the trend towards the publication of content on the basis of Web technologies. However, it eliminates the familiar disadvantages of Web-based business applications.

Disadvantages of HTML

The main disadvantage of HTML-based Web applications is that the Web server must regenerate the pages of an application for almost every user interaction because HTML applications consist of individual pages. Typically, the Web server must reload these pages when a user interaction occurs.

HTML applications cannot run any queries to databases or other Web services in the background in order to integrate them into their display. Each process of this type puts additional strain on the bandwidth and server resources. Because the application logic is completely implemented on the server, the server must be accessed every time data is processed.

Interaction via DHTML

Dynamic HTML (DHTML) describes the client-based dynamization of static HTML pages using JavaScript, which serves as a basis for client-based application logic in DHTML. It takes considerable work to create Web applications that are both visually and functionally attractive. Moreover, it is difficult to implement frameworks that would set the standard in this context because there is no standardized and globally used interpretation of JavaScript as a client-based programming language.

Nevertheless, SAP has always endeavored to support and usefully enhance standards. The following are examples of this.

History of SAP Web technologies

▸ The first SAP business applications were based on DHTML. These applications were provided by the *Internet Transaction Server* (ITS) that used to translate SAP GUI content into HTML pages.

▸ With the introduction of *SAP Web Application Server* (SAP Web AS) SAP-based Web applications became *Business Server Pages* (BSPs). These applicaions allow the use of HTML extensions (*BSP extensions*) which—being HTML extensions—provide tags with new functions. BSP extensions are implemented using classes. Thus, you can create your own extensions from the standard SAP extensions via inheritance and composite definition.

▸ One of the standard BSP extensions provided by SAP is HTMLB (*HTML Business*). HTMLB contains predefined elements that provide a portion of the presentation logic, such as the calendar function as a date help. The annoying screen layout caused by the server-based implemented presentation logic was compensated by the *flicker-free technique*.

The introduction of BSP extensions uncovered a disadvantage of dynamization using DHTML. Because the HTML extensions must run in different Web browsers with different versions and are thus specifically limited by the respective Web-browser technologies, the implementation of even very simple GUI elements is rather laborious. For this reason, the framework uses separate implementations of *cascading stylesheets* and JavaScript files for the different client-based scenarios.

▶ The *Web Dynpro technology* then provided a graphically supported dynamization and data-flow modeling of Web pages. This technology was provided with SAP Web AS 6.30 for Java and was also implemented for ABAP at a later stage.

Despite all those measures, traditional Web applications are not really appealing, and most of the time they aren't very user-friendly either. The possibilities for interacting with the user as a direct reaction to the user's entries are rather limited. The expressiveness is strongly restricted and the *look and feel* is not very sophisticated. The client computer is reduced to the capabilities of the Web browser as presentation platform without its own logic. Effects such as smooth transitions between input templates or *drag-and-drop* functions are entirely missing in pure HTML applications.

Lack of effects

However, it is those very functions that support the users of business applications in carrying out complex tasks, by enabling them to establish intuitive links among the contents displayed. With such functionality, you can design an application's reaction to the user input *effectively*, in the narrowest sense of the word.

True, you can add all those effects using JavaScript, but you then have to implement them in a separate process. This time-consuming method requires a lot of maintenance work and therefore is rarely used to create a client-based SAP application.

If you want such an application to use the capabilities of the Internet for the distribution of data despite all those restrictions, you must use a plug-in for the Web browser in order to overcome the limitations described above. *Java Virtual Machine* and *Flash Player* are such plug-ins.

Accessibility due to plug-ins

To be able to use these extensions the necessary interfaces must be available. SAP NetWeaver 2004s contains the required components.

Thus you can create business applications that contain a wide range of functions and in which the client gains in importance. These applications can respond to user input to a much larger extent than an HTML page would be able to do.

The latest Web technology used in the SAP environment in this context is the support of Adobe Flex. Like client-based applications, Flex applications contain an independent and consistent user interface that can be changed without having to exchange data with a server.

2.2 Rich Internet Applications

At this point of the historical development of business applications Rich Internet Applications (RIAs) come into play. If necessary, a RIA can—among other things—carry out database queries by itself and process the data acquired in this way, or draw new graphics. This way, you can create business applications whose layouts attract the user and which can react directly to a user's input.

2.2.1 Structure

RIAs process the presentation logic

The basic structure of RIAs becomes obvious if you compare the division of the logical layers on the client and server in HTML applications with that of RIAs. In HTML applications, the Web server provides a large portion of the presentation logic. In contrast to that, it is the client that processes the presentation logic in an RIA (see Figure 2.1). Thus, the application can adjust its presentation and functionality without any delay in responding to the current situation.

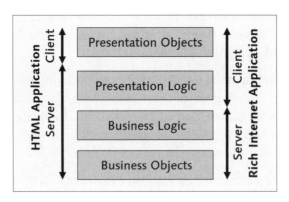

Figure 2.1 Logical Layers of HTML Applications and RIAs

Most of the times, the *model view controller architecture* (MVC) is used to structure RIAs. The origins of the MVC paradigm can be found in the Smalltalk environment. Smalltalk was the first programming language to be used for creating applications based on the MVC design pattern in the 1980s. Today, this language is predominantly used for the development of larger applications that contain a GUI.

MVC architecture

According to the MVC design pattern, an application is divided into three separate areas.

▶ **Model**
The model provides the actual data of the application.

▶ **View**
The view represents the user interface of the application and enables a specific view of the model data.

▶ **Controller**
The application controller manages the interaction options of the user with the program. It decides which functions can be launched, based on the status of the application, and it determines how the application will react to specific user input.

The advantage of this design over the traditional application design is that the three areas are strictly separated from each other. This separation improves the maintainability of applications considerably.

Separation of presentation, control, and content

2.2.2 Advantages

RIAs combine several advantages that were missing in previous concepts in the HTML environment. The primary advantage of an RIA is that the design of its graphical user interface is not subject to any regulation. In contrast to working with HTML applications, you can now combine dynamic user interfaces and animated content without any barriers in one user interface.

Bridging the gap to traditional applications

Moreover, RIAs enable you to save and retrieve content on the client. Due to the separation of the presentation and content layers, you no longer have to transfer the entire context, in particular the presentation context. The interface to the server primarily focuses on transferring the user data of an application. This bridges the gap to traditional clients such as SAP GUI without losing the advantages of Web-based services.

The benefits of RIAs are completely utilized by Adobe Flex. On the client side, this is typically done using the Flash plug-in in any Web browser. The Flash plug-in is a small program that displays the provided Flex contents in a Web browser. However, you can also run the Flex applications without a Web browser so that data is formatted, filtered, saved, and sorted on the client side. This way, you can provide the user with direct feedback for his or her input in Flex applications. Flex enables you to validate data directly without having to send a request to a server.

Drag-and-drop Furthermore, Flex applications enable you to enter into direct interaction with the user. For example, you can implement a drag-and-drop functionality that allows you to change the status of elements, for example in a shop. UI elements such as checkboxes, date-selection fields, list boxes, and data grids can change their appearance and functionality depending on the user input without being reloaded by the Web server. In HTML applications, this is only possible by using JavaScript, as this functionality is not contained in any standard framework.

User guidance Using Flex in the client computer, the user can be notified about the effects of a specific action. And, as in desktop applications, the user can then use this information in order to quickly create different variants of the action in order to check them out. This is possible because the user context is stored on the client computer and because the Flex application responds to user input. The application provides the user with tips for its operation. This way the user has a good overview of everything and is guided through the operational process.

While Web applications so far have more or less copied familiar user interfaces from client-server structures, Adobe Flex—being an RIA—now adds a new interactive component to the SAP environment, whose graphical user interface is hardly restricted in any way.

2.2.3 Limits

By using Flex-based RIAs you can avoid the main drawback of HTML Web applications in that you can use the client as a full-fledged GUI via the runtime environment of the Flash plug-in. This way, you can optimize server requests and process functions of the presentation layer. Because of the integration of the Flex class library, you can easily and efficiently compile sophisticated user interfaces. The library can be extended by additional components. This enables you to add further standard functions to the capabilities of RIAs at any time.

One caveat: The option to interact with the server and the functionality of the Flash plug-in involve some restrictions. On the one hand, such a programming concept is limited by the interaction options with the server and, on the other hand, by the functions made available to an application by the Flash plug-in.

For example, you can only use known protocols in the Web environment. Data transfer protocols that are not XML-based or Web-based cannot be implemented with Flex. Moreover, despite the constant improvement of performance, the presentation of large tables does not reach the quality you know from SAP GUI or Microsoft Excel.

However, with the continuous development of Flex components Adobe is trying to reduce the degree of limitation more and more. You should therefore always take the version of the Flex framework to be used into account. It generally makes sense to use the most current version of the Flash plug-in and Flex components in order to make sure that the Flex application is supported in the best possible way.

The actual limitation of RIAs in Flex, however, is caused by the Flash plug-in of the Web browser. Although today Flash Player is installed in 98 % of all browsers and should therefore not pose any problem for the general acceptance of a Flex-based RIA solution, the Flash plug-in must be available in the specific version required on the client computer where you want to run the application.

Limitation by the Flash plug-in

You can program defensively and make the application downward compatible with older Flash plug-ins, but it is much easier to use the automatic upgrading process and equip the client with the latest version of the plug-in. Whenever a Flash plug-in version is outdated, the user is automatically prompted to install the latest version. This process can also be carried out centrally; e. g., by the system administrator.

2.3   Adobe Flex

Existing develop-
ment evironments
for Flex Adobe Flex provides a programming system and a library of powerful modules that enable you to create and operate RIAs for the Flash
Player. Thus, using Flex enables you to increase the efficiency and
functionality of Web and business applications. For one thing, you
can increase the degree of usability by implementing a standardized
design and dynamic effects; for another, the application can respond
to user input already on the client. You can run queries on Web services and databases and directly analyze these queries. Wait times
caused by page reproductions, as they occur in HTML applications,
are a thing of the past.

2.3.1   Components of a Flex Application

Like BSPs, Flex-based RIAs use a combination of two languages.

MXML ▶ The layout of a Flex-based RIA is defined in MXML (*Macromedia
Extensible Markup Language*; see also Chapter 4). MXML describes
the layout of a Web page and is tag-based, like HTML.

MXML is an XML tag language. Tag languages are frequently used
to define user interfaces, and the most popular of these languages
is HTML. However, because MXML is an XML-based language, it
is much more structured and syntactically more exact than HTML.
In addition, MXML contains more tags than HTML. For example,
you can use tags to define menus, a tree structure, and a table in
MXML. Moreover, you can also add your own tags in MXML, just
as you can in HTMLB.

The MXML files on which Flex applications are based can be created in different types of development environments. The most
simple environment is one where MXML files are created using a
text editor. For software development within a team, you can also
use a file-versioning tool such as Microsoft Visual SourceSafe to
store the MXML files. It is more convenient, however, to create
the applications in an integrated development environment (IDE)
such as Microsoft Visual Studio or Eclipse.

ActionScript ▶ The application logic and data storage are implemented in *Action-
Script* (see also Chapter 4). ActionScript controls the application
both on the server and the client and is based on the same standard as JavaScript, namely the *European Association for Standard-*

izing Information and Communication Systems (ECMA). The close collaboration between Adobe and the ECMA guarantees a standardized advancement of ActionScript.

Since the introduction of Adobe Flex 2.0 in June 2005, this ECMA script language is used in Version 3.0. In this version, ActionScript was complemented with object-oriented programming options.

Within Flash Player, ActionScript is executed in the *ActionScript Virtual Machine* (AVM). As of AVM Version 2, which is implemented in the current Flash Player 9, you can run ActionScript 3.0. Another reason for the advancement of the AVM in addition to object-oriented programming was to optimize performance. As developers use more and more elements including multimedia elements such as video clips for the design of Flex-based RIAs, the performance had to be improved in order to ensure real-time user interaction. To that end, AVM2 processes ActionScript code 10 times faster than its predecessor.

At runtime, the source code is compiled in Flash byte code within a *Small Web Format, Shockwave Flash* (SWF) file. As of Flex Version 2, the compilation process can take place at two different times: either during the development phase, or when a RIA is called. The advantage of carrying out the compilation at a later stage is that you use server-based ActionScript to respond to user input and statuses and to compile the application correspondingly as state-based.

Compiling into SWF format

The SWF file is transferred to the client and run in the Flash plug-in of the browser. The typical size of a SWF file is between 150 and 200 kilobytes. A RIA runs on the client computer as a zero-footprint application; that is, it neither requires a cookie nor has to be installed on the client. The SWF file is executed only in the Flash environment.

Zero-footprint application

There are different ways for a RIA to exchange data with the server at runtime: SOAP, XML, HTTP, or the *Action Message Format* (AMF). The communication options are determined by the Flex Data Services (see Section 2.3.2).

The display of data is another issue that cannot be solved easily in HTML pages. Developing the user interface of a traditional business application represents a big challenge for application designers. There are many different influences and input options that must be

Data display

taken into account. Libraries that are based on JavaScript and *Cascading Styleheets* (CSS) or on Microsoft's *Vector Markup Language* (VML) must be used in order to draw simple charts.

Drilldown effects In Flex applications, you can draw charts and diagrams including 3D effects by integrating the appropriate library. By combining the interactability of Flex with *drilldown effects,* you can provide the user with a straightforward and consistent navigation through charts. The term "drilldown effects" describes the navigation within specific information by means of double-clicking in order to view the structure of elements. It is the use of interactive elements such as the handling of individual objects by means of drag-and-drop that makes the application easy to learn and operate. The user literally "feels" his or her way through the functions of the Flex front end and in this way learns how to use the interactivity.

In HTML applications, this would only be possible by using server-based requests and implementing a comprehensive JavaScript programming. With regard to costs, the use of JavaScript and the like can hardly be recommended.

2.3.2 Flex Product Family

Five components Adobe Flex 2 currently supports the development of RIA with five technological components (see Figure 2.2) that will be described in the following sections.

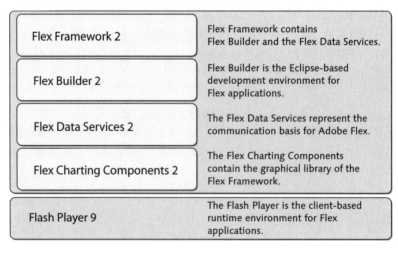

Figure 2.2 Adobe Flex Product Family

Adobe Flex Framework

The Adobe Flex Framework provides the basic structure of a RIA in the form of an ActionScript class library (Version 3.0). Predefined components enable you to design user interfaces. For example, you can use popup buttons, data grids, and a rich-text editor.

Basic structure

Interactive elements such as a drag-and-drop functionality or cross-fading can be used to design the application. The framework contains a skinning and styling architecture that enables you to lay out the appearance of a user interface as per your requirements. In addition, you can implement data flows via specific elements of the framework.

By using the Flex Framework, you can create professional user interfaces that are based on underlying data flows and integrate predefined components. Specific "view statuses" enable you to change the appearance of a RIA with regard to a certain status. An integrated event control enables the interaction with the user.

Adobe Flex Charting Components

Adobe Flex Charting Components 2 enables you to integrate charts in Flex applications. The application programming interface (API) of the charting components makes it easy to use these elements within different applications. If the predefined level of freedom is not sufficient, you can adjust and extend the charting components. Interactive functions such as detail views and view changes provide the user with immediate feedback.

Creating complex charts

Flex Charting Components 2 is fully integrated in the Flex Framework and can therefore also use the enterprise services functions. Depending on the respective navigation within each graphic, a data reload can provide the user with such capabilities as new data-analysis dimensions.

Figure 2.3 shows a sample dashboard application of Flex Builder. On the left, the application displays the temporal development of a company's revenue figures for a selected year. The pie chart in the top right-hand corner shows the annual revenue broken down by different regions. If a user selects a segment of the pie chart, the application displays the development of revenues within this segment for the entire year.

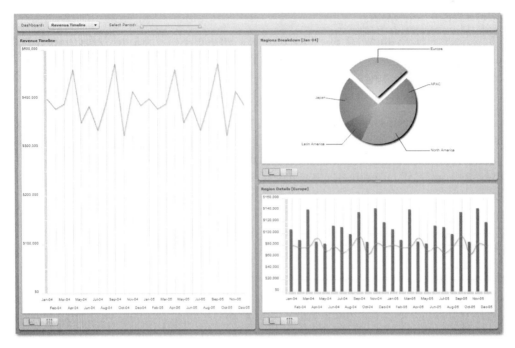

Figure 2.3 Sample Flex Dashboard Application

Adobe Flex Builder 2

Development
environment

Adobe Flex Builder is an IDE application that was specifically designed for the development of Flex applications. Flex Builder supports the user with utilities such as a graphical layout editor, an integrated debugger, and useful coding tips. Flex applications can thus be developed and tested quickly and efficiently. Because Flex Builder 2 is based on the Eclipse platform, many developers don't even need to familiarize themselves with the environment.

Adobe provides Flex Builder as part of the Flex package, and you should generally use this tool to develop your Flex applications. Development under certain conditions can be exceptions to this. For instance, in the SAP environment you can create Flex applications directly in SAP NetWeaver Visual Composer as SAP Analytics applications. Section 8.5 contains an overview of those applications.

Adobe Flex Builder 2 allows you to create both the code and the layout of a Rich Internet Application. Figure 2.4 shows a sample screenshot of Adobe Flex Builder 2 in the source text view. The creation of

ActionScript and MXML code is supported by an integrated code help. Extensive navigation options guide you through the code.

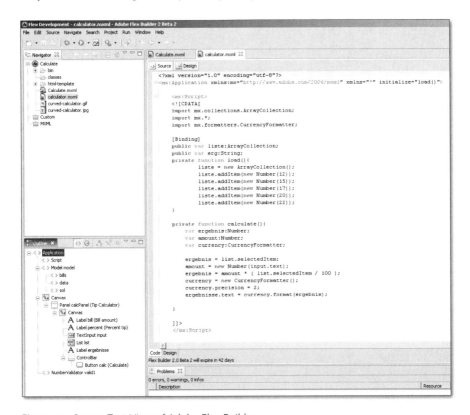

Figure 2.4 Source Text View of Adobe Flex Builder

Flex Builder also contains a powerful debugging tool. The Action-Script Debugger enables you to analyze the application logic at runtime. To validate an application, you can, for instance, display and modify the content of variables, set breakpoints, and execute the code step by step.

Debugging tool

In order to resolve communication problems of a Web application, it is vital that the network traffic can be monitored. Flex Builder allows you to examine the data flow between client and server in a question-and-answer procedure. Variables and data that are exchanged in the individual communication steps can be output.

Moreover, Flex Builder 2 provides visual support for layout creation (see Figure 2.5). You can, for example, view the styles and skins in the design view of a layout. The design view is enabled via an integrated browser within Flex Builder. This means you don't need to call an external Web browser such as Internet Explorer.

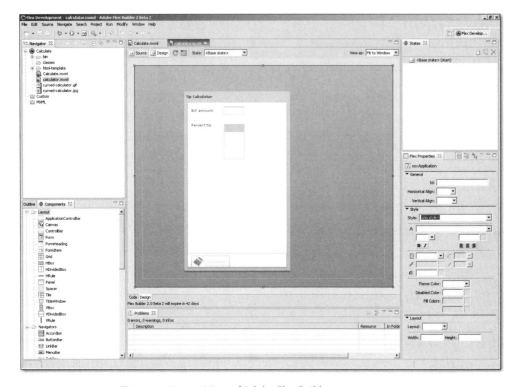

Figure 2.5 Layout View of Adobe Flex Builder

Furthermore, you can use Flex Builder to integrate multimedia elements, such as visual tips on a support page, into the application.

Adobe Flex Data Services

Extending the communication options
Without the Adobe Flex Data Services Flash-based RIAs would only distinguish themselves by their user-friendly GUI. The Flex Enterprise Services provide RIAs with numerous services for the transport and integration of data at runtime.

▸ **RPC services**
Remote Procedure Calls (RPC) are calls of functions that are implemented on another machine. These functions are integrated like local functions that are available within the RIA. This is an easy way of complementing an RIA with the remotely available functions of an infrastructure.

▶ **Flex Message Services**

Flex Message Services control the transport of data between the client and the server. This way you can easily integrate data sources into the application. The services allow you to publish and subscribe to data. The communication among different clients provides new options for collaboration. This technology enables teamwork in Web applications. Flex Messaging Services also enable the integration with existing messaging infrastructures of a company.

▶ **Flex Data Services**

Flex Data Services (FDS) manage data in RIAs. FDS provides a model for synchronizing and controlling data and events. Similar to the *Java Data Objects* (JDO) model, FDS enable you to integrate the presentation layer into the data models and flows of a company. FDS enable the data interaction of a RIA, which serves as a basis for applications that are not constantly connected to a server.

2.3.3 Additional Benefits for SAP Systems due to Flex Applications

The integration layers of SAP NetWeaver—people integration, information integration, and process integration—represent an open integration platform. Both application servers associated with the integration platform (ABAP stack and Java stack) can be connected with Adobe Flex. This enables a smooth integration of Adobe Flex into the SAP NetWeaver integration platform. Flex applications, in turn, provide added value to the people-integration and information-integration layers. With its focus on the SAP NetWeaver Exchange Infrastructure, the process integration layer plays only a minor role in this context because the basic concept of Flex predominantly addresses man-machine communications.

Integration layers of SAP NetWeaver

Figure 2.6 illustrates the individual relationships and the integration of Flex into the different SAP NetWeaver layers.

Flex applications can be integrated very easily into an existing SAP NetWeaver Portal. This holds true for applications that have been created using Adobe Flex Builder as well as for those that have been developed within *SAP NetWeaver Visual Composer*, which has been available since Release SAP NetWeaver 2004s.

SAP NetWeaver Visual Composer

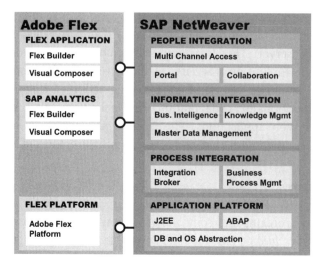

Figure 2.6 Interaction of Adobe Flex and SAP NetWeaver

The Visual Composer enables developers to call the most important Flex functions separately by creating via drag-and-drop an analytical application that is then deployed in Flex.

This way the developer can quickly create portal-integrated Flex reports. The main purpose of the Visual Composer is the creation of reports and their graphical presentations; e. g. meaningful displays of BI charts, as shown in Figure 2.7.

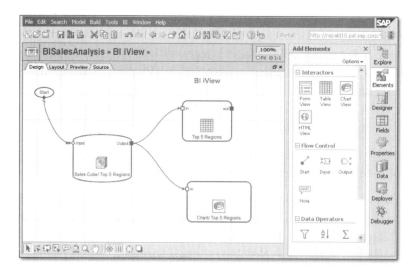

Figure 2.7 SAP NetWeaver Visual Composer

However, you are not obliged to use SAP NetWeaver Visual Composer all the time. As mentioned earlier, you can also use the Eclipse-based Adobe Flex Builder to create applications that can be integrated into SAP NetWeaver Portal. From a developer's point of view, this means that there are numerous different options for creating Flex-based applications.

A multitude of options

The use of Flex is also useful if, for instance, you want to address a wide range of users or if you want to make specific information available to a certain group of users. The added value for SAP customers can be found in the fact that RIA opens up traditional Web applications toward more user interaction and more flexible user interfaces. Moreover, SAP customers benefit from the dynamic display of SAP content in any business-related aspects. Some of these aspects and sample Flex applications are briefly described in the following sections.

Planning and Time Recording

One business application that supports a wide range of users is the time recording and planning of employees, a process that involves every employee within the company. Thus it is very important to keep the recording system as simple as possible. Training costs should be minimized or completely avoided. By using Adobe Flex, you can design the process of recording and changing planning data that used to be based on lists as an interactive process that is graphically much more attractive. Figure 2.8 shows the development of further billable hours in relation to the total number of hours of all employees.

A wide range of users

The online variant of the planning and time-recording system is described in great detail in Chapter 7 and can be implemented easily using the code examples and instructions.

In addition, time recording is a popular offline application. Field sales representatives often record their working hours when they're not connected to the company network. Those offline scenarios can be implemented easily using Flex. The advantage of storing data locally without posing a security risk for the client is one of the essential features of Flex, which makes an offline scenario an interesting alternative as it can now be created cost-efficiently.

Cost-efficient offline applications

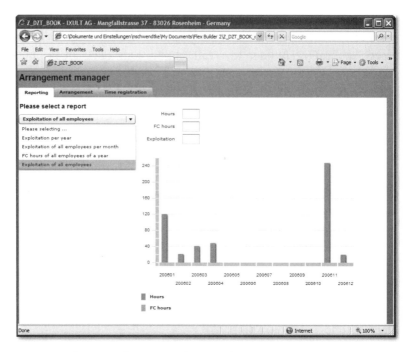

Figure 2.8 Planning and Time Recording as a Flex Application

Process Monitor

Online monitoring
for decision-
makers

Flex applications are particularly useful if you want to actively distribute information. In contrast to traditional Web applications, the
content doesn't need to be specifically updated, given that changing
datasets of the SAP system are presented in real time. This holds true
particularly for process flows such as SAP Workflow scenarios. Individual process steps can be displayed and tracked graphically, so this
function is referred to as a *tracking monitor*.

Workflow
scenarios

Particularly in workflow scenarios, but generally with all business-
relevant activities, it is important to provide each decision maker
with the right presentation. For example, if specific workflow steps
cannot be carried out due to a lack of resources, the decision maker
can draw the right consequences because of a clear presentation of
the matter. Flex is extremely well suited for process monitoring.
Because of the active presentation of changes to the data basis, many
different scenarios are possible. An essential factor in this context is
that the implementation of process monitors using Flex is significantly easier than using any other technology.

Active process monitoring based on a Flex application links process statuses, affects business characteristics and enables forecasting based on retroactive considerations. For example, you can use a monitor to combine open purchase orders and business development with customer information into an overall picture.

As shown in Figure 2.9, you can use Flex especially to combine different pieces of information into groups of information and to present these groups to the user. A list in the upper part of the screen that displays the blocked orders can be used as a basis for a user's further activities. As a decision maker in the workflow scenario, the user can now release purchase orders. The section below the list of orders enables the user to view customer details. In another section below the customer details, the user can check the affected budgets, which are also displayed as a chart in the neighboring pane.

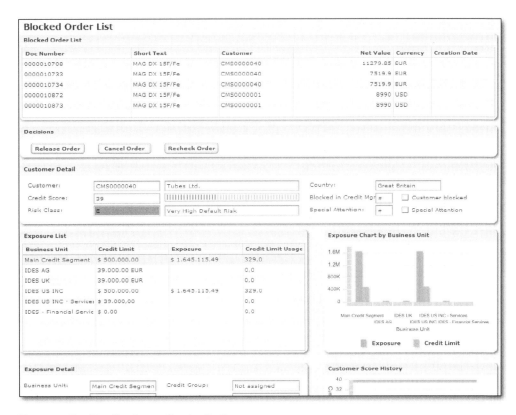

Figure 2.9 Tracking Monitor as Flex Application

Business Information: Sales Activities

Focus on costs Another example is the summary of certain sales activities: a sales board. As shown in Figure 2.10, a sales board is used to assign current revenues and profit margins to individual customers. In addition, the sales board displays threshold values of individual sales activities sorted by employees, as well as orders that have either been lost to competitors or that haven't materialized for other reasons. This information serves as an excellent basis for decisions as it represents an active controlling of the sales division in this graphical version.

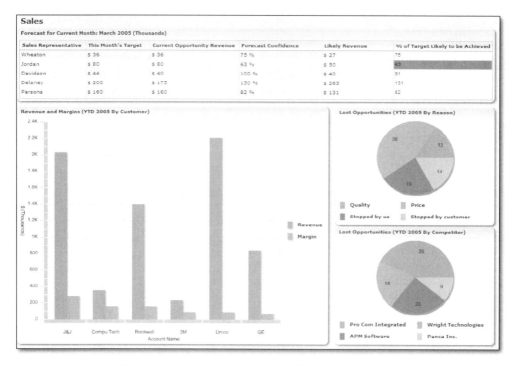

Figure 2.10 Sales Activities as Flex Application

Real-time changes on the screen A real-time monitor that displays the number of pieces sold can be of great help, especially when many individual pieces of goods are sold via electronic media in business-to-consumer (B2C) scenarios. A page that has been updated once does not need to be updated again by the user. Charts and graphics automatically change to reflect changes in the SAP data. This is made possible by the data-push service that's contained in Flex.

2.4   Summary

Originally, SAP and Adobe had entered into a partnership with the objective of using Flex in order to present complex scenarios interactively and in an easy-to-understand manner. A good example of this is a manager's desktop that combines various pieces of information and displays changes in real time.

A new generation of business applications

However, the collaboration between SAP and Adobe means much more for the customer. Using Flex enables users to implement entire applications and scenarios where traditional Web applications have reached their limits for presenting the respective contexts. It is the user-friendliness and the boundless presentation options in particular that make Flex the best choice when it comes to keeping an application as simple as possible and avoiding specific training for that application.

In summary, SAP NetWeaver and Adobe Flex together enable the user to raise SAP-based business applications to a higher level with regard to such capabilities as intuitive operation and flexible adaptation. The open architecture of SAP NetWeaver allows users to benefit from the know-how of many different developers and to use different development environments. The integration of Adobe Flex into SAP NetWeaver enables a robust and highly available application.

This chapter helps you to get started with Adobe Flex Builder, Adobe's development environment for Flex applications. The chapter contains the information necessary to understand and simulate the examples used in the subsequent chapters of this book.

3 Getting Started with Adobe Flex Builder

Adobe Flex Builder is the standard tool used to develop Flex applications for SAP systems. If you have used only SAP GUI until now, you must get familiar with the use of an external tool to develop Flex applications. Although you can develop Flex applications locally within SAP GUI, you should bear in mind that the ABAP development environment does not provide any help for that.

External tool

To be able to use a code check, a tag library, and a WYSIWYG designer, you should therefore use Adobe Flex Builder. Adobe Flex Builder 2.0 is based on the Eclipse development environment. Experienced Web Dynpro developers as well as those who use Flex Builder for the first time should quickly obtain good results. All the examples and screenshots used in this book were created using Adobe Flex Builder 2.0.

3.1 Adobe Flex Builder

Adobe Flex Builder is the development environment for Flex applications. Originally the tool was developed by Macromedia. After Macromedia was acquired by Adobe, Flex Builder was further developed and currently is available in Version 2.0.

Adobe Flex Builder is installed locally on the client. Once you have installed and started Adobe Flex Builder, you will see an initial screen similar to the one shown in Figure 3.1.

Installation

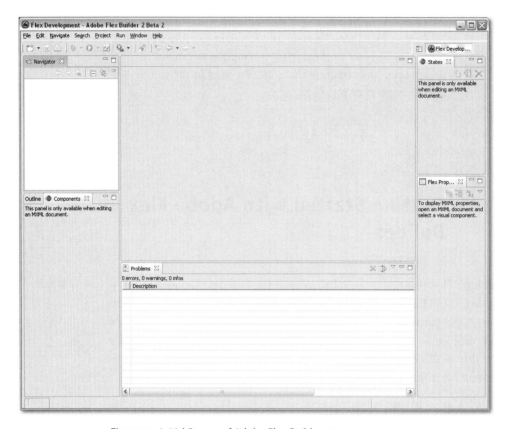

Figure 3.1 Initial Screen of Adobe Flex Builder 2.0

3.1.1 Creating a Project

Project
organization
Flex applications can be developed by different developers and include various documents and components as well as numerous ActionScript files. Usually, development components that are related to each other are organized in a project, and Adobe Flex Builder is no exception to this rule.

Figure 3.2 shows how you can create a project: Select **File • New • Flex Project**.

In the window that opens next (see Figure 3.3), the attributes of your new Flex project to be created are specified in detail. Select **None** for the server technology. You only need the other options if you use additional extensions or products from Adobe such as ColdFusion. Initially—as is true for most other development in the SAP environment—the **None** setting is sufficient.

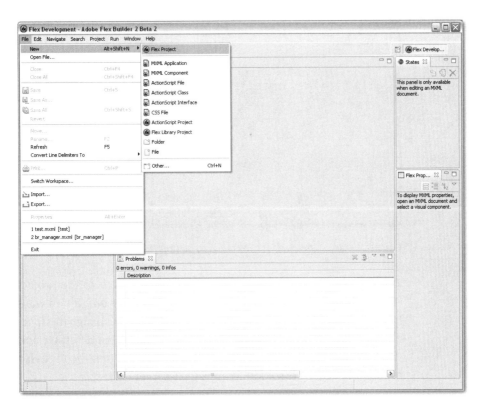

Figure 3.2 Creating a New Project

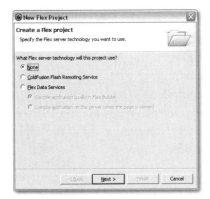

Figure 3.3 Selecting the Flex Server Technology

Then you must assign a name to your first Flex project (see Figure 3.4). In addition, the target path for newly created projects (**Project location**) is stored by default. Typically, this location is on the local host.

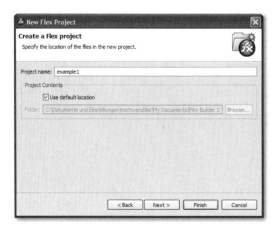

Figure 3.4 Target Location for the Project to be Created

This directory contains all documents that are linked to the project (Flex application, pictures, ActionScript files, and so on). If you want to store the projects centrally on a server, you must change the specification here by deactivating the **Use default location** setting and entering the relevant directory on the server. Note that the user also needs to have authorization to access the server drives.

"Empty" Flex project   Once you have completed the creation of the project by clicking on the **Finish** button, an empty Flex project is displayed on the screen (see Figure 3.5). Technically, the project is not really "empty" because Adobe Flex Builder has already created several documents for the project that are required at this early stage. These are the project file (.*project*), the Flex properties file (.*flexProperties*), the ActionScript properties file (.*actionScriptProperties*), and some directories needed for the graphics, the compiled SWF files, and a settings directory. The files and directories are displayed in the top left section of the screen in the **Navigator** area. However, as far as the application is concerned, the project is indeed empty.

Design vs. code   Initially, Adobe Flex Builder displays the project in the design mode; that is, the source code is implemented by a WYSIWYG editor. If you want to change from the design view into the source code view, you must click on the **Source** or **Code** button located in the middle of the editing pane. In Figure 3.5, that's below the file name **example1.mxml**. Figure 3.6 shows the basic structure of an empty Flex application: the `<mx:Application>` tag. Chapter 4 describes the structure in greater detail.

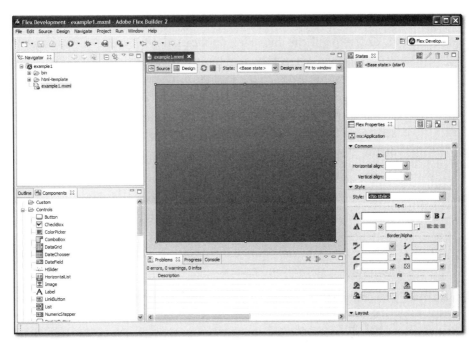

Figure 3.5 Newly Created Project in Adobe Flex Builder (Design View)

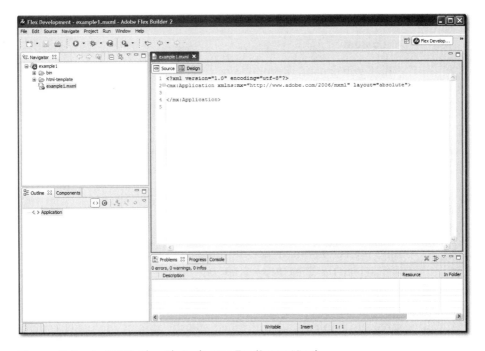

Figure 3.6 Empty MXML File with Application Tag (Source View)

3.1.2   Using the First Flex Component

Components represent the basis

In order to fill the first Flex application with content, you should return to the **Design** view and insert the first layout component into the application. Adobe Flex Builder provides several components in the **Components** tab on the left-hand side. If the tree structure that contains the components does not display on your screen, you can activate it by selecting **Window • Show View • Components** from the menu.

Simply add the components via drag-and-drop. To do that, click on a component, keep pressing the mouse button, and drag the component into the design screen. You should try to use several components here and toggle between the **Design** and **Source** views. You will see that you can immediately refresh and further edit the new components in the source view.

Component tree

The component tree contains the following types of components:

▶ **Layouts**
▶ **Navigators**
▶ **Controls**
▶ **Charts**
▶ **Custom**

When you expand the individual component types, you immediately get an overview of which components have been predefined by SAP so that they can be used right away. Each component consists of MXML and ActionScript.

In order to use a component in an application, you can simply drag it from the components list and drop it into the application. Figure 3.7 shows how the Panel component was inserted into the application.

Title

To assign a title to the Panel component in this example, enter "Address data" in the **Title** property field. To access the property settings for a component, you must highlight the respective component and select the **Flex Properties** tab on the right-hand side of the Adobe Flex Builder screen. Once you have entered the text into the **Title** field and left the field, the design view in the middle of the screen is automatically refreshed and the title of the panel component displays (see Figure 3.8).

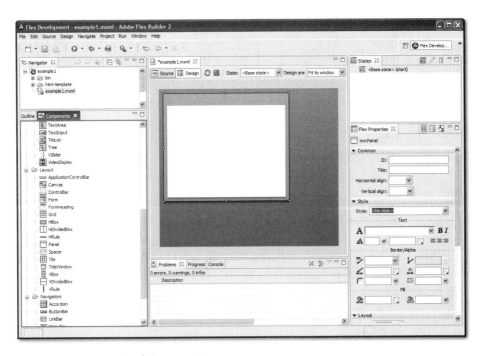

Figure 3.7 Inserting a Panel Component

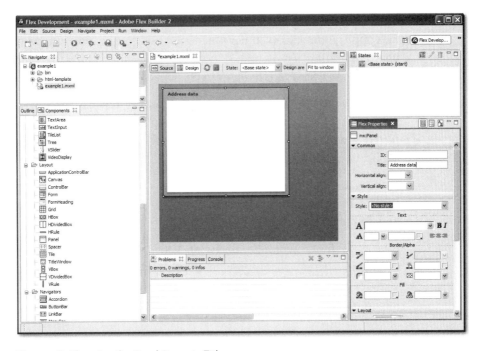

Figure 3.8 Changing the Panel Property Title

Design mode   Similarly, you can define many settings for a component in the design mode, but not all of them. The problem with almost all graphical editors is that it is difficult to operate them when the applications become very complex. This holds also true for Adobe Flex Builder.

The design mode is very useful if you need quick results regarding a demo or a proof-of-concept application. If, however, a user interface contains many components, arranging these components hierarchically becomes an ordeal. This is not due so much to Adobe Flex Builder, but rather because such displays generally pose a problem.

Source mode   If, for instance, you develop a user interface that requires overlapping components that can be shown and hidden via the program control, the display in the design mode is rather difficult. For this reason, it is generally useful to change to the source mode after a few steps and to further process the individual components there. We will also develop the sample application in Chapter 7 predominantly in the source mode and make use of the multiple options of MXML (see Chapter 4) and ActionScript (Chapters 5 and 6).

3.1.3 Testing Flex Applications

Once you have created a project, are using a first component in the Flex application, and even have made the first setting, you can "test" your application. To do that, select **Run • Run <file name>** from the menu or use **Ctrl+F11** (see Figure 3.9).

Because we haven't compiled the application yet, this happens when you run it for the first time. Once the compilation process has completed, a window of your default browser opens up and displays the application (see Figure 3.10).

In this short example, you have learned how to create a Flex project, how to fill the associated Flex application with a component, and how to compile and run the application.

Flex applications typically consist of MXML tags and ActionScript commands. These enable you to develop complex, intuitive, and browser-independent applications, such as those that can be easily integrated into an enterprise portal.

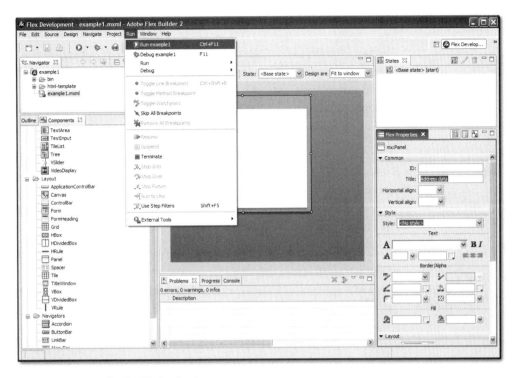

Figure 3.9 Testing the MXML Application

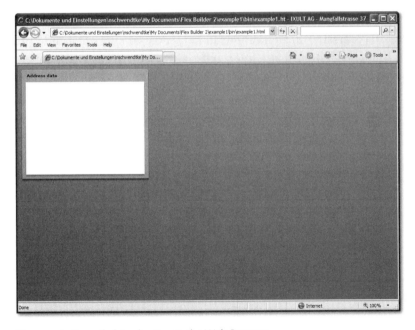

Figure 3.10 Compiled Application in the Web Browser

3.2   Flex Files

Flex files contain the MXML tags and ActionScript codes that are used later for compiling the Flex application. If you already have Web development experience you will probably understand the task comparison "HTML file = MXML file" and "JavaScript file = ActionScript file" even though the technological comparison is not completely appropriate.

Types of Flex files

A Flex project combines different types of Flex files. The following sections describe the different types of Flex files in greater detail. You can define Flex file types just as you define projects by selecting **File • New** in Adobe Flex Builder. The following types of Flex files are available.

▶ **MXML application**

Calling applications separately

MXML applications are Flex files that map a complete application. You can create several MXML applications within a project and call them separately. This can be necessary when you carry out one Flex project but have to develop two different applications; e. g., one for a call center and another one for marketing purposes. MXML applications run independently, and you can execute them using the **Run** call.

▶ **MXML component**

In contrast to an application, an individual component cannot run independently; that is, you must always integrate a component into an application in order to be able to use it.

Developing your own components

Flex allows you to develop your own components using MXML and ActionScript. This gives you the advantage of not having to use the components provided by Adobe so that you can design your own layout. You do not have to restrict the newly created components to graphical elements or a small degree of complexity. On the contrary, they can even contain large parts of the application design. For example, you could use a component to represent an input template for purchase orders that reminds the user of a similar screen in the R/3 system.

You can also implement additional functions and parameters that enable an even higher degree of flexibility and individuality.

▶ **ActionScript file**

You should use ActionScript files whenever you use large Action-Script listings. Although it is possible to integrate ActionScript in MXML files, you should separate the two for clarity's sake.

You can simply integrate and use ActionScript files in Flex applications by using an `include` command. This way you can also develop ActionScript code that can be generally used in different applications.

Integrating ActionScript files

▶ **ActionScript class**

An ActionScript class only consists of plain ActionScript commands, but Adobe Flex Builder supports the creation of classes. Chapter 5 describes the advantages of storing ActionScript classes in separate files and how Adobe Flex Builder can support you in this respect.

Figure 3.11 shows how you can use ActionScript to define a class. To create a new class, select **File • New • ActionScript Class**.

Defining a class

Figure 3.11 Creating a New Class

In Flex, classes are typically summarized into packages. If you have already used Java in the past, you will see some similarities.

In ActionScript, packages also allow you to use classes and class groups within applications that must be specifically integrated.

▶ **ActionScript interface**

Generating an interface

Similarly to defining an ActionScript class, you can generate the interface. Chapter 5 describes the concept of an interface and explains when it is used, and how it is structured. At this point, you only need to know that Adobe Flex Builder supports the program-based definition of interfaces.

There are a few more file types exist that don't need to be described in detail here, such as the CSS file, the ActionScript project, and the Flex library project. For more detailed information on those file types, you should refer to the standard Adobe documentation that can be accessed through the following path: **Help · Welcome · Flex Documentation**.

Standardizing the layout

However, for the examples used in this book and the majority of other applications, you don't need these file types other than the CSS file. As in traditional HTML applications, you can use an existing CSS file to standardize the layout of new and existing Flex applications.

3.3 Flex Samples Explorer

Examples for getting started

For testing purposes and to better understand Flex applications, you should also take a look at the Adobe Flex samples. These examples represent Flex applications of low to medium complexity. Moreover, the examples are specifically designed for quickly getting started with Flex.

You can find the examples under **Help · Welcome** in the menu (see Figure 3.12). The **Welcome** screen of Adobe Flex Builder contains all the important references to sources of information regarding Flex.

You can launch the **Flex Component Explorer** by clicking on it in the middle of the screen. It then should open in a new window of your Web browser and display the individual Flex components, as shown in Figure 3.13. If the components are not displayed on your screen and the background stays dark gray instead, you must install a later version of Flash Player.

Figure 3.12 Adobe Flex Builder Welcome Screen

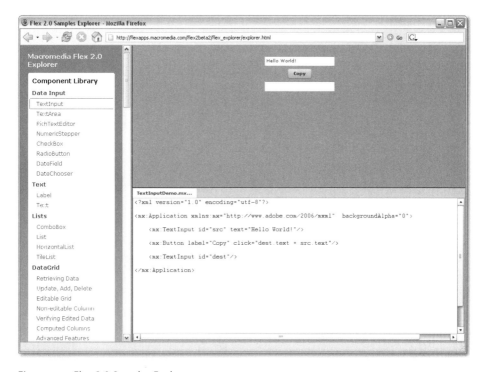

Figure 3.13 Flex 2.0 Samples Explorer

49

The Flex Samples Explorer is designed in such a way that it displays the various components on the left of the screen. The upper right-hand section of the screen displays the example in the same way the end user would also see it. The underlying Flex code is displayed in the lower right-hand area, so that you can see the interdependencies of the example at one glance. If you familiarize yourself with the individual components in this way, you will quickly realize how simple, powerful, and structured a development language Flex is.

MXML is a language based on the XML standard for design-
ing Flex applications. MXML offers tools for such tasks as
creating links between components or loading data from
a server. This chapter explains the basic concepts behind
MXML files and describes individual components that can
be used in a Flex application.

4 MXML

Two languages are generally used to create Flex applications: Multimedia eXtensible Markup Language (MXML) and ActionScript (see
Chapter 5). Like HTML, MXML is a markup language and is based on
the XML standard of the World Wide Web Consortium. MXML is
used to represent the layout of the application, but also to generate
relationships between components, such as the link to data sources
on a server.

Like HTML, MXML consists of *tags*. However, MXML is more struc-   MXML vs. HTML
tured than HTML and consists of more tag elements. Different tags
exist for each individual component in a Flex application, including
the `DataGrid`, `Tree`, `TabNavigator`, or `Accordion` components, which
are introduced in this chapter. You can also expand MXML with your
own components.

One of the most striking differences between MXML and HTML is in
the way they are called. While HTML files can be executed directly in
the Web browser, MXML files require the Flash Player
(*http://www.adobe.com/de/software/flashplayer*) in order to be displayed and executed, because they are compiled as SWF files.
Although Flex applications are based on Flash[1], they do not use the
fundamental Flash concepts such as the timeline. Nevertheless, vari-

---

1 Flash is a development environment that is used to generate "movies" in SWF format: a graphic and animation format based on vector graphics. Flash is widely
used in many Web sites. To be able to view Flash files, you must install a Flash
Player plug-in in your Web browser.

ous components for the Flex application can also be created or modified with conventional Flash development environments.

4.1   Syntax

Most of the MXML tags correspond to the names or attributes of ActionScript classes. MXML file use the following naming convention.

▶ File names must be named in a way similar to that used with ActionScript variables; that is, they must begin with a letter or an underscore (_), and only consist of characters or numbers.

▶ ActionScript classes, component Ids, or the word "application" are not permitted as names for MXML files.

▶ MXML files must end with "mxml."

Composition of MXML files

MXML files themselves have a strictly defined syntax that can be derived from the XML standard. The basic framework of an MXML file will always appear as follows:

```
<?xml version="1.0" encoding="iso-8859-1"?>
<mx:Application
    xmlns:mx="http://www.adobe.com/2006/mxml">
    <!-- Additional MXML tags -->
</mx:Application>
```

Because MXML is based on XML, the file must begin with the <?xml> tag, which is not completed with a closing tag. Specification of the encoding is not mandatory; if it is left out, the ISO-8859-1 encoding is used, which is usually used in US operating systems. To ensure platform independence, we recommend the UTF-8 format, which assigns each symbol a unique number. This ensures platform, language and program independence.

<mx:Application> tag

As well as being the highest node of the Flex application, the <mx:Application> tag also represents the so-called *application container*. A container is a user-interface component that consists of additional components and places these in the layout according to embedded rules. The components are placed as standard beneath the <mx:Application> tag vertically from top to bottom in the page. The nesting of components (see Section 4.3.3) can allow other layouts to be enforced, such as the arrangement of text fields in a row.

An MXML file is essentially an XML file and satisfies the same rules and attributes. The `<mx:Application>` tag contains the required field `xmlns`, which defines the namespace of the MXML tags via a prefix. MXML tags can thus be identified through the prefix `mx`. The namespace MUST be specified.

Characteristics of MXML tags

The `<mx:Application>` tag may only be used in the main file and should be seen in the same way as the `main()` method in other programming languages. It defines the main file of the application, into which additional components can be added.

A MXML application can consist of one or several files. Normally you define a file containing the main application and thus the `<mx:Application>` tag. From this file, additional files are integrated that can consist of MXML tags, ActionScript code or both.

MXML application structure

In practice, it is common to divide a Flex application into functional units (so-called *modules*) and to process each module in a separate file. This has two advantages.

▶ **Easier programming**
Different programmers can develop and test different modules without getting in each other's way. Modules that have been written can also be used in other parts of the application.

▶ **Maintainability**
Errors in the application can be discovered more easily thanks to the modularization. In a Flex application, a module corresponds to an individual component developed in ActionScript or MXML that can be based on further components or can include them.

Furthermore, MXML tags such as XML and HTML tags have so-called *attributes* (also called parameters), as shown in Listing 4.1:

Attributes

```
<mx:HBox>
   <mx:label text="Hello World!"/>
</mx:HBox>
```

Listing 4.1 Text Attribute of the MXML Tag Label

The MXML tag `label` (`<mx:label>`) begins with the namespace here, followed by a colon (:). The attributes that now follow are assigned values through the equals sign (=). Quotation marks ("") must be given here. An open tag must be closed again by its counterpart— here `</mx:HBox>`—though the notation can be shortened by the character combination `/>` at the end of the opening tag. This abbreviation is always used if a tag does not contain any nested child elements, as is the case with `<mx:label [...] />` for example.

Including external files

MXML applications can be based on one or several files; your own components that are written in MXML support ActionScript and Flash files. External files are usually included via the `<mx:Script>` tag with a URL to a referencing file. This reference can be absolute or relative:

▶ **Relative**

```
<mx:Script source="../myscript.as"/>
```

▶ **Absolute**

```
<mx:Script source="http://domain.de/file.mxml"/>
```

In addition to the `<mx:Script>` tag, external files can also be made available to the application through a `HTTPService` (`<mx:HTTPService>`), a `WebService` (`<mx:WebService>`), or a `Style` tag (`<mx:Style>`).

4.2 Layout Components

Dynamic arrangement of the MXML elements

Layout components are used to assign MXML elements according to certain procedures. In this context, we refer to *container components*. Depending on the type of layout component, a dynamic arrangement of the elements can be achieved. The Flex application takes over the positioning and ensures well-balanced page measures for the individual MXML elements.

The following components can be used for the graphic design of the Flex application. For a detailed view of all following MXML examples, you should refer to the MXML documentation under *http://live-docs.macromedia.com/labs/1/flex/langref/index.html*.

4.2.1 Canvas

Set elements through x and y position

The `Canvas` component is a rectangular drawing area. Here, MXML elements can be set through their x and y positions. The call for the `<mx:Canvas>` tag is:

```
<mx:Canvas
    clipContent="true|false"
    defaultButton="No default."
    hLineScrollSize="1"
    hPageScrollSize="5"
    hPosition="0"
    hScrollPolicy="auto|on|off"
    icon="No default."
    label="No default."
    vLineScrollSize="1"
    vPageScrollSize="5"
    vPosition="0"
    vScrollPolicy="auto|on|off"
/>
```

This is a very simple layout component that is used, for example, to represent a background that will make only one drawing interface available.

4.2.2 Panel

Unlike `Canvas`, the `Panel` component—whose sample output is shown in Figure 4.1—has a title bar that can contain a caption. You can also adjust the appearance of the margins. The `<mx:Panel>` tag is called as follows.

Title bar

```
<mx:Panel
    panelBorderStyle="default"
    cornerRadius="3"
    dropShadow="true"
    headerColors="[0xE1E5EB, 0xF4F5F7]"
    headerHeight="28"
    footerColors="[0xF4F5F7, 0xE1E5EB]"
    title="no default"
    titleStyleDeclaration="no default"
    click="eventhandler"
    mouseDownOutside="eventhandler"
    ...
       [Additional MXML tags]
    ...
/>
```

In Listing 4.2, a `Panel` is set to an x-y position. These positions are coordinates to which the individual components can be set on the drawing interface. A width and height are assigned to it through the standard width and height parameters.

```
<mx:Panel x="3" y="5" height="101" width="387"
    title="Panel1"/>
```

Listing 4.2 Panel Component with Header

Figure 4.1 Sample Output for the Panel Component

4.2.3 Grid

Showing components in table layout

The Grid component is used to display MXML components in a table layout, because it consists of column and row tags. The components to be displayed are inserted in the resulting cells. The cells in a row have the same height, but they can have different widths. Conversely, the cells in a column have the same width, but can have different heights.

The <mx:Grid> tag specifies the container. It contains the <mx:Grid-Row> tag for displaying the rows and the <mx:GridItem> tag for specifying the cells, and thus corresponds to the columns. Sample output is shown in Figure 4.2. The complete call is as follows:

```
<mx:Grid
    horizontalGap="8" verticalGap="8">
        <mx:GridRow id="row1">
            <mx:GridItem>
                [Additional MXML tags]
            </mx:GridItem>
        ...
        </mx:GridRow>
    ...
/>
```

Spacing

The horizontalGap and verticalGap parameters of the <mx:Grid> tag specify how many pixels are left between the individual MXML components, to be shown as the spacing for the relevant direction. The standard value is eight pixels as shown.

In Listing 4.3, six buttons are created in three columns and two rows using the Grid component.

```
<mx:Grid>
   <mx:GridRow>
      <mx:GridItem>
         <mx:Button label="Button1"/>
      </mx:GridItem>
      <mx:GridItem>
         <mx:Button label="Button2"/>
      </mx:GridItem>
      <mx:GridItem>
         <mx:Button label="Button3"/>
      </mx:GridItem>
   </mx:GridRow>
   <mx:GridRow>
      <mx:GridItem>
         <mx:Button label="Button4"/>
      </mx:GridItem>
      <mx:GridItem>
         <mx:Button label="Button5"/>
      </mx:GridItem>
      <mx:GridItem>
         <mx:Button label="Button6"/>
      </mx:GridItem>
   </mx:GridRow>
</mx:Grid>
```

Listing 4.3 Six Buttons in a 3x2 Grid Layout

Figure 4.2 Sample Output for the Grid Component

4.2.4 Tile

The Tile component is a means of showing MXML components in a table or network-like structure. Unlike the Grid component, all cells have the same height and width measurements. They can be defined using the tileHeight and tileWidth parameters or adjusted automatically to the MXML components with the greatest measurements in the defined network. The components are each divided according to the direction set.

Displaying
components in a
network structure

The `<mx:Tile>` tag is called as follows:

```
<mx:Tile
   direction="value"
   horizontalAlign="value"
   horizontalGap="value"
   marginBottom="value"
   marginTop="value"
   tileHeight="value"
   tileWidth="value"
   verticalAlign="value"
   verticalGap="value"
   >
   ...
      [Additional MXML tags]
   ...
</mx:Tile>
```

Using the `direction` parameter, you can set the orientation between `horizontal` as the standard value and `vertical`.

For example, six buttons are arranged vertically in Listing 4.4. After a certain number of components, a column is added automatically to ensure uniform arrangement of the components. In this case, an additional column is added automatically after three buttons. Sample output is shown in Figure 4.3.

```
<mx:Tile direction="vertical">
   <mx:Button label="Button1"/>
   <mx:Button label="Button2"/>
   <mx:Button label="Button3"/>
   <mx:Button label="Button4"/>
   <mx:Button label="Button5"/>
   <mx:Button label="Button6"/>
</mx:Tile>
```

Listing 4.4 Tile Layout with Six Buttons Arranged Vertically

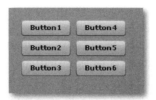

Figure 4.3 Sample Output for the Tile Component

4.2.5 HBox and VBox

The HBox and VBox components depict the contained MXML components in a horizontal or vertical orientation. You can use the components in order to not explicitly specify the orientation of the arrangement via a parameter. Sample output is shown in Figure 4.4. The calls for the tags are as follows:

Displaying components vertically or horizontally

```
<mx:HBox
   ...
       [Additional MXML tags]
   ...
</mx:HBox>
<mx:VBox
   ...
       [Additional MXML tags]
   ...
</mx:VBox>
```

In Listing 4.5, three buttons are shown one below the other.

```
<mx:VBox>
    <mx:Button label="Button1"/>
    <mx:Button label="Button2"/>
    <mx:Button label="Button3"/>
</mx:VBox>
```

Listing 4.5 Three Buttons in the VBox Layout

Figure 4.4 Sample Output for the VBox Component

4.2.6 HDividedBox and VDividedBox

The HDividedBox and VDividedBox components have the same attributes as HBox and VBox. Furthermore, they also have graphic spacers to separate the contained components from each other. The spacers allow the user to actively change the height or width of the resulting cells in the relevant direction. Figure 4.5 displays sample output. The tags required are defined as follows:

Graphic spacers

```
<mx:VDividedBox>
    ...
       [Additional MXML tags]
    ...
</mx:VDividedBox>
<mx:HDividedBox>
    ...
       [Additional MXML tags]
    ...
</mx:HDividedBox>
```

Listing 4.6 shows three buttons in a row. Users can subsequently adjust the widths of the cells as they prefer.

```
<mx:HDividedBox>
    <mx:Button label="Button1"/>
    <mx:Button label="Button2"/>
    <mx:Button label="Button3"/>
</mx:HDividedBox>
```

Listing 4.6 Three Buttons in the HDividedBox Layout

Figure 4.5 Sample Output for the HDividedBox Component

4.3   Navigation Components

Subdivision into context-specific themes

Having gotten to know the layout components in Section 4.2, we now come to the navigation components. They allow the Flex application to be divided into context-specific themes, without having to display the information in a complex way in a screen template.

The following code samples will explain the standard calls using examples. A range of special parameters will also be illustrated. All navigation components are derived from other higher-level components, such as the container component, and thus inherit these components' characteristics and event handlers to take over particular tasks in a Flex application.

4.3.1 Accordion

The Accordion component is known from the Flash area, in particular. It has a defined collection of containers, where only the selected container is displayed. The individual containers appear above each other. You navigate between the individual containers via the container panels, which represent the boundaries between the content of the containers. The container panels appear below each other to show the delimitation of the individual containers. If a container is selected, the subsequent container panels are shown under the content of that container.

Collection of containers

The call for the Accordion component is shown here:

```
<mx:Accordion
   headerHeight="value"
   historyManagement="value"
   marginTop="value"
   marginBottom="value"
   openDuration="value"
   resizeToContent="false|true"
   selectedIndex="value"
   textSelectedColor="value"
   verticalGap="value"
   >
   ...
     [Additional MXML tags]
   ...
</mx:Accordion>
```

The <mx:Accordion> tag has some separate parameters that you can use—for example via selectedIndex—to open the initial container or, with resizeToContent, to dynamically adjust the size to the content. The parameters control the individual behavior of the component.

Listing 4.7 shows a simple call of the component within a Flex application.

```
<mx:Accordion width="397" height="327" id="themes">
   <mx:Canvas label="Panel1" width="100%" height="100%">
     <!-- Add components -->
   </mx:Canvas>
   <mx:Canvas label="Panel2" width="100%" height="100%">
```

```
        <!-- Add components -->
    </mx:Canvas>
</mx:Accordion>
```

Listing 4.7 Accordion Layout with Two Containers

Layout of the containers The component also has the standard parameters `width`, `height`, and `id`, which belong to each component. The added `Canvas` components specify the layout of the containers. Here you can use all the layout components specified in Section 4.2. At the same time, the individual container panels are assigned a label, as you can see in Figure 4.6.

Figure 4.6 Sample Output for the Accordion Component

4.3.2 ViewStack

Including different views in one container The `ViewStack` component is the simplest component for grouping many different views into one container. You can only navigate between the containers explicitly through an event of a different component; for example, using a button that displays the container for a specific index. A `ViewStack` has no headers through which the views are separated.

You use the component with the following call:

```
<mx:ViewStack
    historyManagement="value"
    marginTop="value"
    marginBottom="value"
    resizeToContent="false|true"
    selectedChild="component ID"
    selectedIndex="value"
    >
    ...
        [Additional MXML tags]
    ...
</mx:ViewStack>
```

The `selectedIndex` and `selectedChild` parameters are the most important tools here. Changing one of these parameters allows navigation between the individual containers.

Navigation between the containers

Listing 4.8 shows two `Canvas` components that are embedded into a `ViewStack` component.

```
<mx:ViewStack id="View" width="100%" height="100%">
   <mx:Canvas id="view1" width="100%" height="100%">
      <!-- Add components -->
   </mx:Canvas>
   <mx:Canvas id="view2" width="100%" height="100%">
      <!-- Add components -->
   </mx:Canvas>
</mx:ViewStack>
```

Listing 4.8 Two Canvas Components in the ViewStack Layout

The individual `Canvas` components can be accessed as an event; e.g., by selecting the `id` with the call `selectedChild=view1`.

4.3.3 TabNavigator

You are familiar with the `TabNavigator` component from many other applications. The `TabNavigator` is designed like a kind of card index where you navigate via *tabs*. It is similar to the `Accordion` and, like it, has a number of containers that can be selected individually.

Navigation using tabs

You call the component as follows:

```
<mx:TabNavigator
   horizontalAlign="value"
   horizontalGap="value"
   tabHeight="value"
   tabWidth="value"
   >
   ...
      [Additional MXML tags]
   ...
</mx:TabNavigator>
```

Among other things, you can use the separate parameters of the `<mx:TabNavigator>` tab to adjust the width (`tabWidth`) and height (`tabHeight`) of the tabs.

Listing 4.9 shows a simple call of the component within a Flex application:

```
<mx:TabNavigator width="428" height="327" id="tabnavi">
   <mx:Canvas label="Tab 1" width="100%" height="100%">
      <!-- Add components -->
   </mx:Canvas>
   <mx:Canvas label="Tab 2" width="100%" height="100%">
      <!-- Add components -->
   </mx:Canvas>
</mx:TabNavigator>
```

Listing 4.9 Two Canvas Components in the TabNavigator Layout

As for Accordion, the Canvas component is used for the layout of the containers and for labeling the tabs (see Figure 4.7).

Figure 4.7 Sample Output for the TabNavigator Component

4.3.4 Tree

Tree-like structures

You can build a tree-like structure with the Tree component. It is divided into main nodes and sub-nodes, and you navigate by selecting these. This layout allows a deep classification of the individual subject areas.

The <mx:Tree> tag is described as follows:

```
<mx:Tree
   alternatingRowColors="No default."
   showRoot="true|false"
   labelField="No default."
   dataProvider="No default."
   defaultLeafIcon="No default."
   depthColors="No default."
   firstVisibleNode="No default."
   folderOpenIcon="No default."
```

```
         folderClosedIcon="No default."
         indentation="8"
         openDuration="250"
         openEasing="No default."
         rollOverColor="0xE3FFD6"
         selectedNode="No default."
         selectionColor=#0xCDFFC1"
         cellEdit="event handler"
         cellFocusIn="event handler"
         cellFocusOut="event handler"
         cellPress="event handler"
         change="event handler"
         nodeClose="event handler"
         nodeOpen="event handler"
/>
```

The `Tree` component uses a `dataProvider` to build its structure. The `dataProvider` contains a collection of structured values through which the component is built. Because `dataProviders` are used for many MXML components, we will discuss them in more detail in Chapter 7 and deal with them here in a simple example.

Static and dynamic

The `Tree` component has additional attributes, events, and style parameters for controlling the navigation and appearance. The `selectedNode` parameter specifies which node was selected, and through the event `change` you can use the node as—for example—a navigation instrument to jump to a `ViewStack`.

Listing 4.10 shows the source code for a simple tree structure, which is shown in Figure 4.8. The tree structure is built using a `<mx:XML>` tag.

```
<mx:XML id="treedata">
   <node label="Navigation">
      <node label="Accordion">
         <node label="add component"/>
      </node>
      <node label="ViewStack">
         <node label="add component"/>
      </node>
      <node label="TabNavigator">
         <node label="add component"/>
      </node>
   </node>
```

```
  </mx:XML>
  <mx:Panel id="treePanel" title="Tree Panel">
     <mx:Tree id="navigation" width="285" height="196"
       showRoot="false" labelField="@label">
     <mx:dataProvider>
        {treedata}
     </mx:dataProvider>
     </mx:Tree>
  </mx:Panel>
```

Listing 4.10 Layout of a Tree Structure

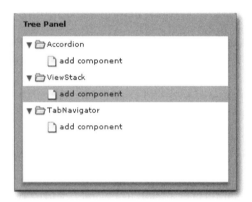

Figure 4.8 Sample Output for the Tree Component

Showing the tree structure

To show the tree structure, the `id` of the XML structure is linked to the `<mx:dataProvider>` tag by the curly brackets (`{}`). The `labelField` parameter is used to specify the field used as the description for the relevant tree node. In this case, the `label` field of the XML node is used as the designation. The `<mx:XML>` tag must be specified outside all representing components, such as the `Panel`.

4.3.5 TabBar and LinkBar

Referencing ViewStacks

`TabBar` and `LinkBar` are both components that use a `dataProvider` to build their navigation structures. They are primarily used to address `ViewStacks`.

The `TabBar` component, similar to the `TabNavigator`, has tabs that you can use to address certain screen templates. However, it cannot directly include new layout components that can display new content through them. In this case, only the tabs are displayed, while the `ViewStack` is missing for the display of other components.

The <mx:TabBar> tag is called as follows:

```
<mx:TabBar
   dataProvider="No default.
   horizontalAlign="left|center|right"
   horizontalGap="6"
   labelField="No default.
   marginLeft="0"
   marginRight="0"
   selectedIndex="0"
   tabHeight="Default from style"
   tabWidth="Default from Label width"
   click="event handler"

   ...
      [Additional MXML tags]
   ...
/>
```

The LinkBar component is also built using a kind of tab arrangement, however these are more like links from the HTML area. The same restrictions apply to displaying screen templates as apply for the Tab-Bar component.

The call for the <mx:LinkBar> is arranged as follows:

```
<mx:LinkBar
   dataProvider="No default.
   horizontalGap="8"
   marginBottom="2"
   marginTop="2"
   rollOverColor="0xE3FFD6"
   selectionColor="0xCDFFC1"
   strokeColor="No default."
   strokeWidth="1"
   verticalGap="8"

   ...
      [Additional MXML tags]
   ...
/>
```

Because neither of the two components has its own ViewStack, the calls of the standard width and height parameters can lead to undesired deformations of the components. In this case you should only fill the parameters with static values, to avoid dynamic size changes.

Deformations

4.3.6 Additional Navigation Components

Additional navigation components are `<mx:MenuBar>`, `<mx:Button-Bar>` or `<mx:ToggleButtonBar>`, though these are predominantly based on those mentioned above. For example, `MenuBar` has a tree- or node-type structure similar to `Tree` and also has similar deformation characteristics when you use the standard parameters such as `TabBar` and `LinkBar`. The `ButtonBar` component is handled in the very same way as the `LinkBar` or `TabBar` component. The additional components can therefore be used in much the same way as the components described above and mainly differ in their design.

4.4   Control Components

Bringing Flex applications to life Having covered the design and navigation capabilities of Flex applications, we will now familiarize ourselves with the content-specific components. Control components are used to prepare data. They offer tools for calculations, allow graphic interpretations, can trigger events, and even have multimedia capabilities.

With the following components you can literally bring your Flex applications to life, by allowing interaction with the user. In Figure 4.9, a number of these components are shown in a form.

Figure 4.9 Sample Output for Control Components

4.4.1 Button

Buttons are the most familiar controls: using a `Button` control, you can trigger an event with your mouse or keyboard. The event can trigger both simple data assignments and complex calculations.

Triggering an event with mouse or keyboard

Calls for a `Button` control in Flex are designed as follows:

```
<mx:Button
    icon="No default."
    label="No default."
    labelPlacement="right|left|bottom|top"
    repeatInterval="35"
    repeatDelay="500"
    selected="false|true"
    toggle="false|true"
    click="event handler"
/>
```

An image file can be assigned to a button via the `icon` parameter, or a caption can be assigned via `label`. The `toggle` parameter defines the button's click behavior. If the parameter takes the value `true`, then when the button is pressed it will not be released again, but will remain pressed. When you press it again, it then returns to its original position. The `click` event calls the button to fulfill the task intended for it.

Listing 4.11 that follows shows a button call for a simple value assignment. Here, the button is assigned a new `Label2` label with the `Label1` label when the `click` event is triggered. Figure 4.10 shows the result.

```
<mx:Button label="Label1" id="button1"
    click="button1.label='Label2'"/>
```

Listing 4.11 Button for Changing a Label Name

Figure 4.10 Sample Output for the Button Component

4.4.2 TextInput

Single-line
text field

The TextInput component is a single-line text field that is used primarily as an input field for text-based or numerical values. The <mx:TextInput> tag call is as follows:

```
<mx:TextInput
    editable="true|false"
    hPosition="0"
    htmlText="No default."
    maxChars="undefined"
    maxHPosition="0"
    password="false|true"
    restrict="null"
    text="No default."
    disabledColor="0xAAB3B3"
    change="event handler"
    enter="event handler"
/>
```

The characters entered can be visually encoded with an asterisk (*) using the password parameter. The characters are held in the text attribute and can be further processed. With restrict, you can enter characters that are exclusively to be used for the input. You can prevent the entry of characters with the addition editable="false" during initialization or at runtime. With the htmlText attribute, you can display the text through HTML formatting, e.g. <h1></h1>. The events can be triggered when you change the entry (change) and by pressing the Enter key (enter).

Numerical and text-based characters are entered in a TextInput control in Listing 4.12. Other characters are excluded from the entry. Figure 4.11 shows the result.

```
<mx:TextInput id="input" text="TextInput 1"
    restrict="A-Z,a-z,0-9"/>
```

Listing 4.12 TextInput Field that Only Allows Entry of Letters and Numbers

Figure 4.11 Sample Output for the TextInput Component

4.4.3   Label

The Label control is a single-line text field that is not ready for input and that is primarily used to describe other controls. Similar to the TextInput control, the text can also be given formatted in HTML.

Describing other controls

You can call the ⟨mx:Label⟩ tag as follows:

```
<mx:Label
    htmlText="No default."
    text="No default."
    disabledColor="0x848384"
    hide="event handler"
    show="event handler"
/>
```

The events hide and show can be triggered when you set the inherited visible attribute. Listing 4.13 shows a Label for describing a TextInputs field.

```
<mx:HBox>
    <mx:Label text="Name"/>
    <mx:TextInput/>
</mx:HBox>
```

Listing 4.13 Label as a Description of a TextInput Field

4.4.4   TextArea

The TextArea control is a multi-line input field, unlike the TextInput control. If the size of the text exceeds the specified size of the control, a vertical scroll bar becomes visible automatically. TextArea controls are mainly used for commentary entries in forms and also can be used in versatile ways.

Commentary entries in forms

The call for the ⟨mx:TextArea⟩ tag is as follows:

```
<mx:TextArea
    editable="true|false"
    hPosition="0 when wordwrap is true."
    hScrollPolicy="auto|on|off"
    htmlText="No default."
    maxChars="undefined"
    maxHPosition="0 when wordwrap is true."
    maxVPosition="0"
```

```
    password="false|true"
    restrict="null"
    text="No default."
    vPosition="0"
    vScrollPolicy="auto|on|off"
    wordWrap="false|true"
    change="event handler"
/>
```

The `TextArea` control has the same attributes as the `TextInput` control. You can use the `hScrollPolicy` parameter to show a horizontal scroll bar.

Listing 4.14 shows a call of the control in a form environment, Figure 4.12 shows the result.

```
<mx:Form width="100%" height="100%">
   <mx:FormItem label="comment">
      <mx:TextArea/>
      <mx:Button label="Submit"/>
   </mx:FormItem>
</mx:Form>
```

Listing 4.14 TextArea Component Within a Form Component

Figure 4.12 Sample Output for the TextArea Component

4.4.5 Text

Displaying texts The `Text` control is the multi-line equivalent to the `Label` control. It is not ready for input and is predominantly used to display texts, though the user cannot make any direct changes.

The call of the `<mx:Text>` tag is as follows:

```
<mx:Text
   marginTop="0"
   marginBottom="0"
   selectable="true|false"
   text="no default"
/>
```

Unlike the `Label` control, the text can be selected in a `Text` control by the `selectable` parameter.

4.4.6   CheckBox

The `CheckBox` control is used to choose options. It has the statuses   Choosing options
`true` and `false`. Depending on whether an option is selected, you can trigger a particular event for further processing. A `CheckBox` group follows the AND principle; that is, you can select all or individual options at the same time.

You can call the `<mx:CheckBox>` tag as follows:

```
<mx:CheckBox
    label="No default."
    labelPlacement="right|left|bottom|top"
    selected="false|true"
    click="event handler"
/>
```

Via the `click` event, you can define events for the selected or removed option. You use the `label` attribute to set a description for the option.

Two `CheckBox` controls are used in the following Listing 4.15. If they are selected, the `label` entry is written to a `Text` control (see Figure 4.13). The event is executed by an ActionScript function. The syntax of ActionScript is explained in detail in Chapter 5.

```
<mx:Script>
    <![CDATA[
    public function createList(){
        list.text="";
        if (software.selected == true)
            list.text+=software.label + "\n";
        if (hardware.selected == true)
            list.text+=hardware.label + "\n";
    }
    ]]>
</mx:Script>
<mx:HBox width="100%" height="100%">
    <mx:VBox width="20%" height="100%">
        <mx:CheckBox label="Software" id="software"
            click="createList()"/>
```

```
      <mx:CheckBox label="Hardware" id="hardware"
          click="createList()"/>
    </mx:VBox>
    <mx:Text id="list" width="200" height="200"/>
</mx:HBox>
```

Listing 4.15 Two CheckBox Components with Event Control

Figure 4.13 Sample Output for the CheckBox Component

4.4.7 RadioButton and RadioButtonGroup

Choosing options

The RadioButton control, in the same way as the CheckBox control, is used to select options. It can also take the values true or false and thus trigger events, but it only allows one value in a group. It therefore uses the OR principle.

The <mx:RadioButton> tag call is as follows:

```
<mx:RadioButton
    data=""
    groupName="No default."
    label="No default."
    labelPlacement="right|left|top|bottom"
    selected="false|true"
    selectedData="No default."
    toggle="false|true"
    click="event handler"
/>
```

Via the groupName attribute, you can specify a group name that applies for several RadioButton controls. In general, there is little point in calling a single RadioButton control, because only in the group can all of the characteristics be used. MXML offers a Radio-ButtonGroup control for this. You can use the chosen RadioButton control without explicitly addressing it.

The call for the <mx:RadioButtonGroup> control is:

```
<mx:RadioButtonGroup
    id="Required - No default."
```

```
    enabled="true|false"
    groupName="No default."
    labelPlacement="right|left|bottom|top"
    selectedData="If the RadioButton does not define
                  the data property, Flex sets
                  selectedData to the value of the label
                  property."
    click="event handler"
    change="event handler"
/>
```

Via the `selectedData` parameter, you can directly access the data element of the selected `RadioButton` control. If this is not assigned, the value of the label is returned.

Listing 4.16 shows a `RadioButtonGroup` with two `RadioButton` controls. If a `RadioButton` control is selected, its label value is copied to a `label` (see Figure 4.14).

```
<mx:RadioButtonGroup id="radiogroup1"
    itemClick="label1.text=
    radiogroup1.selectedValue.toString()"/>
<mx:RadioButton x="89" y="75" label="Button 1"
    groupName="radiogroup1"/>
<mx:RadioButton x="89" y="99" label="Button 2"
    groupName="radiogroup1"/>
<mx:Label x="93" y="140" width="62" id="label1"/>
```

Listing 4.16 RadioButtonGroup Component with Event Control

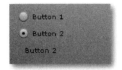

Figure 4.14 Sample Output for the RadioButtonGroup Component

4.4.8 List

The `List` control shows many successive values that can be selected individually or as a multiple selection. It has a vertical scroll bar so that it can show numbers of values that exceed the display length of the `List` control. Optionally, a horizontal scroll bar allows you to show values that are very long.

Vertical scroll bar

The call for the `<mx:List>` tag is:

```
<mx:List
    dataProvider="No default."
    alternatingRowColors="No default."
    change="Event handler; No default."
    marginBotton="0"
    marginTop="0"
    rollOverColor="No default."
    selectionColor="No default."
    selectionDisabledColor="0xDDDDDD"
    selectionEasing="No default."
    selectedIndex="No default."
    selectedIndices="No default."
    selectedItem="No default."
    selectedItems="No default."
    textRollOverColor="0x2B333C"
    textSelectedColor="0x05F33"
    useRollOver="true|false"
```

To fill the control with values, you can copy a `dataProvider`. The `selectedItem` parameter holds the currently selected value. However, you can also use several selected values that are held in the `selectedItems` attribute.

Two lists are shown by the following Listing 4.17. When you make a selection, the selected values of one list are copied to the other list (see Figure 4.15).

```
<mx:List x="29" y="106" id="list1" width="162"
    allowMultipleSelection="true">
    <mx:Array>
        <mx:String>Visa</mx:String>
        <mx:String>MasterCard</mx:String>
        <mx:String>American Express</mx:String>
    </mx:Array>
</mx:List>
<mx:List x="229" y="106" width="162" id="list2"
    dataProvider="{list1.selectedItems}"/>
```

Listing 4.17 Copying Selected Values of a List Component

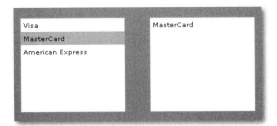

Figure 4.15 Sample Output for the List Component

4.4.9 ComboBox

The ComboBox control has a dropdown list from which a single value   Dropdown list
can be selected. However, the value can also be entered by the user
if the value is not contained in the list.

The <mx:ComboBox> tag call is:

```
<mx:ComboBox
    dataProvider="No default."
    dropdownWidth="Size wide enough to hold text."
    editable="false|true"
    labelField="No default."
    labelFunction="No default."
    rowCount="5"
    selectedIndex="No default."
    selectedItem="No default."
    change="event handler"
    close="event handler"
    enter="event handler"
    itemRollOver="event handler"
    itemRollOut="event handler"
    open="event handler"
    scroll="event handler"
/>
```

You can assign the control a dataProvider that copies dynamic or
static values to the list. You can control the entry of values through
the editable parameter. The number of entries in the list can be limited by the rowCount attribute; the current value is held in the
selectedItem attribute. A number of events are also available to the
ComboBox control for methods of event control, such as triggering of
events when you open the list or when you change the current value.

In Listing 4.18, a `ComboBox` control contains a series of values and the current value is copied to a label (see Figure 4.16).

```
<mx:Label x="35" y="45" id="label1"
    text="{cb.selectedItem}"/>
<mx:ComboBox x="150" y="45" id="cb">
    <mx:Array>
        <mx:String>Visa</mx:String>
        <mx:String>MasterCard</mx:String>
        <mx:String>American Express</mx:String>
    </mx:Array>
</mx:ComboBox>
```

Listing 4.18 Selecting Values with a ComboBox Component

Figure 4.16 Sample Output for the ComboBox Component

4.4.10 Image

Importing graphics

The `Image` control can be used to import graphics or Flash animations into a Flex application. The formats supported are JPEG, SVG, PNG, GIF, and SWF; the transparency of the GIF and PNG format is also supported here.

The `<mx:Image>` tag is formed as follows:

```
<mx:Image
    maintainAspectRatio="true|false"
    source="No default"
/>
```

The `maintainAspectRatio` attribute maintains the page measures. You can specify the source of the graphic to be added via the `source` parameter. We distinguish between two variants here.

▶ Through the `@Embed` addition, the graphic is compiled directly into the SWF file of the Flex application. The advantage of this is that the graphic is loaded very quickly, but the disadvantage is that the SWF file can become very large, depending on the graphic.

▸ In the second variant, a direct URL is copied to the `source` parameter. This can result in a longer load operation, depending on the size of the graphics file. However, the size of the Flex application is not changed by including the graphic.

In Listing 4.19, a graphic is compiled directly into the Flex application and displayed (see Figure 4.17).

```
<mx:Image id="image" source="@Embed('sap.gif')"/>
```
Listing 4.19 Adding a Graphics File with an Image Component

Figure 4.17 Sample Output for the Image Component

4.4.11   DateChooser and DateField

The `DateChooser` control shows the year, the month and the corresponding days in a calendar component. The weeks are each shown here in successive lines. You can navigate through the individual months using the Forward and Back button. The user can select individual, successive, or any number of date specifications, and can also deactivate individual date fields.

Calendar component

The call is performed using the `<mx:DateChooser>` tag:

```
<mx:DateChooser
    dayNames="["S", "M", "T", "W", "T", "F", "S"]"
    disabledDays="No default."
    disabledRanges="No default."
    displayedMonth="Current month."
    displayedYear="Current year."
    firstDayOfWeek="0"
    headerColors="[0xE6EEEE,0xFFFFFF]"
    headerStyleDeclaration="No default."
    monthNames="["January", "February", "March",
                "April", "May", "June", "July",
                "August", "September", "October",
                "November", "December"]"
    rollOverColor="0xE3FFD6"
    selectableRange="No default."
    selectedDate="No default."
    selectionColor="0xCDFFC1"
```

```
    showToday="true|false"
    todayColor=""
    todayStyleDeclaration="No default."
    weekdayStyleDeclaration="No default."
    change="event handler"
    scroll="event handler"
/>
```

Via the disabled* parameter, you can deactivate the date specifications. The display of the days is changed with the dayNames parameter. The showToday parameter pre-selects the current date.

Selecting the date

The DateField control is an interaction between a TextField control and a DateChooser, which is displayed by clicking on a calendar icon. When you select a date, it is shown in the TextField of the Date-Field control depending on the formatting.

The DateField control is called as follows:

```
<mx:DateField
    dayNames="["S", "M", "T", "W", "T", "F", "S"]"
    disabledDays="No default."
    disabledRanges="No default."
    displayedMonth="Month number of the current date."
    displayedYear="Current year."
    firstDayOfWeek="0"
    monthNames="["January", "February", "March", April",
                 "May", "June", "July", "August",
                 "September", "October", "November",
                 "December"]"
    headerColors="[0xE6EEEE,0xFFFFFF]"
    headerStyleDeclaration="No default."
    rollOverColor="0xCDFFC1"
    selectableRange="No default."
    selectedDate="No default."
    selectionColor="0xCDFFC1"
    showToday="true|false"
    todayColor=""
    todayStyleDeclaration="No default."
    weekdayStyleDeclaration="No default."
    change="event handler"
    close="event handler"
    open="event handler"
    scroll="event handler"
/>
```

A format can be copied to the `DateFormatter` class for the date display. This is also described in more detail in Chapter 6 when we discuss ActionScript.

The following Listing 4.20 shows a `DateField`. When you click on the calendar icon, the calendar opens and another date can be selected, based on the current date shown in the field (see Figure 4.18). The date is given in the standard format `MM/DD/YYYY`.

```
<mx:DateField id="date1" width="100"/>
```
Listing 4.20 DateField Component with Date Display

Figure 4.18 Sample Output for the DateField Component

4.4.12 DataGrid

The `DataGrid` control allows you to format data in the form of tables. The system supports the adjustment of the column width, the rendering of non-text data, drag-and-drop, and multiple data selections.

Table-like data formatting

The call for the `<mx:DataGrid>` tag contains the following options:

```
<mx:DataGrid
   cellEditor="No default."
   cellRenderer="No default."
   columns="No default."
   columnName="No default."
   dataProvider="No default."
   editable="false|true"
   focusedCell="No default."
   headerColors="[0xE6EEEE, 0xFFFFFF]"
   headerHeight="20"
   headerStyle="No default."
   hGridLineColor="#666666"
   hGridLines="false|true"
```

```
        resizableColumns="true|false"
        rollOverColor="#0xE3FFD6"
        selectable="true|false"
        selectionColor="#0xCDFFC1"
        showHeaders="true|false"
        sortableColumns="true|false"
        vGridLineColor="#666666"
        vGridLines="false|true"
        cellEdit="event handler"
        cellFocusIn="event handler"
        cellFocusOut="event handler"
        cellPress="event handler"
        columnStretch="event handler"
        headerRelease="event handler"
/>
```

With `columnName`, you can specify several column headers. As with the `List` control, with `DataGrid` you can also copy a `dataProvider`. Furthermore, many different event handlers are offered; e. g., to trigger an event when you are editing a cell using `cellEdit`.

Column headers   Listing 4.21 shows a three-column `DataGrid` control. A field of data objects is copied to the `DataGrid` here. The objects each consist of three data attributes, which are shown as column headers. The respective data that is assigned is displayed in the rows. Figure 4.19 shows the output of this sample.

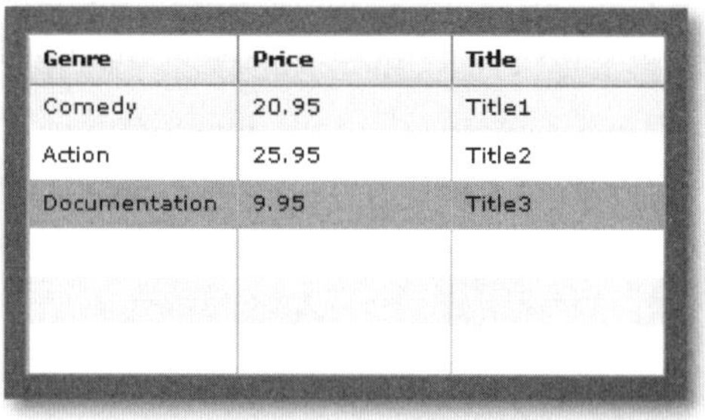

Genre	Price	Title
Comedy	20.95	Title1
Action	25.95	Title2
Documentation	9.95	Title3

Figure 4.19 Sample Output for the DataGrid Component

```
<mx:DataGrid x="103" y="429">
    <mx:Array>
        <mx:Object Title="Title1" Price="20.95"
                   Genre="Comedy"/>
        <mx:Object Title="Title2" Price="25.95"
                   Genre="Action"/>
```

```
      <mx:Object Title="Title3" Price="9.95"
                 Genre="Documentation"/>
   </mx:Array>
</mx:DataGrid>
```

Listing 4.21 Displaying a Table Using a DataGrid Component

ActionScript is used to implement the application logic in Flex applications. This chapter introduces you to the basic principles involved in doing that. Note, however, that the chapter is not intended to be a reference work for Action-Script. It only describes the most important functions and language elements that you will need, in particular in the SAP environment.

5   ActionScript

While the previous chapter described the use of MXML in great detail, we will now focus on ActionScript. ActionScript is the programming language for Flex applications and was provided for the first time with Flash Version 4.0 in 1999. In contrast to the markup language MXML, ActionScript enables the implementation of the application logic on both the client and the server. Combined with MXML, ActionScript also allows you to develop complex and at the same time intuitively operable user interfaces.

Difference from MXML

ActionScript is based on ECMA standards (*http://www.ecma-international.org*) and is currently available in Version 3.0. Compared to ActionScript 2.0, the most important new features are the enhanced object orientation and the improved performance.

Especially in the SAP environment, it is often necessary to present complex aspects as simply as possible without forgoing the corresponding functionality. However, in traditional Web applications (HTML/Java) the implementation already fails when it comes to presenting those aspects. Moreover, costs used to play an important role in the past and it often happened that they finally impeded the implementation.

In addition to providing better functionality, one of the main goals of ActionScript and hence the application logic based on it is to reduce the costs that accrue during and after the development stage. Those of you who already have been involved in Web-development projects in the SAP environment will probably know that functions

Objective: Cost reduction

such as sorting, filtering, or the editing of tables are very important, but that the task of implementing such functions with traditional methods in the user interface is complex.

Because of the use of ActionScript, Flex enables both the presentation via MXML files and the implementation of logic at the same time. This logic is needed, for instance, if you want to create complex list outputs that are similar to ALV grids in the SAP system, or if you want to control screen sequences or carry out arithmetical operations.

Thus the basic principles of ActionScript are the focus of this chapter. These basics help you to better understand the structure of the following examples as well as the sample application in Chapter 7. Whenever you need more detailed information on ActionScript, you should refer to the Adobe documentation. You can access the documentation in Adobe Flex Builder under **Help**. It describes the individual components of ActionScript in a clearly structured and very detailed way.

5.1 Syntax

Close relationship to Java

The ActionScript syntax can basically be compared to Java, even though there are many differences. If you already have experience with Java, you won't have a problem using ActionScript. On the other hand, if you don't have any Java experience, it won't take you much longer to become familiar with ActionScript than it would if you were Java-literate.

ActionScript is not a "difficult" programming language, as the syntax is easily readable and transparent. It is rather the complexity of the application that creates problems for the developer. The development environment of Adobe Flex Builder supports you in many respects, as it contains numerous utilities such as an automatic code supplementation function. These utilities provide you with a degree of programming comfort.

5.1.1 Comments

Comments help you to make code readable

Clearly, you should insert comments into your own source code or external code. Nevertheless it is surprising to see how carelessly many developers handle the use of comments in practice. However, comprehensible comments within programming code also prove the quality of the developer: It doesn't help to develop a smart program if it is missing comments that would have enabled third parties to interpret the program adequately.

This is particularly important with regard to applications that collaborate across different platforms. Not only do we want to comment on the source code in our sample applications but also on the communication interfaces between the SAP system and the Flex framework. This way, we can enable third parties to understand the source code and the overall program sequence. If you combine different development techniques (ABAP Objects, Business Server Pages, Adobe Flex) into a functioning entity, you must also provide comments that clearly enable any person to see how those components work together.

To a large extent, the syntax of comments is based on the following familiar HTML specifications.

Specifications

▶ **Single-line comments**

```
// This comment stretches across one line
/* This one also reaches to the end of the line */
Location = "Chicago"; // comment at end of the line
```

▶ **Multiline comments**

```
/* Beginning of a multiline comment
-- Change of program structure, AL 20051206 --
Multiline comments are no problem at all.
However, you should only use them if they
make sense.
-- End of program structure, AL 20051206 --
*/
```

The comments in ActionScript should be based on the development guidelines already being used. If these development guidelines are insufficient or only geared towards ABAP, you should complement them with the new options provided by ActionScript. This includes the interfaces of Flex and SAP applications as well as instructions on how to insert comments in them. This way you can facilitate the creation of cross-application documentation and the interdisciplinary collaboration between ABAP and Flex developers, if that work is not done by the same person.

Interdisciplinary development

Some functions of the ABAP Workbench such as versioning, the modification wizard, and so on, are either not available in the Flex development environment or can only be used by integrating additional software products. For this reason, it is even more important to include harmonized comments in the code.

Program header It often happens that a common program header is used in those cases. This program header contains the description of the code as well as information on the author, the creation date, or a project ID. Listing 5.1 shows an example of a program header.

```
/* projekt key:     E3.1.1
   product line:    HIVE
   product module: DDIC Dynamics
   version:         1.12
- - - - - - - - - - - - - - - - - - - - - - - - - - - - - - - - - - - - - -
   description: distribute data in HIVE engine
   author:      D. Knapp, F. Sonnenberg
   email:       dk@ixult.de, fs@ixult.de
   created:     04/22/2006
- - - - - - - - - - - - - - - - - - - - - - - - - - - - - - - - - - - - - -
   last changed
   by:                at:              reason:
   FSONNENBERG        04/25/2006       add SQL_EXCEPTION
   DKNAPP             04/29/2006       added fieldname
   ALORENZ            04/29/2006       added population
*/
```

Listing 5.1 Example of a Program Header

5.1.2 Case Sensitivity

ActionScript is case sensitive In contrast to ABAP, ActionScript is case sensitive; that is, it makes a difference whether you use uppercase or lowercase letters. Because ActionScript was developed on the basis of the ECMA-262 standard, you must make sure that you use uppercase and lowercase letters consistently.

Listing 5.2 shows how you can declare variables. Note, however, that variables should always begin similarly, either with an upper case or a lower case letter.

```
var supplier = "Miller";
var order    = "1234567";
var order    = "00004711";
```
Listing 5.2 Case-Sensitive Declaration of Variables

5.1.3 Blanks

In ActionScript, blanks, tabulators, and line separators are treated in the same way as in ABAP. These characters are more or less ignored as long as they don't separate the key words and identifiers contained in the code.

Blanks, tabulators, and line separators are particularly useful if you want to make the code optically more readable. Please note that the appearance of code tells you a lot about the quality, experience, and knowledge of the programmer. You should therefore keep the structure of the code as straightforward as possible in order to facilitate editing the code.

Designing clear code

Listing 5.3 shows how you can design a clear assignment of values to variables.

```
var supplier = "Miller";
var customer = "0000000001";
var matno    = "000000000000000001";
```
Listing 5.3 Clear Code Structure Because of the Use of Blank Characters

5.1.4 Dot Syntax

The use of dot syntax in ActionScript is implemented in more or less the same way as you know it from other object-oriented programming languages. The dot syntax is a good way to separate objects from properties or methods. In ABAP, you can compare this to the character combinations => and -> when calling methods, or to the minus sign (-) when accessing properties and attributes.

Dot syntax as a separator for properties and methods of objects

▶ **Dot syntax for properties**
  Nearly all objects in Flex contain specific properties that can be changed. To be able to access the properties they must be addressed using the dot syntax. The general syntax is structured as follows:

```
[object].[attribute] = value;
```

The following sample coding shows you how to access the property of a TextInput control.

```
<mx:TextInput x="10" y="10" id="first name"/>
var first name = firstname.text;
```

In this way you can access all the properties of an object which can be changed in order to adjust the properties to the respective requirements. The only thing you must make sure of in this context is that the data types are compatible.

▶ **Dot syntax for methods**
As is the case with the properties, you can access and execute methods using a dot syntax. However, you also can transfer specific arguments to a method. The general syntax is structured as follows:

```
[object].[method](arguments);
```

In the following example, we call the calculateTax() method of the invoice object:

```
invoice.calculateTax(amount.text);
```

To be able to carry out the calculation, the method must also be assigned the amount. This amount is contained in a TextInput field whose properties you can also access via a dot syntax. Not only can you transfer individual values but also entire objects. The following chapters will describe this aspect in more detail.

5.1.5 Curly Brackets

Curly braces
In ActionScript you use curly brackets for more than grouping blocks.

▶ **Block grouping**
As in other programming languages, you can use curly-bracket punctuation marks to form blocks. This facilitates structuring the source code so that it becomes more readable:

```
onClick() {
firstname.text = "";
}
```

▶ **Generating objects**
Curly brackets also enable you to generate objects. Thus you can also use the operator instead of the new Object() statement:

```
// Generate object
customer = { name: "Armin Lorenz", city: "Rosenheim" };
customerName = customer["name"];
```

▶ **Generating arrays**

In addition, you can use curly brackets for a facilitated creation of arrays. The commonly used `new Array()` statement can thus be replaced by curly brackets:

```
// Generate array
customerList = { customer1 : "Armin Lorenz",
                 customer2 : "Daniel Knapp" };
customerOne = customerList["customer1"];
```

5.1.6 Semicolons

As in many other programming languages, the semicolon (;) terminates a statement in ActionScript similar to the period (.) in ABAP. ActionScript also allows you to terminate a statement with a line break, but for better readability and also in order to simplify the source code, you should make sure that each statement terminates with a semicolon.

Semicolons conclude a statement in ActionScript

There are, however, other exceptions to that. Statement blocks and control structures must not end with a semicolon. The inclusion of additional ActionScript files represents a special case. This technique enables you to include and use external ActionScript files in your own program. Although the `#include` can be interpreted as a statement, you must not terminate it with a semicolon.

Listing 5.4 shows the correct use of an `#include` statement.

```
// Correct statement
#include "home.as"
name = "Thomas";
// Incorrect statement
#inlcude "home.as";
```

Listing 5.4 The #include Statement as a Special Case

5.1.7 Parentheses

First of all, parentheses can be interpreted as in mathematics; that is, you can use them to define processing sequences (see Listing 5.5).

Parentheses determine the processing sequence

```
firstValue = 10 * 2 + 3;
secondValue = 10 * (2 + 3);
```
Listing 5.5 Using Parentheses for Processing Sequences

When you call a function, the required transfer parameters are transferred in parentheses. This is similar to the `PERFORM` statement in ABAP. Listing 5.6 shows how parentheses are used in method calls in ActionScript and how the parentheses can be transferred within the parameters.

```
invoice.calculateTax(amount.text);
```
Listing 5.6 Using Parentheses for Method Calls

5.1.8 Keywords

Keywords must not be used as identifiers

Like ABAP, ActionScript contains a multitude of keywords. These keywords are reserved words that must not be used as identifiers in ActionScript. Table 5.1 contains a list of keywords that should not be used as declaration names.

as	break	case	catch	class
const	continue	default	delete	co
else	extends	false	finally	for
function	if	implements	import	in
instanceof	interface	internal	is	native
new	null	package	private	protected
public	return	super	switch	this
throw	to	true	try	typeof
use	var	void	while	with

Table 5.1 Keywords in ActionScript

5.1.9 Constants

Constants do not differ from regular variables

Using constants is a good way to make applications and parts of programs configurable. This way you can reduce considerably the required maintenance and customizing work. If you define constants always in the same location, you can easily identify them during a development project and store them centrally in a profile file.

There are two different types of constants: ActionScript already contains constants that don't need to be defined any further. An example of this is the number pi that can be retrieved via the `Math` library:

```
Number = Math.PI;
```

In addition, you can also create custom constants. Note that in ActionScript, the structure of constants differs little from the assignment of a variable.

Listing 5.7 shows that you can only determine from the context whether you are dealing with a constant or a variable assignment. The constant "Author" is assigned the value "Daniel Knapp."

```
Author = "Daniel Knapp";
```

Listing 5.7 Sample Value Assignment for a Constant

5.2   Data Types

In ActionScript, you must distinguish data types in the same way as you would do in other programming languages. There are several basic data types that differ in their behavior and properties. The basic data types are assigned their values directly. The basic data types include the following types, most of which should be familiar from the ABAP environment:

ActionScript uses data types that don't exist in the SAP system

- ▶ String
- ▶ Number
- ▶ Boolean
- ▶ Null
- ▶ Undefined
- ▶ Array
- ▶ MovieClip
- ▶ Functions

Those of you who have been using ABAP will be able to use the first data types of the preceding list without any problem, even though ABAP does not distinguish between "null" and "undefined." The basic data type "MovieClip", however, is completely new to SAP developers.

Because Flex is closely related to Flash, and ActionScript is also used for programming Flash, ActionScript contains many command sets that are required to process and control movie clips. Because you develop business applications and won't have much to do with this basic data type, we will focus on the data types relevant to you. Nevertheless, if you are interested in those data types, we would like to refer you to the wide range of information available on the Internet and in the documentation section of Adobe Flex Builder (**Help • Welcome**).

5.2.1　String

Strings can contain almost any value

A string can consist of letters, numbers, and special characters. In contrast to ABAP, where you can limit the length of strings (for example CHAR10), ActionScript does not contain this restriction option. Apart from that, the ABAP data type String can be compared to the basic data type of the same name in ActionScript.

Listing 5.8 shows that the String data type is processed with quotation marks.

```
customerFirstname = "Armin":
customerLastname = 'Lorenz';
```
Listing 5.8 Strings with Different Quotation Marks

Specialty about quotation marks

You may have noticed that ActionScript uses different types of quotation marks. This is a special feature of this programming language. You cannot combine the different types of quotation marks with each other, and opening and closing quotation marks must be identical.

Experienced ABAP developers will probably prefer single quotation marks (inverted commas) in order to keep the different syntaxes of ABAP and ActionScript as similar as possible and to avoid confusion. ABAP uses double quotation marks for line-restricted commenting.

Defining a line break

The example in Listing 5.9 illustrates how you can define a line break within a string: If the opening and closing quotation marks are not located within the same line, the interpreter will generate an error message. At this point you must use the escape sequence \n.

```
customerPhrase = 'Welcome!\nWe hope...';
```
Listing 5.9 Forcing a Line Break Within a String

If you want to use the quotation mark a second time within the same string, you must place a backslash (\) in front of the duplicate instances (see Listing 5.10).

```
customerPhrase = 'You can\'t beat the feeling';
```
Listing 5.10 Prefixing a Backslash to Insert Quotation Marks

An easier way here is to replace the quotation mark; that is, if you want to use a single quotation mark within the string, you can place the double quotation marks at the beginning and end of the string. This is not always possible. You cannot always know upfront whether the quotation mark you want to use is already being used in the text, especially when you merge different strings dynamically. Therefore, you should always analyze the text and insert backslash characters wherever that's necessary.

String Processing

If you use strings and CHAR fields in ABAP, the most frequently used processing method is the CONCATENATE command. ActionScript also allows numerous methods to be used for the basic data type. Listing 5.11 shows how you can concatenate two strings using a blank-space character.

There are numerous string processing methods available

```
// Concatenate strings
customerFirstname = 'Armin';
customerLastname = 'Lorenz';
customerName = customerFirstname + , , +
                customerLastname;
```
Listing 5.11 Concatenating Strings and Blank Spaces

If you want to stay closer to the ABAP standard when using Action-Script, you can use the concat() method whose name you should be familiar with (see Listing 5.12).

95

```
// Concatenate strings
customerTitel = 'Mr. ';
customerFirstname = 'Armin';
customerLastname = 'Lorenz';
customerCompleteName =
  customerTitel.concat(customerFirstname,
                          customerLastname);
```

Listing 5.12 Concatenating Strings Using concat()

Case sensitivity Please note that strings are case sensitive. In ActionScript, you cannot automatically convert a mixture of uppercase and lowercase letters into capitals. In the SAP Dictionary, this is controlled via the domain field.

Table 5.2 provides an overview of other string-processing methods.

Method	Description
String.concat	Concatenates two strings: `str.concat(string1, string2)`
String.charAt	Returns a character in a specific position: `str.charAt(i)`
String.charCodeAt	Returns the number of the character in the specified position as a 16-bit integer: `str.charCodeAt(i)`

String.indexOf	Determines a substring within a string element:
	`customerName.lastIndexOf(substring`
	`  [startindex]);`

String.lastIndexOf	Determines the last substring within a string element:
	`customerName.lastIndexOf(substring`
	`  [startindex]);`

String.slice	Extracts a substring: `customerName.slice(start, [end]);`
String.split	Uses a separator to divide the string into substrings: `customerName.split(separator, [limit]);`
String.substr	Returns a part of the string: `customerName.substring(from,to);`
String.substring	Returns a part of the string: `customerName.substring(from,to);`

Table 5.2 String Methods

Method	Description
String.toLowerCase	Implements the string in lower case letters: customerName.toLowerCase();
String.toUpperCase	Implements the string in upper case letters: customerName.toLowerCase();
String.length	Returns the length of a string: customerName.length();

Table 5.2 String Methods (cont.)

If you need to process large quantities of data from SAP systems in other applications, you will sooner or later run into the problem of leading zeros that are contained in customer, order, or purchase-order numbers. You need to decide on which side of the development you want to process the leading zeros. Let's suppose you want to send customer numbers from the SAP system into a Flex application and write them back again. There are two options: Either you remove the leading zeros and complement missing ones on the side of the SAP system, or you do that in the Flex application.

Leading zeros

Unfortunately, there is no silver bullet. However, it makes more sense to process the leading zeros on the SAP side because the data must be validated in any case (for authorization, consistency, unit, and so on) before you can further process it in the SAP system.

Escape Sequences

Escape sequences are needed whenever you use characters within strings which carry out an operation or mark the end of the string. There are numerous examples of using escape sequences; Table 5.3 contains a list of the most frequently used ones.

Escape sequences enable you to map special characters

Escape sequence	Character
\n	Line feed
\r	Carriage return
\b	Backspace
\t	Tabulator
\"	Double quotation mark

Table 5.3 Escape Sequences

Escape sequence	Character
\'	Single quotation mark
\\	Backslash

Table 5.3 Escape Sequences (cont.)

If you already use Unicode in your SAP system and also want to use Unicode to process strings in Flex applications, you should take Table 5.4 into account.

Escape sequence	Character
\000 – \377	Octal byte value
\x00 – \xFF	Hexadecimal byte value
\u0000 – \uFFFF	16-bit Unicode character (hexadecimal notation)

Table 5.4 Escape Sequences in Unicode

If you use Unicode consistently, you should note that you can display Unicode in Flash Player only as of Version 6.x. At the time this book was written, Flash Player Version 9 was available. This version is used for all examples provided in this book.

5.2.2 Numbers

Numbers can be calculated or stored as constants in the Math class

This basic data type comprises integers and floating-point numbers. A special characteristic of ActionScript is that floating-point numbers can be stored in the same way as integers. Listing 5.13 shows how you can assign variables to numbers. To do that, you do not need to use inverted commas, as is the case in ABAP.

```
customerClassification = 20;
customerValue          = 2000.50;
```

Listing 5.13 Assigning Numbers

As in ABAP, the point is used to separate decimal places. However, you don't need to use inverted commas because ActionScript uses the semicolon instead of a period to terminate a command. In addition, you can assign the number values to a variable in hexadecimal and scientific notation.

The `Math` object we already mentioned earlier is particularly interesting, as it enables you to carry out difficult and complex mathematical calculations. Table 5.5 provides an overview of the most important methods for the `Math` object.

Complex
mathematical
calculations

Method	Description
Math.abs	Calculates the absolute value
Math.acos	Calculates the arccosine
Math.asin	Calculates the arcsine
Math.atan	Calculates the arctangent
Math.atan2	Calculates the angle between the x axis and a specific point
Math.ceil	Rounds a number up to the next integer
Math.cos	Calculates the cosine
Math.exp	Calculates the exponential value
Math.floor	Rounds a number down to the next integer
Math.log	Calculates the logarithm
Math.max	Returns the bigger of two integers
Math.min	Returns the smaller of two integers
Math.pow	Calculates x to the power of y
Math.random	Returns a random number between 0 and 1
Math.round	Rounds to the next integer
Math.sin	Calculates the sine
Math.sqrt	Calculates the square root
Math.tan	Calculates the tangent

Table 5.5 Methods of the Math Object

In addition, the `Math` object contains numerous properties, as shown in Table 5.6.

Property	Description
Math.E	Eulerian constant
Math.LN2	Logarithm of 2

Table 5.6 Properties of the Math Object

Property	Description
`Math.LOG2E`	Logarithm of e to the basis 2
`Math.LN10`	Logarithm of 10
`Math.LOG10E`	Logarithm of e to the basis 10
`Math.PI`	Circumference by diameter
`Math.SQRT1_2`	Reciprocal value of the square root of 1/2
`Math.SQRT2`	Square root of 2

Table 5.6 Properties of the Math Object (cont.)

Mathematical errors

If an error occurs during a mathematical function, for example in a division by zero, ActionScript does not return a runtime error, as is the case in ABAP. Instead, you can gather from the result that this "exception" has occurred.

The following example in Listing 5.14 could be divided by 0 without any prior check if the `orderQuantity` variable contains the value 0.

```
unitprice = orderNetval / orderQuantity;
```
Listing 5.14 Sample Division Operation in ActionScript

If the value of the `orderQuantity` variable was 0, ABAP would return a runtime error unless you caught that error upfront. However, in ActionScript the program continues, and even the `unitprice` variable contains a value: `NaN` ("Not a number"). If you compared `NaN` with another number value, you would always determine that the values are not equal even if you compared the value with itself.

Division by 0

To make sure that the value of a calculation is not `NaN`, you must use the function `isNaN()` instead of carrying out a comparison. Listing 5.15 shows how you can catch a division by 0.

```
if (isNaN(orderNetwr/orderQuantity)) {
Unitprice = 0;
}
else {
unitprice = orderNetval / orderQuantity;
}
```
Listing 5.15 Example of Using the isNaN() Function

Sometimes it is necessary to output numbers as strings, especially if you want to process numbers in text. For those cases, the `Number` object provides two useful methods (see Table 5.7).

Property	Description
`Number.toString`	Returns the `Number` object as a string
`Number.valueOf`	Returns the basic value of a `Number` object

Table 5.7 Number Object

5.2.3 Boolean

The `Boolean` data type can have the values `true` or `false` in ActionScript. Alternatively, you can also use the values 1 (true) and 0 (false), as in other programming languages. ActionScript will interpret these entries correctly. Thus, the two listing lines that follow have the same effect:

True, false

```
customerDeleted = true;
customerDeleted = 1;
```

5.2.4 Objects

Objects primarily consist of attributes and methods. If you have ABAP Objects programming experience, you will be familiar with this aspect. However, you only need a little basic knowledge of object-oriented programming for the examples in this book.

Instantiated objects are the most frequently used type of variables in applications

▶ **Attributes**

Objects generally contain various different attributes. The attributes can be filled initially using a constructor, or they can adapt themselves at runtime. The following two lines show how you can assign values to class attributes.

```
customer.firstname = 'Armin';
customer.lastname  = 'Lorenz';
```

▶ **Methods**

In addition to attributes, the methods of classes play a major role. The following sections illustrate how clearly structured you can program the functionality of an application by using object-oriented programming.

To call methods of objects, you must use the following syntax:

```
customer.create();
customer.delete();
customer.select();
```

The following sections describe the use of objects in more detail, particularly the use of associative arrays (see Section 5.7.2).

5.2.5 Null and Undefined

"Null" is not the same as "undefined"

ActionScript contains two basic data types of which you could think that they mean the same. However, null and undefined are two different things.

In ABAP, this difference exists only if you consider both field symbols and variables at the same time. Field symbols are defined at the beginning of a program, function module, or method in ABAP, and must then be assigned using the ASSIGN command. If they are not assigned and an access to the field symbols occurs, ABAP returns a runtime error.

▶ **Undefined**

The undefined data type behaves exactly like the assignment of a field symbol: If a non-existing variable or object property is accessed, the return value is undefined. If this return parameter is then transferred to a string variable, "undefined" will be displayed in the text.

▶ **Null**

In contrast to undefined, the accessed variable does actually exist in the ActionScript code, but it hasn't been assigned a value yet; technically speaking, null is an object. If a variable has the value null, it is very likely that it doesn't contain any valid array, object, number, string, or any other type of content.

The null value can occur in the following scenarios:

▷ An expected parameter is missing

▷ A variable does not contain any value

▷ A variable has not yet been assigned any value

▷ A function has not returned any value

▷ A variable has been assigned this value

5.3   Variables

In ActionScript, variables work much as they do in ABAP. There are, however, some differences regarding the variable names, assignments, and existing data types, which we'll describe in the following sections.

The most commonly used way of processing values dynamically

In ABAP, variables are predominantly defined using a data type that exists in the ABAP Dictionary. This has the advantage that an adjustment of the data type automatically involves the adjustment of the variable in all programs that reference this data type.

Flex does not provide this convenient method of defining data types in a data dictionary and reusing these data types. Thus in ActionScript, variables can be of the following types: string, number, Boolean, object, or MovieClip. The MovieClip type is only briefly treated in this book, as it plays only a minor role in SAP application development.

5.3.1   Naming Variables

Typically, the variable names in ActionScript differ considerably from those used in ABAP. That's partly because of the different "language styles" of ABAP and ActionScript, and partly because ActionScript contains fewer technical restrictions than ABAP. The following list provides an overview of the criteria to be considered when assigning names to variables.

Variable names are subject to restrictions in ActionScript

- ▸ The names are not case sensitive.
- ▸ Names must not begin with numbers.
- ▸ Names must begin with a letter or the $ character.
- ▸ There is no length restriction for names.
- ▸ Names must not contain blank spaces.
- ▸ Names must be single-line.
- ▸ Names must not contain any reserved words.

Listing 5.16 shows types of names you can use for variables.

```
customerFirstname = 'Armin';
$profit           = 4000;
```

103

```
_purchaseOrder     = '4500000001';
tab_count          = 1000;
```
Listing 5.16 Sample Declaration Names

After all it is completely up to you what kind of names you want to assign to your variables. If a company has already established some guidelines for developments, these guidelines should also include elements for Flex applications now. Also, there's no issue that argues against naming the variables in ActionScript in the same way as they already exist in the SAP environment. This facilitates troubleshooting because you use the same variable names, dictionary terms, or table names.

Memory area   In ActionScript, variables are stored in the memory. In contrast to other programming languages, the programmer does not need to bother about the memory area, as this task is completely carried out by the interpreter.

5.3.2   Declaring Variables

In order to notify the interpreter about the fact that a variable is being declared, you must use the var command in ActionScript. Similar to the DATA statement in ABAP, the required portion of the memory is reserved and made accessible via the name. In Listing 5.17, we declare three variables of the String type.

```
var customer:String;          // Customer
var purchaseOrder:String;     // Purchase order
var incomingInvoice:String;   // Incoming invoice
```
Listing 5.17 Declaration of String Variables

If you want to declare several variables at the same time, you must use the comma notation in ActionScript, as shown in Listing 5.18.

```
var customer, purchaseOrder, incomingInvoice;
```
Listing 5.18 Simultaneous Declaration of Several Variables

5.3.3 Dynamic Variable Names

In real life, applications are often very complex. Sometimes you may need to access variables dynamically. The following example illustrates the dynamic access to variables (see Listing 5.19). First a general variable is assigned the declaration name of another variable (second line). Then you can use the keyword `this` in order to change the value of the `NAMEV` variable without directly accessing it.

Dynamic variable names help to carry out complex operations

```
var NAMEV:String;
var sapCustomerFirstname    = 'NAMEV';
this[sapCustomerFirstname] = 'Armin';
```

Listing 5.19 Using Dynamic Variable Names

5.3.4 Types of Variables

ActionScript primarily distinguishes between global and local variables. This facilitates program development considerably. The more comprehensive the written code, the more often you access the different types of variables.

ActionScript supports both local and global variables

▶ **Local variables**

Local variables are defined in a statement block and lose their validity when the block ends. The advantage of this is that you can declare variables with the same names in each statement block. If you differentiate the naming of variables by the variable type, this reduces the level of complexity of the variable declaration within the entire source code.

Limited validity

The following code example declares a local variable that applies only to the area included in the curly brackets.

```
function createCustomer() {
  var lv_customerFirstname:String = 'Armin';
}
```

You can basically say that local variables must always be defined in a `function` statement block. Subordinate statement blocks do not affect the access to the local variables in any way. The following code example shows that all variables within the function are defined locally and that they can be accessed from within the function. Thus, local variables always belong to a function.

```
function blockTest (testArray:Array) {
  var numPos:int = testArray.length;
```

```
    if (numPos > 0) {
        var elemStr:String = "Element #";
        for (var i:int = 0; i < numPos; i++) {
            var valueStr:String = i + ": " + testArray[i];
            trace (elemStr + valueStr);
        }
        trace (elemStr, valueStr, i);// still valid
    }
    trace (elemStr, valueStr, i);
}

blockTest(["Earth", "Moon", "Sun"]);
```

▶ **Global Variables**

The advantage of global variables is that they don't lose their validity. This means that you can use and edit global variables in any statement block. To avoid confusion, you should make sure during declaration that the name of a variable provides information on its type.

In the following example, we'll define a global variable `global-Custno` of the `String` type.

```
var globalCustno:String;
function createCustomer() {
    ...
}
```

If a global and a local variable are declared using the same identifier, the variable that is declared last will be accessed. Within a function, this means that the local variable is accessed. Outside of the function it is the global variable that's accessed. The following example illustrates this:

```
var str1:String = "Global";
function scopeTest () {
    var str1:String = "Local";
    trace (str1); // Output: Local
}
scopeTest();
trace (str1); // Output: Global
```

The `str1` variable that has been declared outside of the function contains the value `Global`, even outside of the function. Within the function, a variable has been declared with the same name. This means that within the function, the globally defined variable is overridden with the locally defined one so that the variable value is `Local` within the function. The value outside of the function does not change.

When you define variables in ActionScript, you don't need to place them at the beginning. You can even assign values to a variable prior to defining it. The compiler does the work here.

In the compilation process, all variables are placed at the beginning of a function before the source code is compiled. This procedure is referred to as *hoisting*. Make sure you do not confuse it with *hosting*. Listing 5.20 illustrates the hoisting effect. The variable `num` is assigned the value 5 before it is declared.

Hoisting

```
num = 5;
trace(num); // Output: 5
var num:Number = 10;
trace(num); // Output: 10
```
Listing 5.20 Hoisting Effect in ActionScript

However, as a developer you should take into account that the readability of a program decreases substantially if the variable declarations are not always located at the beginning of a statement.

5.3.5 Initial Values of Variables

If you define different types of variables and use them in the program later on, you will often have to check whether the variables have been assigned any values or if they still have their initial values. Table 5.8 shows the initial values of variables after their declaration.

Different
initial values

Data type	Initial value
Boolean	False
Int	0
Number	NaN
Object	Null
String	null
uint	0

Table 5.8 Initial Values of Declared Variables

Data type	Initial value
Not declared	Undefined
All other classes	null

Table 5.8 Initial Values of Declared Variables (cont.)

5.3.6 Converting Data Types

ActionScript uses numerous conversion routines

ActionScript provides several types of data conversion. You must distinguish between the automatic, or implicit, conversion and the deliberate, or explicit, conversion.

▶ **Implicit conversion**

In many scenarios, values are automatically converted into target variables. These scenarios include the following:

▷ Value assignments

▷ Transfer of function attributes

▷ Processing of return values (e. g., functions)

▷ as expressions

▷ Expressions containing operators (e. g., "+")

The following code example shows the implicit conversion of simple data types:

```
class A {}
class B extends A {}

var objA:A = new A();
var objB:B = new B();
var arr:Array = new Array();

objA = objB; // successful
objB = arr; // erroneous
```

▶ **Explicit conversion**

In order to increase the data quality and stability of the application, you often need to carry out both the implicit and explicit data conversion. The following example shows how values are transferred from a string variable to an integer variable. In this case, however, the transfer results in a runtime error:

```
var quantityField:String = "3";
var quantity:int = quantityField; // Runtime error
```

Instead you should use the following statement:

```
var quantityField:String = "3";
var quantity:int = int(quantityField);
```

ActionScript allows you to convert any data type into an int, uint, or Number value. You will have to decide whether this is appropriate in each case. What is important here is that a failure does not abort the program, as the target variable then contains the initial value.

Casting int, uint, Number

Table 5.9 lists the values that are returned in case of an erroneous assignment. If Boolean type variables are transferred to a Number data type, true turns into 1 and false into 0.

Data Type	Result for Erroneous Assignment
int	0
uint	0
Number	NaN

Table 5.9 Return Values for Erroneous Conversion of int, uint, and Number

Listing 5.21 provides a brief overview of the behavior of different data types. If the myBoolean variable is assigned the value true (=1), all other data types also receive the value 1. If you change the value of the myBoolean variable to false (=0), the other data types will also adopt the value 0.

Behavior of different data types

```
var myBoolean:Boolean = true;
var myUINT:uint = uint(myBoolean);
var myINT:int = int(myBoolean);
var myNum:Number = Number(myBoolean);
trace(myUINT, myINT, myNum); // Output: 1 1 1
myBoolean = false;
myUINT = uint(myBoolean);
myINT = int(myBoolean);
myNum = Number(myBoolean);
trace(myUINT, myINT, myNum); // Output: 0 0 0
```

Listing 5.21 Converting the Boolean Data Type into Number Data Types

You can successfully convert string variables if they consist of numbers. In this context you can also process strings that contain negative numbers and hexadecimal content.

Floating point numbers

For strings containing floating point numbers, you should note that the decimal place gets truncated in case of an assignment to the int data types. However, if you convert a string that contains floating-point numbers into a Number object, the decimal places are preserved.

Listing 5.22 shows the behavior of the different string variables.

```
trace(uint("5"));          // Output: 5
trace(uint("-5"));         // Output: -5
trace(uint("27"));         // Output: 27
trace(uint("3.7"));        // Output: 3
trace(int("3.7"));         // Output: 3
trace(int("0x1A"));        // Output: 26
trace(Number("3.7"));      // Output: 3.7
```

Listing 5.22 Sample String Conversion

Casting Boolean

If different data types are assigned to a Boolean value, most of the information is reduced significantly (to 0 and 1 or true and false respectively). What is interesting here is the way in which the respective content is converted. The following examples show how the conversion works.

Listing 5.23 illustrates how you can convert negative and positive values into the Boolean data type.

```
var myNum:Number;
for (myNum = -1; myNum<2; myNum++) {
  trace ("Boolean(" + myNum +") is " + Boolean(myNum));
}
```

Listing 5.23 Test Routine for Converting Numbers into the Boolean Data Type

The result of the calculation carried out in Listing 5.23 is as follows:

```
Boolean(-1) is true
Boolean(0) is false
Boolean(1) is true
```

Listing 5.24 shows the behavior of the different string values.

```
var str1:String;        // String = null
trace(Boolean(str1));   // Output: false
```

```
var str2:String = "";   // Blank string
trace(Boolean(str2));   // Output: false

var str3:String = " "; // Only blank spaces
trace(Boolean(str3));   // Output: true
```

Listing 5.24 Output of the "For" Loop

If string variables are assigned, this will always cause a `false` output if he string itself is `null` or blank (`""`). In all other cases the value `true` is assigned. Listing 5.25 shows how you can assign objects.

```
var myObj:Object;        // Object is null
trace(Boolean(myObj));  // Output: false

myObj = new Object();   // Instantiated object
trace(Boolean(myObj));  // Output: true
```

Listing 5.25 Conversion of a String to the Boolean Data Type

Table 5.10 provides an overview of the resulting data types and their effects on the `Boolean` values.

Data type	Result after conversion
String	`false` **if the string is** `null` **or blank (`" "`), otherwise** `true`
null	`false`
Number, int, **or** uint	`false` **if the value is 0, otherwise** `true`
Object	`false` **if the instance is 0, otherwise** `true`

Table 5.10 Overview of Rules for Conversions into Boolean Data Type

Most of the time, the conversion into a `String` data type does not entail any loss of data. Because `String` can include and display all other data types, there shouldn't be any problem.

Casting string

The following example (see Listing 5.26) shows the results to be expected after a conversion.

```
var myArray:Array =
  ["one", "two", "three"];
trace(String(myArray));
  // Output: one,two,three

var myDate:Date = new Date(2005,6,1);
```

```
trace(String(myDate));
   // Output: Fri Jul 1 00:00:00 GMT-0700 2005
```

Listing 5.26 Conversion of Different Data Types into a String

Table 5.11 summarizes the results to be expected.

Data type	Result after conversion
Array	String containing all values of the array
Boolean	true or false
Date	Date as a string
null	null
Number, int, or uint	Number as a string
Object	If the instance is null, then null; otherwise [object Object]

Table 5.11 Overview of Rules for Conversions into String Data Type

5.4 Operators

Operators are used differently depending on the data type

Operators are special functions used for various activities in order to return a value. For example, operators can be used to calculate values. The two operators used in the following code example carry out an addition (+) and a multiplication (*):

```
var sumNumber:uint = 2 + 3 * 4; // uint = 14
```

Depending on the context, some operators can have different functions. The example in Listing 5.27 shows the behavior of the + operand with the Number data type and with the String data type.

```
trace (5 + 5);     // Output: 10
trace ("5" + "5"); // Output: 55
```

Listing 5.27 Different Behavior of the Same Operator with Number and String Data Types

Processing the operator leads to different results. The result returned by an operator completely depends on the data types you use.

5.4.1 Basic Calculating Operations

The operators for the basic calculating operations do not differ significantly from those used in other programming languages, particularly in ABAP (see Table 5.12). However, in contrast to ABAP, there are no synonyms available for these operators (such as `DIV`, for example) that you could use in the same way.

No synonyms

Operator	Processing
+	Addition
-	Subtraction
*	Multiplication
/	Division
%	Modulo

Table 5.12 Overview of Operators for Basic Calculating Operations in ActionScript

5.4.2 Ranking Order and Associativity

In addition to processing operators (addition, subtraction, and so on), the ranking order also plays an important role. You probably remember the basic rules from your math lessons. These mathematical ranking orders are also used in ActionScript (see Listing 5.28).

```
var sumNumber:uint = (2 + 3) * 4; // uint == 20
```
Listing 5.28 Defining Ranking Orders Using Parentheses

As shown in the example, you can use parentheses in ActionScript to define the processing sequence within a statement. Not only is the processing sequence used for arithmetical operations, but also to run comparisons. The following example shows that relational operators are processed from left to right.

Setting parentheses

```
trace (3 > 2 < 1);   // Output: false
trace ((3 > 2) < 1); // Output: false
```

In contrast, the following example shows that the statement receives the value `true` if you set the parentheses differently.

```
trace (3 > (2 < 1)); // Output: true
```

5.4.3 Primary Operators

Primary operators are used to generate arrays and objects, instantiate classes, access properties, and so on. Table 5.13 provides a brief overview of these operators.

Operator	Processing
[]	Array is initialized
{x:y}	Object is initialized
()	Grouping
f(x)	Function call
new	Constructor call
x.y x[y]	Access to a property

Table 5.13 Overview of Primary Operators

5.4.4 Postfix Operators

Downstream execution

Postfix operators execute their statements after the lines have been interpreted; that is, in a downstream execution. Listing 5.29 shows the way a postfix operator works.

```
var ixNumb:Number = 0;
trace (ixNumb++); // Output: 0
trace (ixNumb);   // Output: 1
```
Listing 5.29 Sample Postfix Operator

This example shows clearly that the addition is not executed until the operation has ended (postfix). Table 5.14 lists the available operators.

Operator	Processing
++	Variable is increased by 1
--	Variable is decreased by 1

Table 5.14 Overview of Postfix Operators

5.4.5 Unary Operators

Upstream execution

In contrast to the postfix operators, unary operators first carry out the addition or subtraction process. The example in Listing 5.30 illustrates this.

```
var ixNumb:Number = 0;
trace (++ixNumb); // Output: 1
trace (ixNumb);   // Output: 1
```
Listing 5.30 Sample Unary Operation

Depending on the individual case, it may be necessary to increase or decrease a variable up front.

5.4.6 Bit Operators

Bit operators enable the movement by individual bits to the right or left. Table 5.15 lists the operators required for that.

Operator	Processing
<<	Per-bit shift to the left
>>	Per-bit shift to the right

Table 5.15 Overview of Bit Operators

5.4.7 Relational Operators

Relational operators are very often used; effectively, every if query uses them. Whereas you can use letter combinations in ABAP (LT, GT, and so on) instead of relational characters such as <, >, and so on, this is not possible in ActionScript. Table 5.16 contains the possible relational operators that are used most frequently.

Small combinations of letters

Operator	Processing
<	Smaller than
>	Bigger than
<=	Small than or equal to
>=	Bigger than or equal to
==	Equal to
!=	Not equal to
===	Strictly equal to
!==	Strictly unequal to
as	Data type is being checked

Table 5.16 Overview of Relational Operators

Operator	Processing
in	Object property is being checked
is	Data type is being checked

Table 5.16 Overview of Relational Operators (cont.)

5.4.8 Logical Operators

Logical operators help you to combine several criteria with each other. To do this, you can mainly use the two logical operators shown in Table 5.17.

Operator	Processing
&&	AND
||	OR

Table 5.17 Overview of Logical Operators

5.4.9 Assignment Operators

Changing variables of different data types

Assignment operators are used whenever you need to change variables of different data types. The most commonly used assignment operator is the equals sign. However, ActionScript provides a number of additional variants. Table 5.18 contains a list of assignment operators and the related abbreviated notations.

Operator	Processing
=	Simple assignment
*=	Multiplication and assignment
/=	Division and assignment
%=	Modulo and assignment
+=	Addition and assignment
-=	Subtraction and assignment
<<=	Assignment per bit, left
>>=	Assignment per bit, right
&=	AND assignment per bit

Table 5.18 Overview of Assignment Operators

Operator	Processing
^=	XOR assignment per bit
!=	OR assignment per bit

Table 5.18 Overview of Assignment Operators (cont.)

5.5 Control Structures

Control structures are used in almost any larger program. You can use control structures to respond to specific statuses and to control the program flow systematically. ActionScript basically uses the following three different types of control structures:

Control structures enable the control of a flow logic

▶ if ... else
The most simple form of a control structure compares the return value of a term. The program components to be executed are combined into blocks. You can recognize this by the including curly brackets ({ }):

```
if (x > 20) {
    trace ("x is > 20");
}
else {
    trace ("x is <= 20");
}
```

▶ if ... else if
This type of control structure complements the above simple form with an additional criterion. Both variants are also implemented in ABAP and are used in almost the same manner. The following sample code illustrates the use of the if-else if statement:

```
if (x > 20) {
    trace ("x is > 20");
}
else if (x < 0) {
    trace ("x is negative");
}
```

▶ switch
You can use the switch statement to simplify complex nestings with if-else statements. The switch statement carries out the same task as the CASE statement in ABAP. The following example illustrates the switch syntax that's used in ActionScript:

```
var someDate:Date = new Date();
var dayNum:uint = someDate.getDay();
switch(dayNum) {
    case 0:
       trace("Sunday");
       break;
    case 1:
       trace("Monday");
       break;
    case 2:
       trace("Tuesday");
       break;
    case 3:
       trace("Wednesday");
       break;
    case 4:
       trace("Thursday");
       break;
    case 5:
       trace("Friday");
       break;
    case 6:
       trace("Saturday");
       break;
    default:
       trace("Invalid");
}
```

5.6   Loops

Loops are used for iterative execution of statements

Loops allow the iterative execution of code blocks. We distinguish between different types of loops: Loops can be terminated after a certain number of cycles or via a condition.

▶ for **Loop**
The simple for loop is used to achieve a certain number of cycles. In order to use the for loop, you must use three parameters that control the number of cycles via a relational expression.

The following code example shows that the initial value of the i variable of the int type (integer) is 0 and that this value increases by 1 in each cycle. When i reaches the value 5, the loop terminates.

```
var i:int;
for (i = 0; i < 5; i++) {
```

```
    trace (i);
}
```

► for-in **Loop**

The for-in loop is is an advancement of the for loop. It is primarily used to read out values in a dynamic object or in an array. This way you can access parameters whose names you don't know. For instance, you may have to find a specific value within a property, but you don't know the attribute name.

The following lines illustrate how you can do this by using the for-in loop.

```
var myObj:Object = {x:20, y:30};
for (var i:String in myObj) {
    trace (i + ": " + myObj[i]);
}

// Output:
// x: 20
// y: 30

var myArray:Array = ["one", "two", "three"];
for (var i:String in myArray) {
    trace (myArray[i]);
}

// Output:
// one
// two
// three
```

► while **Loop**

The while loop behaves like an if statement that is executed repeatedly until the value true is output. Note that in a while loop the statement is checked prior to the block execution.

The following example illustrates how you can use the while loop in the program. The condition is checked before the loop starts. If the condition is true, the loop is executed as often as necessary until the condition is false.

```
var i:int = 0;
while (i < 5) {
    trace (i);
    i++;
}
```

▶ do-while **Loop**

The do-while loop behaves like a while loop, with the difference that the expression is checked at the end, not at the beginning. You should use the do-while loop when you need at least one loop cycle, as illustrated in the following example. The listing shows that despite the initial value 5 of variable I, the loop is cycled once. After that, the loop terminates when the check has been performed (i<5).

```
var i:int = 5;
do {
    trace (i);
    i++;
} while (i < 5);

// Output: 5
```

5.7   Arrays

Arrays can take up and dynamically process large quantities of inter-related data

Arrays allow you to include several values in one variable. This can be necessary to combine related information logically and technically. Thus, arrays serve as containers for many different types of information that can be accessed conveniently and dynamically. Strictly speaking, arrays are simply objects.

You can use arrays as simple, indexed arrays that can be read out using an int value. You also can use associative arrays. These arrays enable to you access values via attribute names. Arrays can also become multidimensional. In the context of SAP objects, you can regard arrays as internal tables that can also be multidimensional (table type as structure element).

5.7.1   Indexed Arrays

Integer value

The simplest type of arrays is indexed arrays. You can access the individual values via an integer value that always begins with 0 for the first element.

Listing 5.31 shows how you can declare, fill, and process an array.

```
// Call the array constructor.
var myArray:Array = new Array();
myArray.push("one");
```

```
myArray.push("two");
myArray.push("three");
trace (myArray); // Output: one,two,three

// Call the array with literal.
var myArray:Array = ["one", "two", "three"];
trace (myArray); // Output: one,two,three
```

Listing 5.31 Indexed Arrays, Example

5.7.2 Associative Arrays

Instead of an index, associative arrays use a keyword to process the
contents. The array contains name-value pairs whose sequence is not
sorted within the array.

Keyword

As mentioned earlier, arrays are also objects. This becomes obvious
when you declare arrays. The following example shows how you can
declare and edit associative arrays (see Listing 5.32).

```
var screenInfo:Object = {Type:"Flat Panel",
                         Resolution:"1024 x 768"};
trace (screenInfo["Type"], screenInfo["Resolution"]);

// Output: Flat Panel 1024 x 768
```

Listing 5.32 Declaring and Assigning Associative Arrays

If no content is needed or available at the time of declaration, you
can also create an empty array using the Object constructor (see Listing 5.33).

```
var screenInfo:Object = new Object();
```

Listing 5.33 Creating an Array Using an Object Constructor

If you want to fill the array with values afterwards, you can do that as
shown in the lines in Listing 5.34.

```
screenInfo["aspect_ratio"] = "16:10";
screenInfo.colors = "16.7 million";
trace (screenInfo["aspect_ratio"],
  screenInfo.colors);

// Output: 16:10 16.7 million
```

Listing 5.34 Assigning and Reading Values in Associative Arrays

You should make sure that you use parameter names that don't contain any blank space characters, such as `aspect_ratio` in Listing 5.34.
You also could have used `screenInfo["aspect ratio"]`, but then you
wouldn't be able to use dot syntax in order to access the array.

5.7.3   Multidimensional Arrays

Multidimensional arrays are used particularly often to process XML
documents or Web services. You can create multidimensional arrays
as index-based or associative arrays. Because associative arrays are
used more often in practice, we'll focus on this type here as well.

Listing 5.35 shows how you can declare and edit multidimensional
associative arrays. The example illustrates that the number of values
can vary.

```
var taskList:Object = new Object();
taskList["Mon"] = ["Washing up"];
taskList["Tue"] = ["Washing up", "electrician"];
taskList["Wed"] = ["Washing up", "gardener"];
taskList["Thu"] = ["Washing up"];
taskList["Fri"] = ["Washing up", "kindergarten"];
taskList["Sat"] = ["Washing up", "carwash"];
taskList["Sun"] = ["Washing up", "mowing"];
```
Listing 5.35 Declaration of Multidimensional Arrays

Indexed multidimensional arrays behave similarly, the only difference being that they are addressed via `Integer` values (see Listing
5.36).

```
trace(taskList[2][1]); // Output: gardener
```
Listing 5.36 Accessing Individual Values via Indexes

5.7.4   Functions

Functions are self-contained code blocks that perform certain tasks,
during values are imported and exported frequently. Program support as it is provided by the function modules in an SAP system is not
contained in ActionScript.

Functions are often mistaken for methods. The reason for this is that
the definitions of methods and functions are identical, and you can

only gather from the context whether you are dealing with a method or a function.

Listing 5.37 shows how you can define a function and transfer parameters to it. As you can see, the transferred parameters are treated like local variables.

```
function addPosno(xPos:int, yPos:int) {
    xPos++;
    yPos++;
    trace(xPos, yPos);
}

var xValue:int = 10;
var yValue:int = 15;
trace(xValue, yValue);        // Output: 10 15
addPosno(xValue, yValue);     // Output: 11 16
trace(xValue, yValue);        // Output: 10 15
```

Listing 5.37 Declaring and Calling Functions

5.8   Objects and Classes

We do not intend in this section to provide you with a complete introduction to object-oriented programming. It contains, rather, the necessary basic principles that you need to understand the sample application in Chapter 7 and to get started with ActionScript, MXML, and ABAP.

5.8.1   Class Definition

The SAP development environment requires you to act within a relatively rigid framework. Both functions and classes are maintained and managed using specific transactions. In ActionScript, classes are always defined via the program code itself. The example in Listing 5.38 shows you how to declare a simple class.

```
public class Shape {
    var visible:Boolean = true;
}
```

Listing 5.38 Creating a Class Called Shape

In this example, we used the keyword `visible` for the class definition. Other keywords and their meanings are listed in Table 5.19.

Attribute	Description
`internal`	Visible in the same package
`private`	Visible in the class
`protected`	Visible in the class and in derived classes
`public`	Completely visible
`prototype`	Indicates the affiliation to a `prototype` class
`static`	Visible in the class (across instances)
`UserDefinedNamespace`	Separate user-defined namespace

Table 5.19 List of Possible Class Attributes

5.8.2 Class Methods

Methods in classes are defined like functions

Basically, class methods correspond to functions that have been declared within a class. The class methods cannot be used outside of their instance.

Listing 5.39 shows how you can define a class method. As you can see, the method is also defined using the keyword `function`. Because this happens within a class definition, however, we are dealing with a method instead of a function.

```
public class Shape {
    var visible:Boolean = true;
    public function getShape() : String {}
}
```

Listing 5.39 Declaring a Class Method

▶ **Constructor**
Classes often require a constructor. A constructor is used to run the code initially when an object is instantiated.

Defining a constructor

To define a constructor, you don't need a special keyword, but the method must have the same name as the class. This way, the constructor is defined. The following example shows how you can define a constructor.

```
class Example {
    public var status:String;
    public function Example (){
        status = "initialized";
    }
}

var myExample:Example = new Example();
trace (myExample.status); // Output: initialized
```

▸ **Static methods**

Static methods enable you to call even non-instantiated classes and objects. In ActionScript, you can declare static or instance-independent methods using the keyword, `static`. The following example shows how you can declare static methods within a class.

Declaring static methods

```
class customer {
    public var subrc:String;
    static function customerSearch (){
    }
}
```

▸ **Instance methods**

In contrast to static methods, you can use instance methods for instantiated objects only. This procedure is used whenever a method without instantiation doesn't make sense.

Declaring instance methods

For example, suppose you want to create a sales order in a method. To do that, you must have a customer number; i.e., an instantiated `customer` object. Then you also want to be able to create a sales order for the customer number.

You declare an instance method without using the keyword, `static`. The following example shows you how to declare such a method.

```
public function customerCreate () {
    .. ;
}
```

5.8.3   Interfaces

Interfaces allow the communication between objects that are not directly related to each other. Without going into too much detail about the usefulness of interfaces in general, we want to describe the declaration of an interface using the following example (see Listing 5.40).

Declaring interfaces

```
public interface IEventDispatcher {
    function addEventListener(type:String,
            listener:Function,
            useCapture:Boolean=false,
            priority:int=0):void;
    function removeEventListener(type:String,
            listener:Function,
            useCapture:Boolean=false):void;
    function dispatchEvent(event:Event):Boolean;
    function hasEventListener(type:String):Boolean;
    function willTrigger(type:String):Boolean;
}
```

Listing 5.40 Declaring an Interface

Listing 5.40 shows how interfaces contain different functions that are required to perform specific tasks. You can also see how to use an event listener object in order to transfer an event to another object. This option is needed if you want a program to react to drag-and-drop functions. You will certainly use the IEventDispatcher interface in many applications as it represents a standard communication method.

ActionScript is an object-oriented application language. It provides a wide range of options: to present multimedia data, to carry out specific tasks within a certain period, to perform arithmetic calculations, or to change the presentation of graphical components.

6   ActionScript Extensions

Multimedia components play an important role in modern applications. They not only enhance the quality of the content presentation considerably in Web applications, but also in business applications. Applications in which users can only process text-based information are increasingly dying out.

Growing importance of multimedia applications

In this chapter, we'll complement the basic principles of ActionScript introduced in Chapter 5 with their actual meanings, as they are known from the Flash world. You will learn how to use different media formats, text fields, and even mathematical functions in ActionScript. Based on this knowledge, you will then be able to process complex application scenarios in a Flex application.

6.1   Audio and Video Objects

ActionScript enables you, among other things, to integrate audio and video files into a Flex application. These media formats are particularly useful in online stores and help portals in order to provide the user with information both in images and on a multimedia level. The `flash.media` package provides Flex developers with important classes that enable the integration of such media formats (see Table 6.1).

Integrating audio and video files

Class	Description
`public class Sound`	Control class for the integration of sounds in a Flex application
`public class SoundLoaderContext`	Class that controls the loading behavior of an audio file
`public class SoundChannel`	Class to play an audio file
`public class SoundMixer`	Class that enables you to mix different sounds within a SWF file
`public class SoundTransform`	Class that modifies the properties of an audio playback, such as the volume or audio panning[1]
`public class Video`	Class that enables you to play FLV files (*Flash Video*) within a Flex application

Table 6.1 Classes of the flash.media Package

6.1.1 Audio Files

The `flash.media.Sound` class enables you to integrate an audio file into a Flex application. Moreover, it provides information on the sound that has been loaded, such as the length of the file or the size in bytes of the audio file you have loaded.

To instantiate an object of this class, you must use the following constructor:

```
public function Sound(stream:URLRequest = null,
  context:SoundLoaderContext = null)
```

Buffer The `stream` parameter is an object of the `flash.net.URLRequest` type that allows you to address an external file via an HTML request. The request actually addresses the data of this file, which can then be loaded by the sound object using the `load()` method. The `context` parameter is an object of the `SoundLoaderContext` class and is responsible for providing a buffer for the audio file if the audio file is not loaded completely into the sound object at the time of playback. The buffer, which is specified in milliseconds, stores the required data for playback during the loading process. Thus the sound object is able to stream audio data.

---

1 Panning describes the mapping of movements into sounds and pictures from one place to another.

Table 6.2 provides an overview of the properties of the sound object.

Property	Description
bytesLoaded:int [read-only]	Specifies the current number of loaded bytes of the sound object
bytesTotal:int [read-only]	Returns the size of the sound object
id3:Array [read-only]	Provides access to the metadata of an MP3 file
isBuffering:Boolean [read-only]	Specifies whether the buffer is used for an external audio file
length:Number [read-only]	Specifies the length of the current sound in terms of milliseconds

Table 6.2 Properties of the Sound Class and Their Meanings

Because the Sound class is directly derived from the flash.events.EventDispatcher class, it enables you, among other things, to capture the events listed in Table 6.3 by using an event listener. In addition, the class contains important methods (see Table 6.4).

Event	Description
complete	Is triggered when data has been loaded
id3	Is triggered if the id3 metadata of an MP3 file is available
ioError	Is triggered if the data stream cannot be accessed
progress	Is triggered when the data is being loaded
soundComplete	Is triggered when the sound playback has completed

Table 6.3 Events of the Sound Class and Their Meanings

Method	Description
close():void	Closes the data stream in order to delete all data of the sound object that has been loaded

Table 6.4 Methods of the Sound Class and Their Meanings

Method	Description
load(stream:URLRequest, context:SoundLoaderContext = null):void	Loads audio data from a specific URL (similar to the constructor call)
play(startTime:Number = 0, loops:int = 0, sndTrans-form:SoundTransform = null):SoundChannel	Creates a new audio track and starts playback You can use starttime to set the starting point. The loops parameter controls the repetitions, while you can use the sndtransform parameter to manipulate the playback properties.

Table 6.4 Methods of the Sound Class and Their Meanings (cont.)

Sound track In addition to the load() method, the play() method is responsible for starting the sound playback. When the sound playback is started, an object of the SoundChannel class is instantiated. This object provides the option to create a sound track for the playback of the sound object. During the playback, the SoundChannel object provides the properties listed in Table 6.5.

Property	Value	Description
leftPeak:Number [read-only]	▶ 0 = no volume ▶ 1 = full volume	Current volume of the left channel
Position:Number [read-only]		Current playback time in terms of milliseconds
rightPeak:Number [read-only]	▶ 0 = no volume ▶ 1 = full volume	Current volume of the right channel
soundTransform: SoundTransform [read-write]		Plays the SoundTransform object of the current sound track

Table 6.5 Properties of the SoundChannel Class and Their Meanings

Volume The SoundTransform object enables you to control the volume and the distribution of the volume to the left and right loudspeakers. To do that, the properties listed in Table 6.6 must be set.

Property	Value	Description
leftToLeft:Number [read-write]	▶ 0 = no signal ▶ 1 = full signal	Indicates which portion of the left inbound signal is directed to the left loudspeaker

Table 6.6 Properties of the SoundTransform Class and Their Meanings

Property	Value	Description
`leftToRight:Number` [read-write]	▸ 0 = no signal ▸ 1 = full signal	Indicates which portion of the left inbound signal is directed to the right loudspeaker
`pan:Number` [read-write]	Range from -1 (full left-hand panning) to 1 (full right-hand panning)	Left-hand/right-hand panning of audio signals
`rightToLeft:Number` [read-write]	Range from -1 (full left-hand panning) to 1 (full right-hand panning)	Left-hand/right-hand panning of audio signals
`rightToRight:Number` [read-write]	▸ 0 = no signal ▸ 1 = full signal	Indicates which portion of the right inbound signal is directed to the right loudspeaker
`volume:Number` [read-write]	Range from 0 (minimum) to 1 (maximum)	Volume

Table 6.6 Properties of the SoundTransform Class and Their Meanings (cont.)

In Listing 6.1 we load an MP3 file in a Flex application. Buttons enable you to play and stop the audio file as well as to control the volume (see Figure 6.1).

MP3 files

```
<mx:Script>
<![CDATA[
  import flash.media.Sound;
  import flash.media.SoundChannel;
  import flash.media.SoundTransform;
  var s:Sound;
  var song:SoundChannel;
  var vol:SoundTransform = new SoundTransform();

// Method for playback
public function startSound(){
  var url:URLRequest = new URLRequest ("sound.mp3");
  s = new Sound( url );
  song = s.play();
}

// Method for stopping the playback
```

```
public function stopSound(){
  song.stop();
}

// Method for turning up the volume
public function volumeUp(){
  vol.volume = vol.volume + 0.1;
  song.soundTransform = vol;
}

// Method for turning down the volume
public function volumeDown(){
  vol.volume = vol.volume - 0.1;
  song.soundTransform = vol;
}
]]>
</mx:Script>

<mx:Canvas id="canvas" width="100%" height="100%">
  <mx:Button x="27" y="35" label="Start" id="start"
    click="startSound()"/>
  <mx:Button x="90" y="35" label="Stop" id="stop"
    click="stopSound()"/>
  <mx:Button x="150" y="35" label="Up" id="up"
    click="volumeUp()"/>
  <mx:Button x="208" y="35" label="Down" id="down"
    click="volumeDown()"/>
</mx:Canvas>
```

Listing 6.1 Controlling an MP3 File Using ActionScript

Figure 6.1 Screen Display for Controlling an MP3 File Using ActionScript

6.1.2 Video Files

Streaming videos

The `flash.media.Video` class enables you to play Flash Video (FLV) files within a Flex application without having to embed the video directly into a SWF file. Thus you can stream the video in the same way as when using the `flash.media.Sound` class. In addition, the `flash.media.Video` class provides the option to stream a video directly from a Web cam.

You can instantiate objects of this class using the following constructor:

```
public function Video(width:uint = 0, height:uint = 0)
```

The `width` and `height` parameters indicate the width and height of the output in terms of pixels. Furthermore, the class contains the properties listed in Table 6.7.

Property	Description
`deblocking:int` [read-write]	Indicates the type of the deblocking filter that is used for post-editing decoded videos
`smoothing:Boolean` [read-write]	Indicates whether the video is to be smoothed (interpolated) during scaling
`videoHeight:uint` [read-only]	Indicates the height of the video object in terms of pixels
`videoWidth:uint` [read-only]	Indicates the width of the video object in terms of pixels

Table 6.7 Properties of the Video Class and Their Meanings

As of Flash Player Version 8.x, the deblocking filter supports two codec types: the *Sorenson Spark Codec,* and the *On2 VP6 Codec.* These filters affect the playback performance of the video as well as the picture quality. The `deblocking` property can contain the values from 0 to 5 described in Table 6.8. Moreover, you can use the methods listed in Table 6.9 if you use the `Video` class.

Deblocking filter

Value	Description
0 (default)	Leaves it up to the video compressor to decide whether or not an another filter should be added
1	No deblocking filter is used
2	Only the Sorenson filter is used
3	The On2 filter is used (without the use of a de-ringing filter which reduces picture artefacts)
4	The On2 filter is used (with a fast de-ringing filter)
5	The On2 filter is used (with a slower de-ringing filter of a better quality)

Table 6.8 Values of the deblocking Property and Their Meanings

Method	Description
attachCamera(camera:Camera):void	Specifies a video stream from a camera, which is to be displayed within the video object in an application (this must be an object of the flash.media.Camera type)
attachNetStream(netStream: NetStream):void	Specifies a video stream which is to be displayed within the video object in an application (this must be an object of the flash.net.Netstream type)
clear():void	Deletes the picture that is currently displayed in the video object

Table 6.9 Methods of the Video Class and Their Meanings

play(), pause(), close()

In the following example (see Listing 6.2), we'll display a video object in a Flex application via a NetStream object. Buttons enable you to carry out the play(), pause(), and close() methods in the NetStream object. These methods allow you to start, pause, resume, and stop the video stream.

```
// VideoStream.as
package classes{
   import flash.events.NetStatusEvent;
   import flash.events.IEventDispatcher;
   import flash.events.SecurityErrorEvent;
   import flash.media.Video;
   import flash.net.NetConnection;
   import flash.net.NetStream;
   import flash.util.trace;
   import mx.core.UIComponent;
   public class VideoStream extends UIComponent {
     private var videoUrl:String = "video.flv";
     public  var stream:NetStream;
     public function VideoStream() {
       var connection:NetConnection = new
         NetConnection();
       var video:Video = new Video(360, 240);
       configListeners(connection);
       connection.connect(null);
       stream = new NetStream(connection);
       configureListeners(stream);
       stream.publish(false);
       video.attachNetStream(stream);
```

```
        stream.play(videoUrl);
        addChild(video);
      }

// Event listener to capture events
      private function
        configListeners(dispatcher:
          IEventDispatcher):void {
          dispatcher.addEventListener(
            NetStatusEvent.NET_STATUS,
            netStatusHandler);
          dispatcher.addEventListener(
            SecurityErrorEvent.SECURITY_ERROR,
            securityErrorHandler);
      }
      private function
        netStatusHandler(event:
          NetStatusEvent):void {
          trace("netStatusHandler: " + event);
          var info:Object = event.info;
          for(var i:String in info) {
            trace(i + " : " + info[i]);
          }
      }
    private function
      securityErrorHandler(
        event:SecurityErrorEvent):void {
        trace("securityErrorHandler: " + event);
        }
    }
}

// Flex application
<?xml version="1.0" encoding="utf-8"?>
<mx:Application
  xmlns:mx="http://www.adobe.com/2006/mxml" xmlns="*">
  <mx:Script>
  <![CDATA[
  import classes.VideoStream;
  var video:VideoStream;
  public function playVid(){
    video = new VideoStream();
    canvas.addChild(video);
  }
  public function pauseVid(){
    if (video != null)
```

```
            video.stream.pause(true);
   }
   public function stopVid(){
     if (video != null)
       video.stream.close();
   }
]]>
```

```
</mx:Script>
<mx:Canvas id="canvas" width="100%" height="100%">
  <mx:Button x="79" y="257" label="Play" id="play"
    click="playVid()"/>
  <mx:Button x="138" y="257" label="Pause" id="pause"
    click="pauseVid()"/>
  <mx:Button x="212" y="257" label="Stop" id="stop"
    click="stopVid()"/>
</mx:Canvas>
</mx:Application>
```

Listing 6.2 Integrating an FLV Video in a Flex Application

In the preceding Listing 6.2, the video display is stored in the Video-Stream class, which inherits properties from the mx.core.UICompo-nent type in order to enable the display in the Flex application. The NetStream and video objects are then instantiated in the constructor of this class, which also starts the video.

Event listeners Event listeners are used to capture events In the MXML application; you then can integrate the class via import classes.VideoStream and use the buttons to control the playback behavior (see Figure 6.2).

Figure 6.2 Screen Display of an FLV Video

136

6.2   Date Objects and Timer Objects

You can also use date and timer objects in Flex applications. The date object is used to create and process date and time values. The information can be called in relation to the coordinated universal time (UTC) or to the time in the operating system Flash Player is running on. The timer object is used to automatically trigger specific events during a given period of time.

Creating date and time values

6.2.1   Date Objects

The `Date` class is directly derived from the main class `Object` of the ActionScript class hierarchy. It does not contain any static methods, but only instance methods. The sole exceptions are the methods `Date.parse()` and `Date.UTC()`. The automatic changeover to Daylight Savings Time for a current date and time information depends on the operating system and the Flash Player version.

As described in Chapter 5, the objects of the `Date` class are also instantiated via the constructor. You can call the constructor as follows:

```
Date(yearOrTimevalue:Object, month:Number,
  date:Number = 1, hour:Number = 0, minute:Number = 0,
  second:Number = 0, millisecond:Number = 0)
```

Instantiating without explicitly specified parameters causes the creation of a date object of the current time. When you specify parameters, you must at least transfer the year and the month, as otherwise the system will use the default time: January 1 1970, 0:00:00 UTC.

Current time

Table 6.10 lists the most important properties of this object. You can access these properties by using `get` and `set` methods.

Property	Value	Description
date:Number [read-write]	Integer from 1 to 31	Day of the month for the specified date object according to the local time

Table 6.10 Overview of Properties of the Date Class

Property	Value	Description
dateUTC:Number [read-write]	Integer from 1 to 31	Day of the month for the specified date object according to the universal time
day:Number [read-only]	▶ Sunday = 0 ▶ Monday = 1 ▶ Tuesday = 2 ▶ Wednesday = 3 ▶ Thursday = 4 ▶ Friday = 5 ▶ Saturday = 6	Weekday according to local time
dayUTC:Number [read-only]	▶ Sunday = 0 ▶ Monday = 1 ▶ Tuesday = 2 ▶ Wednesday = 3 ▶ Thursday = 4 ▶ Friday = 5 ▶ Saturday = 6	Weekday according to universal time
fullYear:Number [read-write]	e.g., 2006	Complete year according to local time
fullYearUTC:Number [read-write]	e.g., 2006	Complete year according to universal time
Hours:Number	Integer from 0 to 23	Indication of hours as integer according to local time
hoursUTC:Number [read-write]	Integer from 0 to 23	Indication of hours as integer according to universal time
milliseconds:Number [read-write]	Integer from 0 to 999	Indication of milliseconds according to local time
millisecondsUTC:Number [read-write]	Integer from 0 to 999	Indication of milliseconds according to universal time
minutes:Number [read-write]	Integer from 0 to 59	Indication of minutes according to local time
minutesUTC:Number [read-write]	Integer from 0 to 59	Indication of minutes according to universal time

Table 6.10 Overview of Properties of the Date Class (cont.)

Property	Value	Description
`Month:Number` [read-write]	▶ January = 0 ▶ February = 1 ▶ March = 2 ▶ April = 3 ▶ May = 4 ▶ June = 5 ▶ July = 6 ▶ August = 7 ▶ September = 8 ▶ October = 9 ▶ November = 10 ▶ December = 11	Month of the year according to local time
`monthUTC:Number` [read-write]	▶ January = 0 ▶ February = 1 ▶ March = 2 ▶ April = 3 ▶ May = 4 ▶ June = 5 ▶ July = 6 ▶ August = 7 ▶ September = 8 ▶ October = 9 ▶ November = 10 ▶ December = 11	Month of the year according to universal time
`seconds:Number` [read-write]	Integer from 0 to 59	Indication of seconds according to local time
`secondsUTC:Number` [read-write]	Integer from 0 to 59	Indication of seconds according to universal time
`time:Number` [read-write]	Integer	Number of miliseconds that have passed since January 1, 1970 (00:00:00)
`timezoneOffset:Number` [read-only]	Integer	Difference between the local time of the computer and the universal time in minutes

Table 6.10 Overview of Properties of the Date Class (cont.)

In addition, the Date class provides the following methods for presenting the properties (see Table 6.11).

Method	Description
toDateString()	Indicates the date as a string containing abbreviated weekday names (e. g., "Thu"), month names (e. g., "Jan"), the day as an integer, and the year as an integer without specifying the time and time zone
toLocaleDateString()	Indicates the date as a string (like toDateString())
toLocaleString()	Indicates the date as a string (like toDateString()) and specifies the time as HH:MM:SS including the local time without the time zone
toString()	Indicates the day, date, time, and time zone
toLocaleTimeString()	Indicates the time as HH:MM:SS including the local time without specifying the date and time zone
toUTCString()	Indicates the day, date, and time according to universal time

Table 6.11 Methods of the Date Class and Their Meanings

Changing the value of a date object
The static Date.UTC() method enables you to change the value of a date object. You can call this method as follows:

```
public static function UTC(year:Number, month:Number,
  date:Number = 1, hour:Number = 0, minute:Number = 0,
  second:Number = 0, millisecond:Number = 0):Number
```

The call via parameters basically corresponds to the call of the constructor; the only difference is that here you cannot omit the parameters in order to determine the current date. The function returns the number of milliseconds that have passed in the period from January 1 1970 (00:00:00 universal time) and the time specified in the parameters. You can use the setTime(millisecond:Number) method to transfer this return value to a date object.

To format the output of the date object, you can use the DateFormatter class that is contained in the mx.formatters package. This class is an MXML class. You can call the constructor as follows:

```
DateFormatter()
```

The DateFormatter class contains the formatString property and the format() method, which are declared as follows:

▶ `formatString:String`

The formatting pattern specifies the format in which the date   **Formatting pattern**
object is to be returned. You can use the following characters:

- ▶ Y: year
- ▶ M: month
- ▶ D: day of month
- ▶ E: weekday
- ▶ A: local time (a.m./p.m.)
- ▶ J: hour (0–23)
- ▶ K: hour (0–11 a.m./p.m.)
- ▶ L: hour (1–12 a.m./p.m.)
- ▶ N: minute
- ▶ S: second

▶ `format(value:Object):String`

This method formats the date object according to the formatting
pattern and returns it as a string.

Listing 6.3 illustrates how to use the `Date` and `DateFormatter` classes
including the integration into a Flex application. Here we use the
date of April 10, 2006. A button enables you to trigger the formatting of the date into "04/10/2006." Figure 6.3 shows the output.

```
<mx:Script>
<![CDATA[
import mx.formatters.DateFormatter;
var datum:Date = new Date (2006, 4, 10);
public function formatActDate(){
  var datef:DateFormatter =  new DateFormatter();
  datedisplay.text = datef.format(datum);
}
]]>
</mx:Script>
<mx:Canvas id="canvas" width="100%" height="100%">
  <mx:Label x="33" y="31" id="datedisplay"
    text="{datum.toDateString()}"/>
  <mx:Button x="177" y="29" label="Format"
    id="formatDate" click="formatActDate()"/>
</mx:Canvas>
```

Listing 6.3 Formatting a Date Output

Figure 6.3 Display of a Formatted Date Output

6.2.2 Timer Objects

Executing source code within a specific period

The Timer class enables you to instantiate timer objects that allow you to execute source code within a specific period. The class is contained in the flash.util package and is directly derived from the event handler class, flash.events.EventDispatcher.

You can start the timer using the start() method. When you do so, a timer event is triggered at a specific point in time. This timer event can be captured using an event listener.

You can instantiate the timer object via the following constructor:

```
Timer(delay:Number, repeatCount:uint = 0)
```

The delay property represents a time delay in milliseconds that indicates the period after which the timer event is triggered. The repeat-Count property indicates how often the timer event is to be triggered. If the value of this property is 0, the timer event is triggered repeatedly until the timer is stopped. In addition, the timer contains the properties, methods, and events listed in Table 6.12.

Property	Description
currentCount:uint	Number of timer events called after it has been triggered using the start() method
running:Boolean	Returns true in running mode
Method	**Description**
reset():void	Stops the running timer and sets currentCount to 0
start():void	Starts the timer if it is not in running mode
stop():void	Stops the running timer
Event	**Description**
timer	Created once the time interval delay has been reached
timerComplete	Created once the timer has reached the number of repetitions specified in repeatCount

Table 6.12 Properties, Methods, and Events of the Timer Class

In order to capture the timer event, you must transfer an event listener to the timer object. You can do that by using the following
inherited method:

```
addEventListener(type:String, listener:Function,
  useCapture:Boolean = false, priority:int = 0):void
```

The important parameters in this method are `type`, which specifies
the type of event, and `listener`, which is assigned the function that
processes the event. This method can only contain an object of the
`flash.events.Event` type as a parameter and no return value.

In Listing 6.4, we start a timer once the Flex application has been
started. The timer outputs the current time to a label for a period of
10 seconds. For this purpose, the `delay` property is assigned the
value 1,000, while `repeatCount` is assigned 10. The `dateTimerHan-`
`dler(event:TimerEvent)` function is responsible for updating the
time.

```
<?xml version="1.0" encoding="utf-8"?>
<mx:Application
  xmlns:mx="http://www.adobe.com/2006/mxml" xmlns="*"
  creationComplete="init()">
<mx:Script>
<![CDATA[
import flash.util.Timer;
import flash.events.TimerEvent;
var datum:Date;
var myTimer:Timer;

public function init(){
  myTimer = new Timer(1000, 10);
  myTimer.addEventListener(TimerEvent.TIMER,
    dateTimerHandler);
  myTimer.start();
}
public function dateTimerHandler(event:TimerEvent){
  datum = new Date();
  currentDate.text = date.toLocaleTimeString();
}
]]>
</mx:Script>
<mx:Canvas id="canvas" width="100%" height="100%">
  <mx:Label x="33" y="31" id="currentDate"/>
```

```
</mx:Canvas>
</mx:Application>
```
Listing 6.4 Display of the Current Time via Timer Control

6.3 Mathematical Functions

Common mathematical operations and values

The Math class contains several methods and constants that represent frequently used mathematical operations and values (see also Section 5.2.2). The Date class is directly derived from the main class Object of the ActionScript class hierarchy. All methods are static. For this reason, you do not need to generate an object of this class.

You can call the methods using Math.method(parameter), and the constants via Math.constant. The Math class provides the constants and methods listed in Tables 6.13 and 6.14 respectively. The values specified for the constants are approximate values.

Constant	Description
static E:Number = 2.71828182845905	Mathematical constant for the basis of the natural logarithm, notated as e
static LN10:Number = 2.302585092994046	Mathematical constant for the natural logarithm of 10, represented by loge10
static LN2:Number = 0.6931471805599453	Mathematical constant for the natural logarithm of 2, represented by loge10
static LOG10E:Number = 0.4342944819032518	Mathematical constant for the logarithm to the basis 10 of constant e (Math.E), represented by log10e
static LOG2E:Number = 1.442695040888963387	Mathematical constant for the logarithm to the basis 2 of constant e (Math.E), represented by log2e
static PI:Number = 3.141592653589793	Mathematical constant for the ratio between the circumference of a circle and its diameter
static SQRT1_2:Number = 0.7071067811865476	Mathematical constant for the square root of 1
static SQRT2:Number = 1.4142135623730951	Mathematical constant for the square root of 2

Table 6.13 Overview of Mathematical Constants of the Math Class

Static Method	Description
`static abs(val:Number):Number`	Calculates an absolute value for the number specified in the `val` parameter and returns this value
`static acos(val:Number):Number`	Calculates the arccosine for the number specified in the `val` parameter and returns the arccosine as a radian
`static asin(val:Number):Number`	Calculates the arcsine for the number specified in the `val` parameter and returns the arcsine as a radian
`static atan(val:Number):Number`	Calculates the value of the angle whose tangent is defined in the `val` parameter in the radian
`static atan2(y:Number, x:Number):Number`	Calculates the angle of the point `y/x` in the radian, measured anti-clockwise from the x-axis of a circle (`0,0` being the center of the circle)
`static ceil(val:Number):Number`	Returns the upper limit of the specified number or term
`static cos(angleRadians:Number):Number`	Calculates the cosine of the specified angle and returns it as a radian
`static exp(val:Number):Number`	Returns the value of the basis of the natural logarithm (e) to the power of the exponent specified in the `val` parameter
`static floor(val:Number):Number`	Returns the lower limit of the number or term specified in the `val` parameter
`static log(val:Number):Number`	Returns the logarithm of the `val` parameter
`static max(val1:Number, val2:Number):Number`	Analyzes `val1` and `val2` and returns the bigger of the two values
`static min(val1:Number, val2:Number):Number`	Analyzes `val1` and `val2` and returns the smaller of the two values
`static pow(val1:Number, val2:Number):Number`	Calculates `val1` to the power of `val2` and returns the result
`static random():Number`	Returns a pseudo random number n, whereby the following condition applies: $0 <= n < 1$
`static round(val:Number):Number`	Rounds the value of the `val1` parameter up to the next integer and returns this integer

Table 6.14 Overview of Static Methods of the Math Class

Static Method	Description
`static sin(angleRadians: Number):Number`	Calculates the sine of the specified angle and returns it as a radian
`static sqrt(val:Number):Number`	Calculates the square root of the specified number and returns the square root
`static tan(angleRadians: Number):Number`	Calculates the tangent of the specified angle and returns the tangent

Table 6.14 Overview of Static Methods of the Math Class (cont.)

In Listing 6.5, we'll determine the sine of a 45-degree angle. Prior to that, the radian must be calculated using the following term: `45 * Math.PI/180`.

```
var sin_value:Number = Math.sin( 45*Math.PI/180 );
```

Listing 6.5 Calculating the Sine Value

6.4 Keyboard Events

Responding to keyboard entries

To be able to respond to keyboard entries, you can use the `Keyboard-Event` class that is contained in the `flash.events` package. This class contains two events that can be responded to within a Flex application: `KeyboardEvent.KEY_DOWN` to respond to the pressing of a key, and `KeyboardEvent.KEY_UP` to respond to the pressing of a key after the key has been pressed. Furthermore, the class contains the properties listed in Table 6.15.

Property	Description
`charCode:uint`	Contains the ASCII character of the pressed key
`ctrlKey:Boolean`	Indicates whether or not the control key was pressed (`true` or `false`).
`keyCode:uint`	Contains the key code of the pressed key
`keyLocation:uint`	Contains the keyboard position of the pressed key
`shiftKey:Boolean`	Indicates whether or not the **Shift** key was pressed (`true` or `false`).

Table 6.15 Properties of the KeyboardEvent Class and Their Meanings

The class contains the `updateAfterEvent():void` method that enables you to refresh the display once the event has been processed and when a new graphical component has been added by the processing of the event.

Refreshing the display

In order to instantiate an object of this class, you must use the `public function KeyboardEvent()` constructor. You can call this constructor as follows:

```
KeyboardEvent(type:String, bubbles:Boolean = true,
  cancelable:Boolean = false, charCode:uint = 0,
  keyCode:uint = 0, keyLocation:uint = 0,
  ctrlKey:Boolean = false, altKey:Boolean = false,
  shiftKey:Boolean = false)
```

Here you must at least specify the event type `type` including the `KEY_DOWN` and `KEY_UP` values. The `bubbles` parameter indicates whether the event object is processed in the bubbling[2] phase of the event sequence. The `cancelable` parameter indicates whether the event can be canceled. In the MXML environment, many display components already use the events of this class, so that you only need to assign an event listener to those objects.

The key code of those keyboard characters that cannot be directly determined via the ASCII code can be requested using the static constants of the `Keyboard` class in the `flash.ui` package. These include, among others, `Keyboard.BACKSPACE`, `Keyboard.ENTER`, `Keyboard.TAB`, and constants for the arrow keys and function keys.

Listing 6.6 shows a `<mx:TextInput>` component in which the string is copied into a `<mx:List>` component once the string has been entered and confirmed by pressing the **Enter** key (see Figure 6.4).

Copying a string

```
<mx:Script>
<![CDATA[
var array:Array = new Array();
public function enter(event:KeyboardEvent):void{
  if (event.keyCode == Keyboard.ENTER){
```

---

2 The bubbling phase is one in which events are controlled. During this phase, the events moves upwards n the object hierarchy like a bubble. In this context, a check is carried out for all objects that are superior to the triggering object in order to see if an event handler exists that captures this event.

```
        array.push(input.text);
          list.dataProvider = array;
}
]]>
</mx:Script>
<mx:Canvas id="canvas" width="100%" height="100%">
  <mx:TextInput x="21" y="22" id="input"
    keyDown="enter(event)"/>
  <mx:List x="209" y="22" id="list"/>
</mx:Canvas>
```

Listing 6.6 Copying a Text Using the Keyboard

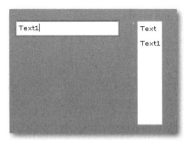

Figure 6.4 Screen Output for Copying a Text via the Keyboard

6.5 Text Fields and Text Formats

Stylesheets and layouts

The ActionScript package `flash.text` contains classes that enable you to use text fields, format text, manipulate the dimensions of text elements within a text field, and use stylesheets and different layouts. The package contains the classes listed in Table 6.16.

Class	Description
AntiAliasType	Class containing static anti-aliasing values for the `flash.display.TextField` class
ColorType	Class providing the static values DARK_COLOR and LIGHT_COLOR for the colors of the `flash.text.TextRenderer` class
FontStyle	Class providing the static font style values for the `flash.text.TextRenderer` class
GridFitType	Class providing static values for the `flash.display.Text-Field` class in order to attain a useful grid adjustment

Table 6.16 Classes of the flash.text Package and Their Meanings

Class	Description
StyleSheet	This class enables you to create a stylesheet object that contains text formatting rules for the size of a text, its color, and so on
TextFormat	Class that contains information on character formats
TextFormatAlign	Class that contains static values for the alignment of text; the values can be used by the TextFormat class
TextLineMetrics	Class that contains information on the text position and dimensions of a text line within a text field
TextRenderer	This class contains extended anti-aliasing functions for embedded fonts
TextSnapshot	TextSnapshot objects enable you to use static text in a movie clip

Table 6.16 Classes of the flash.text Package and Their Meanings (cont.)

You can apply the resulting text properties to text fields of the flash.display.TextField type. The TextField class can be used to create areas for the entry and display of text, and it contains many properties and methods for presenting text. All dynamic text fields and input text fields in a SWF file are instances of the TextField class. However, Flex applications predominantly use the Label, Text, TextArea, and TextInput components as well as their formatting classes. But you can use the TextField class in order to implement your own text component classes.

Presentation of text

The following sections describe some of the properties and methods. For a more detailed view, you should refer to the **ActionScript and MXML Language Reference** that you can find at the following address: *http://livedocs.macromedia.com/labs/1/flex/langref/flash/display/TextField.html*.

You can instantiate an object of this class using the following constructor:

```
public function TextField()
```

In addition, the class contains the properties listed in Table 6.17. The methods listed in Table 6.18 enable you to change the properties of the text field.

Property	Description
antiAliasType:String [read-write]	Contains the anti-aliasing type for the text field
backgroundColor:uint [read-write]	Contains the background color of the text field
border:Boolean [read-write]	Indicates whether the text field contains a visible border (true or false)
borderColor:uint [read-write]	Contains the color of the border
caretIndex:int [read-only]	Contains a flashing starting point to insert text
defaultTextFormat:TextFormat [read-write]	Contains an object of the flash.text.Textformat type
embedFonts:Boolean [read-write]	Indicates whether or not embedded fonts are to be used for the presentation
gridFitType:String [read-write]	Indicates the type of grid adjustment used for this textfield instance
html:Boolean [read-write]	Boolean value that specifies whether or not the text field contains HTML data
htmlText:String [read-write]	If the text field is an HTML text field, this property contains the HTML presentation of the text field content
length:int [read-only]	Specifies the number of characters in a text field
multiline:Boolean [read-write]	Indicates whether the text field contains multiple lines
password:Boolean [read-write]	Indicates whether the text field is a password text field
restrict:String [read-write]	Specifies the characters a user may enr into the text field
selectable:Boolean [read-write]	Boolean value that specifies whether the text field can be selected
styleSheet:StyleSheet [read-write]	Adds a stylesheet to the text field
text:String [read-write]	Indicates the current text in the text field

Table 6.17 Properties of the TextField Class and Their Meanings

Property	Description
textColor:uint [read-write]	Indicates the color of the text in the text field
textHeight:Number [read-only]	Indicates the height of the text
textWidth:Number [read-only]	Indicates the width of the text
type:String [read-write]	Specifies the type of text field
wordWrap:Boolean [read-write]	Boolean value that specifies whether the text field contains a line break

Table 6.17 Properties of the TextField Class and Their Meanings (cont.)

Method	Description
appendText(newText: String):void	Adds a new text to the end of the current text
getImageReference(id: String):DisplayObject	Returns a DisplayObject (bitmap file or movie clip) for a specified id; the Display-Object transferred in HTML format using the <img> tag
getLineLength(lineIndex: int):int	Returns the number of characters contained in a specific line of text
getLineMetrics(lineIndex: int):TextLineMetrics	Returns information on the text position and dimensions of a text line as a textlinemetrics object
getLineText(lineIndex: int):String	Returns the text of a specific text line
getTextFormat(beginIndex:int = 0, endIndex:int = 0x7FFFFFFF):TextFormat	Returns a text-format object for a character, a string of characters, or for an entire textfield object
removeTextField():void	Removes the text field
replaceSelectedText(value: String):void	Replaces the current selection with the content of the value parameter
replaceText(beginIndex:int, endIndex:int, newText: String):void	Replaces several characters in the specified text field that are identified by the beginIndex and endIndex parameters with the content of the newText parameter

Table 6.18 Methods of the TextField Class and Their Meanings

Method	Description

`setTextFormat(format:`
`TextFormat, beginIndex:`
`int = 0, endIndex:`
`int = 0x7FFFFFFF):void`
	Assigns the text formatting specified by `Text-`
	`Format` to parts of the text or the complete
	text

Table 6.18 Methods of the TextField Class and Their Meanings (cont.)

In Listing 6.7 we assign a `TextFormat` object to a text field. In addition, a border is specified and color values are set, as shown in Figure 6.5.

```
// TextFieldFormat.as
package classes {
  import flash.display.TextField;
  import flash.text.TextFormat;
  import mx.core.UIComponent;
  public class TextFieldFormat extends UIComponent {
    public var label:TextField;
    public function TextFieldFormat() {
      var format:TextFormat = new TextFormat();
      format.font = "Arial";
      format.size = 14;
      format.color = 0xFF01FF;
      label = new TextField();
      label.text = "TextField";
      label.width = 200;
      label.height = 20;
      label.y = 20;
      label.border = true;
      label.borderColor = 0xFFDDFF;
      label.background = true;
      label.backgroundColor = 0x00DDFF;
      label.setTextFormat(format);
      addChild(label);
    }
  }
}

// Flex application
<?xml version="1.0" encoding="utf-8"?>
<mx:Application
  xmlns:mx="http://www.adobe.com/2006/mxml" xmlns="*"
  creationComplete="init()">
<mx:Script>
```

```
<![CDATA[
  import classes.TextFieldFormat;
  public function init(){
    canvas.addChild(new TextFieldFormat());
  }
]]>
</mx:Script>
<mx:Canvas id="canvas" width="100%" height="100%"/>
</mx:Application>
```

Listing 6.7 Text Field with Formatting

Figure 6.5 Screen Output for the Text Field with Formatting

6.6 Other ActionScript Packages

In addition to the ActionScript packages described in this chapter, many other useful packages are available. These are listed in Table 6.19.

Useful and versatile

Package	Description
flash.accessibility	Contains classes that provide access to Flash content and applications
flash.display	Contains classes that enable Flash Player to create graphics on the screen
flash.errors	Contains general error classes
flash.events	Supports the new DOM event model and contains some classes for triggering these events
flash.external	Contains the externalInterface class that you can use to communicate with Flash Player
flash.filters	Contains classes that you can use for bitmap-filtering effects (supported as of Flash Player Version 8.x)
flash.geom	Contains a geometry class for points, rectangles, or transformation matrices
flash.net	Contains classes for sending and receiving packages on a network
flash.print	Contains classes for starting print processes

Table 6.19 ActionScript Packages and Their Functions

Package	Description
flash.system	Contains classes that enable you to access system functions
flash.ui	Contains user interface classes that enable you, for instance, to interact with the keyboard or mouse
flash.util	Contains additional tool classes, functions, and interfaces
flash.xml	Contains classes that enable you to access XML documents

Table 6.19 ActionScript Packages and Their Functions (cont.)

In this chapter, we'll develop a sample application step by step. The first part of the chapter contains a description of the application and a definition of the requirements. The subsequent sections then describe the individual programming steps in the SAP and Flex environments.

7   Developing a Sample Application

The sample application that is developed in great detail in this chapter focuses on planning and recording of working hours, including their analysis.

The advantage of Flex and Flash applications is that to a large extent you can develop the SAP logic and the front-end presentation separately, provided you have defined a common interface. In order to clearly point out the separation of front-end and back-end components, we'll treat the development in the SAP environment and in the Flex development environment separately once we have designed the concept of the application.

Separation of back end and front end

7.1   Concept

Before you can start the actual development work, you must design a concept. For the application used here, you must define the minimum requirements to be met by a time-planning and time-recording tool, as well as the data model that meets these requirements, and also the way in which the interfaces must be defined. Moreover, you should roughly describe the layout of the application.

7.1.1   General Requirements of the Application

Time planning and time recording are supposed to enable employees of a company to efficiently and effectively record their working hours and to plan their subsequent activities based on this data. As a result, both project managers and personnel planning will know

Objective

exactly at what time a certain employee works on a specific project and how the subsequent activities of this employee can be scheduled further. The time-recording component then enables you to analyze the working hours of the employees and facilitates the creation of an invoice to the customer.

The application must meet the following general requirements.

▶ **Intuitiveness, with easy usability**
Planning is an activity carried out with regard to the future, whereas time recording refers to the past. To be able to carry out both activities efficiently and effectively, the application must be easy to use and it must be intuitive. You therefore should avoid using graphical animations for the data entry.

▶ **Small data transfer volume**
An aspect that's closely related to the previous one involves the interface of the application. The transfer of data between the SAP system and the Flex framework is supposed to guarantee the efficiency of the application. For this reason, you should keep the data volume to be transferred as small as possible.

▶ **Functionality to customize and maintain the application for system-specific requirements**
Furthermore, it must be possible to customize the application for different purposes in order to be able to respond to system-specific properties (holiday calendar ID, company code, and the like). It must be possible to enter activities to be planned directly from Flex into the SAP system. If this is the case, the application can usually also be maintained without any problem.

▶ **Logical naming convention**
A very important aspect in the development of the application is that you maintain a logical naming convention. The naming convention facilitates the readability of the source text and thus speeds up maintenance times. Moreover, you can use *SAP Code Inspector*[1] to automatically check the naming convention. SAP Code Inspector detects any non-adherence to the naming convention. In addition, you should make to insert comments in the source text.

---

1 You can access SAP Code Inspector using Transaction SCI. In addition to automatically checking predefined naming conventions, SAP Code Inspector is primarily used to test ABAP code. You can find further information in the SAP Library.

▶ **Development close to the standard**
The application should not create any complex workarounds in order to provide basic functions. You should rather use Business Application Programming Interfaces (BAPIs) and other similar functions provided by SAP.

Restrictions

Because this is only a sample application, we'll avoid developing complex user input options and other specific requirements. The application is supposed to exemplify *how* you can implement basic requirements; you can develop other advanced control elements individually to fit your requirements.

7.1.2 Specific Requirements of the Application

The activities of recording and planning working hours allow scheduling and time recording for one activity per day in order not to make the application too complex. Furthermore, the degree of accuracy of working hours to be recorded is set to one hour in order to avoid additional development work regarding troubleshooting user input and also to avoid having to implement additional conversion routines. These can be easily implemented and will be briefly discussed later in this chapter.

Properties

The following specific requirements must be met:

Specific requirements

▶ **Pre-assignment of time recording during planning**
In order to facilitate time recording after the planning process, the time-recording function is pre-assigned the planned activity during the planning of one workday. If the planning process has been carried out accurately, time recording can be done without further editing.

▶ **Month-end closing**
To prevent data from being changed and manipulated once it has been entered, it must be possible to close a month. This means that as soon as a month has been closed, it can no longer be edited. In this context, the recorded working hours should be checked for plausibility.

> ▶ **Defining whether an activity can be billed to a customer**[2]
> For management consultants in particular, project work is one of the most important activities, as this work is (directly or indirectly) linked to their performance-related bonuses. Consequently, it must be possible to mark activities as bonus-relevant. Employees who work at customer sites thus enter their work for activities that cannot be billed to the customer; i. e., work that is not bonus-relevant. A separation into billable and non-billable hours is particularly important with regard to reporting (concerning the utilization of an employee's capacity). As a result, the application must allow you to maintain the bonus relevance of an activity.

> ▶ **Useful analyses**
> The analysis of recorded working hours plays a central role for a company. It is important to know which employees have worked on a specific project for which part of the fiscal year and, also, what is the current capacity utilization of the company (in relation to the total number of working hours and the billable hours of the employees). For this reason, the following useful analyses will be used in the sample application.

> > ▶ Capacity utilization of an employee per calendar year

> > ▶ Capacity utilization of all employees per month

> > ▶ Capacity utilization of all employees per calendar year

> The analyses defined in this way are then to be evaluated graphically within the front end.

7.1.3   Data Model

To be able to implement the requirements defined in the previous section, you must design an appropriate data model. The data model should be simple but efficient and it should not increase the volume of data to be transferred.

Data elements   Our application is based on one data element only, which identifies the activity. In order to ensure a sufficient number of activities and to combine (8-digit) PSP element IDs and (4-digit) absence types, the activity is defined as a 12-digit data element.

---

2   In consulting, the term "billable hours" describes the working hours that can be billed to a customer.

The application requires four tables. One of the tables is responsible for storing the planning data (planning table), and another one is needed for storing the time recording data (time-recording table). To meet the general requirement of customizability, we need a customizing table, while an activity table enables us to manage the activities and to set the bonus-relevance. The tables contain the following information:

▸ **Planning table (ZDZTB_001)**

The planning activity must be performed by each employee. Because we want to plan only one activity per day the combination of personnel number (PERSNO) and date (DATE) is a fully qualifying primary key. In addition to the personnel number and the date, the activity (ACTIVITY) must be recorded, and a flag must be available to indicate whether a month has been closed or can still be edited (FINISHED).

▸ **Time-recording table (ZDZTB_002)**

The time-recording table can be implemented in a similar way. You can use the same fully qualifying primary key as in the planning table, consisting of the personnel number (PERSNO) and the date (DATE). In addition to the activity (ACTIVITY), there are fields that contain the hours (HRS_COMPL) and the potentially existing billable hours (HRS_BILL). As in planning, a finished flag (FINISHED) is provided.

▸ **Customizing table (ZDZTB_003)**

To a large extent, the structure of the customizing table is standardized and contains name-value pairs (NAME and VALUE). Here you can make settings for the holiday calendar ID, relevant company codes, and the like.

▸ **Activity table (ZDZTB_004)**

The settings for the activities are contained in the activity table. Note that these settings are limited to the bonus-relevance aspect. In the sample application we use one flag for this (BONUS). This flag indicates whether or not an activity (ACTIVITY) is bonus-relevant. For other applications, you can consider using formulas for bonus determination.

No table is needed for reporting, but the interface to be designed should be simple and reusable, which is why we define a structure that includes reporting. The structure consists of the personnel number (PERNR) and the activity (ACTIVITY), both of which are populated with data in the case of individual reporting (individual employee, individual activity). The period (PERIOD) indicates whether a month (M) or a year (Y) is being analyzed. Moreover, to be able to easily determine whether an existing report refers to *one* (S) or *multiple* employees (M) the PERSNO_NO flag was added. The working hours entered are listed under the HRS (recorded working hours) and HRS_ BILL (bonus-relevant working hours) components.

7.1.4 Defining the Interface

The interface must present the data from the SAP system in a concise manner so that the data volume to be transferred is kept small.

XML interface

The interface itself is implemented on the basis of XML. In the Flex application, the XML files are addressed via a URL, and their content is determined and processed at runtime. Interface files are required for the following cases:

▶ Adding a planning (*)

▶ Reading planning data

▶ Adding time recording (*)

▶ Reading time-recording data

▶ Closing a month (*)

▶ Reporting data

▶ Application-relevant data

▶ Login data (*)

The cases marked with an asterisk (*) are necessary in order to recognize errors when adding data and to troubleshoot those errors. For example, you can use appropriate error message texts in the XML file to publish errors in the back end to the front end (adding a planning when a month has been closed, for instance).

Adding data/login

The XML interface for adding data must be defined for the following cases: "adding a planning," "adding time recording," "closing a month," and "login data." The XML interface can have the following format:

```
<error_text></error_text>
```

To read planning data from the back-end system, it is useful to provide the XML file with the following structure (see Listing 7.1):

```
<result>
   <head>
      <persno></persno>
   </head>
   <pos>
      <entry>
         <date></date>
         <activity></activity>
         <finished></finished>
      </entry>
   </pos>
</result>
```
Listing 7.1 XML Interface for Planning Data

To keep the data-transfer volume small, the personnel number is output only once in the head section of the structure although it is stored for each data record. All other information of the entries is contained in the pos section of the XML file. Both sections are summarized in a <result> tag.

To read-time recording data from the back-end system, it is useful to provide the XML file with a structure similar to the one used for the planning data (see Listing 7.2):

```
<result>
   <head>
      <persno></persno>
   </head>
   <pos>
      <entry>
         <date></date>
         <activity></activity>
         <hrs_compl></hrs_compl>
         <hrs_bill></hrs_bill>
         <finished></finished>
      </entry>
   </pos>
</result>
```
Listing 7.2 XML Interface for Time Recording Data

Similarly to planning, the personnel number is also output only once in the head section of the structure in order to minimize the volume of data to be transferred. All other information of the entries is contained in the pos section of the XML file. Both sections are summarized in a <result> tag. In addition to the planning data, time recording also contains the time data (hours and billable hours).

Reporting data The presentation of the reporting data is to be identical for each reporting case. For this purpose, the structure of the XML file should be based on the data model (see Listing 7.3).

```
<report>
   <entry>
      <persno></persno>
      <activity></activity>
      <period></period>
      <persno_no></persno_no>
      <hrs></hrs>
      <hrs_bill></hrs_bill>
   </entry>
</report>
```

Listing 7.3 XML Interface for Reporting Data

Like the structure defined in the data model, all elements of the structure are contained in the XML file of the interface. Additional calculations such as a conversion in percentages and so on, are performed at a later stage on the client.

Application-relevant data Application-relevant data includes content of drop-down boxes in the Flex application, such as personnel numbers, activities, and so on. The content is to be transferred to the front end and always in the same structure (see Listing 7.4).

```
<data>
   <type></type>
   <entry>
      <name></name>
      <value></value>
   </entry>
</data>
```

Listing 7.4 XML Interface of Application-Relevant Data

The type (`type`) indicates what kind of data is being processed (activities, personnel numbers, absence types, and so on). The individual values are then listed within the `<entry>` tag.

7.1.5 Application Layout

The layout of the application should be simple, straightforward, and easy to use. For this purpose, we'll use separate tabs (also referred to as tabstrips) to bundle the core functions. Another step towards intuitive usability is to avoid using too many control elements such as buttons, icons, and so on.

As core functions, planning and time recording require drop-down boxes for the activities, an input field for the working hours, and a calendar component for entering the date. Furthermore, data that has already been entered—for example, in a table—must be displayed and be editable.

Planning and time recording

For reporting purposes, the selection of an employee (drop-down box) or the entry of the employee's personnel number as well as the required period represents a basic characteristic. Moreover, the user must be able to select the type of reporting he or she wants to execute.

Reporting

We'll describe more layout details in the section that treats the development of the front end (see Section 7.3).

7.2 Developing in the SAP Environment

This section describes the developments that are necessary in the SAP system. Here we define the basic structure of the application, implement the data model, create necessary function modules, and define the interface. Short tests at the end of the section are intended to demonstrate that the solution is operable.

The application in the SAP system is implemented as a Business Server Page (BSP) application that provides data from the SAP system via XML files.

Type of implementation

Basically, Flex can be integrated in two different ways: via an XML interface or as an implementation using Java classes. The solution described here is based on the implementation of an XML interface via a BSP application. The main argument in favor of this solution is that the development is very transparent, which can be essential when using the application on the customer's side. The source text of the BSP application is open and thus transparent. In contrast to this, Java classes are not permanently integrated in the SAP system and are written by using internal and external tools such as Eclipse or SAP NetWeaver Developer Studio. Moreover, Java is still not entirely accepted by customers.

The BSP application is based on an application class that contains the information required at runtime. Necessary operations for creating and reading SAP information are carried out by function modules that are called in the BSP application.

MVC model   The advantage of Rich Internet Applications (RIAs) is that they have been written in compliance with the MVC model (see Section 2.2). The MVC model can also be used for the back-end application in the SAP system, which is pretty useful for more complex applications. However, because the sample application described here is not very complex and is merely supposed to convey the basic procedure when designing RIAs, we do not implement it in the SAP system according to the MVC model.

7.2.1   Creating the Basic Structure

The basic structure of the application comprises the required function groups, the BSP application, and its application class, in a package specifically created for this purpose.

Creating a package   To create the basic structure, you must go to the ABAP Workbench (Transaction SE80). There, you must create a package in the customer namespace (Z_DZT_BOOK) and an associated transport request.

Function groups   To structure the logic of the application in a useful way, you should create different function groups that will take up the function modules. In our case, the following structure id is helpful. The function group ZDZTB_ACQUISITION is used to take up function modules from the planning and time recording area. The ZDZTB_OTHER group hosts other function modules (login data, application data), and the ZDZTB_REPORTING group takes up reporting-relevant function modules (see Figure 7.1).

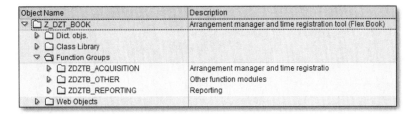

Figure 7.1 Creating Function Groups

After that, you must create a class that will later become the applica-   **Application class**
tion class of our BSP application (see Figure 7.2). The class consists of
the following attributes: DATA (data required for the application),
PLAN (planning data in a table), ERROR_TEXT (errors that have occurred
during processing), REPORT (reporting data as a structure), REPORT_
TABLE (more detailed reporting data in a table), and TR (time recording data in a table).

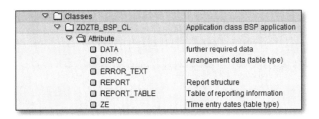

Figure 7.2 Creating the Application Class

You can use the default settings for the properties of the class. As
we'll describe the associated attributes of the class at a later stage,
you don't need to create them now.

7.2.2   Implementing the Data Model

The first step towards implementing the data model requires the data
element of the activity (see Section 7.1.3). The data element consists
of a 12-digit character field so that it can display both PSP elements
(8-digit) and absence types (4-digit). This results in a CHAR12 primary
key (see Figure 7.3).

Once you have maintained the field names, you can use the data element.

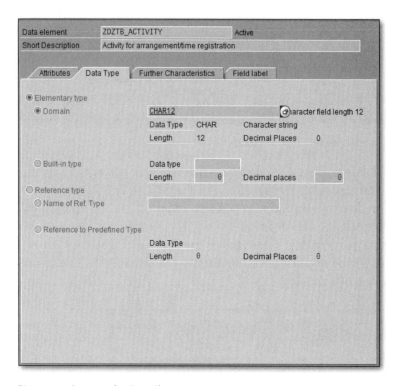

Figure 7.3 Creating the Data Element

Then you can implement database tables according to the definition of the data model in Section 7.1.3. The table to be used to store planning data is assigned the name ZDZTB_001 and has the structure shown in Figure 7.4. The fields must be created in accordance with the data model and consist of the primary key fields client (MANDT), personnel number (PERSNO), and the date (DATE), as well as the non-key fields ACTIVITY (activity of the planning) and the FINISHED flag (month closed).

Field	Key	Initi...	Data element	Data Ty...	Length	Deci...	Short Description
MANDT	✓	✓	MANDT	CLNT	3	0	Client
PERNR	✓	✓	PERSNO	NUMC	8	0	Personnel number
DATUM	✓	✓	DATS	DATS	8	0	Field of type DATS
ACTIVITY			ZDZTB_ACTIVITY	CHAR	12	0	Activity for arrangement/time registration
FINISHED			FLAG	CHAR	1	0	General Flag

Transp. table ZDZTB_001 Active
Short Description Arrangement data

Attributes / Delivery and Maintenance / Fields / Entry help/check / Currency/Quantity Fields

Srch help   Built-in type   1 / 5

Figure 7.4 Table for Storing Planning Data

The technical settings are supposed to contain the data type APPL0 and size category 0. You can make these settings via the menu item, **Technical Settings** that is located directly above the table name. Figure 7.5 shows the settings made. For more complex applications that can be used in live systems, you naturally must choose a higher category.

Technical settings

Name	ZDZTB_001		Transparent Table
Short text			
Last changed	DKNAPP	20.11.2006	
Status	Active	Saved	

Logical storage parameters

Data class	APPL0	Master data, transparent tables
Size category	0	Data records expected: 0 to 19.000

Buffering
- ● Buffering not allowed
- ○ Buffering allowed but switched off
- ○ Buffering switched on

Buffering type
- ☐ Single records buff.
- ☐ Generic area buffered   No. of key fields
- ☐ Fully buffered

☐ Log data changes

Figure 7.5 Setting the Technical Data of the Table

The table to be used to store time-recording data is assigned the name ZDZTB_002 and has the structure shown in Figure 7.6. Similar to the planning data table, this table contains the fields MANDT, PERSNO, DATE, ACTIVITY, and FINISHED. It also contains the fields HRS_COMPL for the exact calculation of the working time in terms of hours, and HRS_BILL for working hours that can be billed to the customer. Here as well you can set the technical settings to the data type APPL0 and size category 0.

The customizing table used to store application-relevant data is assigned the name ZDZTB_003 and has the structure shown in Figure 7.7. It consists of the NAME and VALUE fields and is used to store system and application-related data.

Here you must set the technical settings to APPL2 (Customizing) and size category 0. You can use these settings also in live systems.

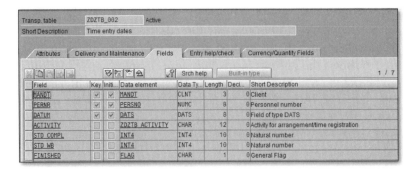

Figure 7.6 Table for Storing Time-Recording Data

Transp. table	ZDZTB_002	Active
Short Description	Customizing table	

Attributes | Delivery and Maintenance | Fields | Entry help/check | Currency/Quantity Fields

1 / 3

Field	Key	Initi...	Data element	Data Ty...	Length	Deci...	Short Description
MANDT	✓	✓	MANDT	CLNT	3	0	Mandant
NAME	✓	✓	CHAR100	CHAR	100	0	Charakter 100
VALUE			CHAR100	CHAR	100	0	Charakter 100

Figure 7.7 Customizing Table of the Application

The table to be used to store activities and their settings is assigned the name ZDZTB_004 and has the structure shown in Figure 7.8. The activity table requires the key field of the activity (ACTIVITY), a description of the activity (DESCR), and the flag that indicates the bonus relevance (BONUS).

Transp. table	ZDZTB_004	Active
Short Description	Activity table	

Attributes | Delivery and Maintenance | Fields | Entry help/check | Currency/Quantity Fields

1 / 4

Field	Key	Initi...	Data element	Data Ty...	Length	Deci...	Short Description
MANDT	✓	✓	MANDT	CLNT	3	0	Client
ACTIVITY	✓	✓	ZDZTB_ACTIVITY	CHAR	12	0	Activity for arrangement/time registration
DESCR			CHAR100SM	CHAR	100	0	Charakter 100
BONUS			FLAG	CHAR	1	0	General Flag

Figure 7.8 Table of Activities and Their Properties

Here you must set the technical settings to APPL0 and size category 0. You can use these settings also in live systems.

During the further course of the development we'll need additional DDIC objects such as structures and table types, which are briefly described below. The structures and table types are required for the planning and time recording data and are assigned names according to the following naming convention:

Additional DDIC objects

- ZDZTB_001_STRU, ZDZTB_002_STRU, ZDZTB_003_STRU

- ZDZTB_001_TAB, ZDZTB_002_TAB, ZDZTB_003_TAB.

The format of the structures is exactly the same as that of the corresponding tables, as shown in Figure 7.9. Thus, they consist of the following fields: MANDT, PERSNO, DATE, ACTIVITY, and FINISHED.

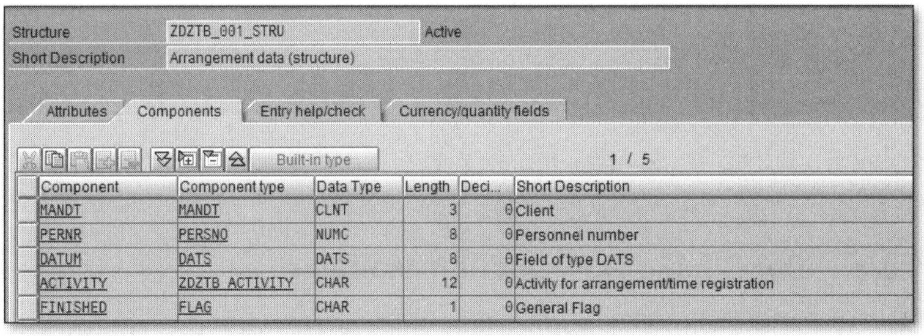

Structure	ZDZTB_001_STRU		Active		
Short Description	Arrangement data (structure)				

Attributes / Components / Entry help/check / Currency/quantity fields

Built-in type   1 / 5

Component	Component type	Data Type	Length	Deci...	Short Description
MANDT	MANDT	CLNT	3	0	Client
PERNR	PERSNO	NUMC	8	0	Personnel number
DATUM	DATS	DATS	8	0	Field of type DATS
ACTIVITY	ZDZTB_ACTIVITY	CHAR	12	0	Activity for arrangement/time registration
FINISHED	FLAG	CHAR	1	0	General Flag

Figure 7.9 Structure of Planning Data

The reporting structure defined in Section 7.1.3 is important. It is implemented as shown in Figure 7.10. The structure consists of the year/month combination (YEARMON), the personnel number (PERSNO), the activity of the planning or time recording (ACTIVITY), the period (PERIOD; Y=year or M=month), the number of analyzed personnel numbers (PERSNO_NO; S=single or M=multi), and the total amount of hours (HRS) and billable hours (HRS_BILL).

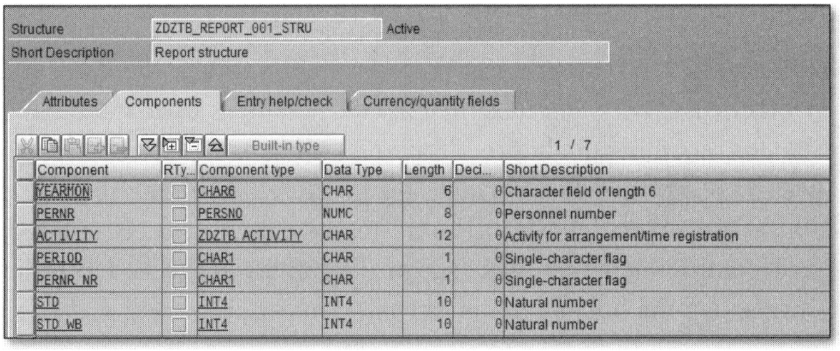

Reporting structure

Structure	ZDZTB_REPORT_001_STRU		Active		
Short Description	Report structure				

Attributes / Components / Entry help/check / Currency/quantity fields

Built-in type   1 / 7

Component	RTy...	Component type	Data Type	Length	Deci...	Short Description
YEARMON	☐	CHAR6	CHAR	6	0	Character field of length 6
PERNR	☐	PERSNO	NUMC	8	0	Personnel number
ACTIVITY	☐	ZDZTB_ACTIVITY	CHAR	12	0	Activity for arrangement/time registration
PERIOD	☐	CHAR1	CHAR	1	0	Single-character flag
PERNR_NR	☐	CHAR1	CHAR	1	0	Single-character flag
STD	☐	INT4	INT4	10	0	Natural number
STD_WB	☐	INT4	INT4	10	0	Natural number

Figure 7.10 General Reporting Structure

Once you have successfully created and activated all DDIC objects, the application contains the elements shown in Figure 7.11.

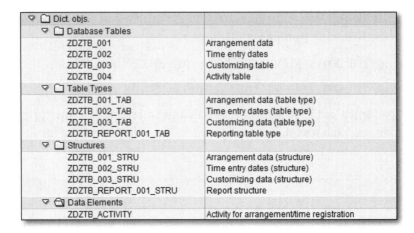

▽ ☐ Dict. objs.	
▽ ☐ Database Tables	
ZDZTB_001	Arrangement data
ZDZTB_002	Time entry dates
ZDZTB_003	Customizing table
ZDZTB_004	Activity table
▽ ☐ Table Types	
ZDZTB_001_TAB	Arrangement data (table type)
ZDZTB_002_TAB	Time entry dates (table type)
ZDZTB_003_TAB	Customizing data (table type)
ZDZTB_REPORT_001_TAB	Reporting table type
▽ ☐ Structures	
ZDZTB_001_STRU	Arrangement data (structure)
ZDZTB_002_STRU	Time entry dates (structure)
ZDZTB_003_STRU	Customizing data (structure)
ZDZTB_REPORT_001_STRU	Report structure
▽ ☐ Data Elements	
ZDZTB_ACTIVITY	Activity for arrangement/time registration

Figure 7.11 DDIC Objects of the Planning Tool

7.2.3 Developing the Function Modules

The actual logic of the application that carries out the creation of planning and time-recording functions can be controlled via function modules that are stored in the function groups described earlier in this chapter.

Planning and Time-Recording Modules

Creating a planning module

You can only create a planning module if the month has not been closed, which can be determined via the FINISHED field in Table ZDZTB_001. However, you must also check the corresponding flag in Table ZDZTB_002 to see if the month has been closed there, because planning data does not necessarily have to exist in that table.

In planning, you must transfer the personnel number, the date, and the planned activity. Because the planned activity is used as a default value for recording the hours, a time-recording data record is created once the planning data record has been entered. The time-recording data record pre-assigns eight hours to the activity that is entered. Furthermore, the bonus-relevance of the activity is checked in order to pre-assign the billable hours as well, if necessary.

The modification of a planning module is carried out in the same way as the creation of a planning and is automatically processed using a MODIFY statement.

The function module ZDZTB_PLAN_ADD adds a planning module in the manner described above and is a component of the function group ZDZTB_ACQUISITION. If an error occurs during processing, the error is returned by the function module and then transferred from the BSP application to the frontend for display purposes; otherwise PE_ERROR_TEXT is assigned the value OK. Listing 7.5 shows the corresponding source text.

```
FUNCTION ZDZTB_PLAN_ADD.
*"----------------------------------------------------------
*"*"Local interface:
*"  IMPORTING
*"     REFERENCE(PI_PERSNO) TYPE   PERSNO
*"     REFERENCE(PI_DATE) TYPE   DATS
*"     REFERENCE(PI_ACTIVITY) TYPE   ZDZTB_ACTIVITY
*"  EXPORTING
*"     REFERENCE(PE_SUBRC) TYPE   SY-SUBRC
*"     REFERENCE(PE_ERROR_TEXT) TYPE   STRING
*"----------------------------------------------------------

   DATA: it_dztb_001 TYPE TABLE OF zdztb_001,
         it_dztb_002 TYPE TABLE OF zdztb_002,

         wa_dztb_001 LIKE LINE OF it_dztb_001,
         wa_dztb_002 LIKE LINE OF it_dztb_002,

         l_finished  TYPE flag,
         l_month     TYPE string,
         l_bonus     TYPE flag.

* Has month been closed? -> Forbid planning
   CONCATENATE pi_date(6) '%' INTO l_month.

   CLEAR l_finished.
   SELECT * FROM zdztb_001 INTO TABLE it_dztb_001
      WHERE persno = pi_persno
        AND date LIKE l_month.

   LOOP AT it_dztb_001 INTO wa_dztb_001
      WHERE finished = 'X'.
      IF wa_dztb_001-finished = 'X'.
```

```
            l_finished = 'X'.
              EXIT.
          ENDIF.
      ENDLOOP.

* Also check time recording if month has been closed
    IF l_finished IS INITIAL.
        SELECT * FROM zdztb_002 INTO TABLE it_dztb_002
           WHERE persno = pi_persno
             AND date LIKE l_month.

        LOOP AT it_dztb_002 INTO wa_dztb_002
           WHERE finished = 'X'.
           IF wa_dztb_002-finished = 'X'.
              l_finished = 'X'.
              EXIT.
           ENDIF.
        ENDLOOP.
    ENDIF.

* No finished entry found
    IF l_finished IS INITIAL.

* Add planning
        CLEAR wa_dztb_001.
        wa_dztb_001-persno = pi_persno.
        wa_dztb_001-date = pi_date.
        wa_dztb_001-activity = pi_activity.

* Check for billable hours
        CLEAR l_bonus.
        SELECT SINGLE bonus FROM zdztb_004 INTO l_bonus
           WHERE activity = pi_activity.

        IF l_bonus IS NOT INITIAL.
           wa_dztb_002-hrs_bill = 8.
        ENDIF.

* Add ti recording (default values)
        CLEAR wa_dztb_002.
        MOVE-CORRESPONDING wa_dztb_001 TO wa_dztb_002.
        wa_dztb_002-hrs_compl = 8.

* Insert/change previous entry
        MODIFY zdztb_001 FROM wa_dztb_001.
        MODIFY zdztb_002 FROM wa_dztb_002.
```

```
    pe_subrc = sy-subrc.
    pe_error_text = 'OK'.

  ELSE.
    pe_subrc = 8.
    pe_error_text = 'Month has already been closed,
                     Planning impossible!'.
  ENDIF.
ENDFUNCTION.
```

Listing 7.5 Function Module ZDZTB_PLAN_ADD

For a personnel number, the planning information is read out on a monthly basis. The relevant information for a personnel number and a month is loaded from the planning table. After that, the information is returned by the function module.

Reading out planning data

The function module used to read out planning data is called ZDZTB_PLAN_GET. It is also contained in function group ZDZTB_ACQUISITION, as shown in Listing 7.6.

```
FUNCTION zdztb_plan_get.
*"----------------------------------------------------
*"*"Local interface:
*"  IMPORTING
*"     REFERENCE(PI_PERSNO) TYPE  PERSNO
*"     REFERENCE(PI_MONTH) TYPE  CHAR6
*"  TABLES
*"      PET_PLAN STRUCTURE  ZDZTB_001
*"----------------------------------------------------

  DATA: l_month TYPE string.

  CONCATENATE pi_month '%' INTO l_month.
  CONDENSE l_month NO-GAPS.

  FREE pet_plan.
  SELECT * FROM zdztb_001 INTO TABLE pet_plan
    WHERE persno = pi_persno
      AND date LIKE l_month.

ENDFUNCTION.
```

Listing 7.6 Function Module ZDZTB_PLAN_GET

The function module used for creating a time-recording module works similarly to that used for creating the planning. First a check is run to see whether the month to which you want to add the time recording has been closed (FINISHED flag in Table ZDZTB_002). Moreover, the planning table is also checked in order to see if the month has been closed there.

The activity entered is checked for bonus relevance and the corresponding data record is created for Table ZDZTB_002. If an entry exists already, this entry is overwritten with the newly recorded activity. Then the new data record is added to the time-recording table. If an error occurred during the creation of the data record, this error is transferred to the front end by using a variable.

The function module ZDZTB_TR_ADD adds time recording in the manner described above and is also a component of the function group ZDZTB_ACQUISITION. Listing 7.7 shows the corresponding source text.

```
FUNCTION zdztb_tr_add.
*"----------------------------------------------------
*"*"Local interface:
*"  IMPORTING
*"     REFERENCE(PI_PERSNO) TYPE  PERSNO
*"     REFERENCE(PI_DATE) TYPE  DATS
*"     REFERENCE(PI_ACTIVITY) TYPE  ZDZTB_ACTIVITY
*"     REFERENCE(PI_HRS) TYPE  INT4
*"  EXPORTING
*"     REFERENCE(PE_SUBRC) TYPE  SY-SUBRC
*"     REFERENCE(PE_ERROR_TEXT) TYPE  STRING
*"----------------------------------------------------

   DATA: it_dztb_002 TYPE TABLE OF zdztb_002,
         it_dztb_001 TYPE TABLE OF zdztb_001,

         wa_dztb_002 LIKE LINE OF it_dztb_002,
         wa_dztb_001 LIKE LINE OF it_dztb_001,

         l_finished  TYPE flag,
         l_month     TYPE string,
         l_bonus     TYPE flag.

* Has month been closed? -> Forbid time recording
   CONCATENATE pi_date(6) '%' INTO l_month.
```

```
    CLEAR l_finished.
    SELECT * FROM zdztb_002 INTO TABLE it_dztb_002
       WHERE persno = pi_persno
         AND date LIKE l_month.

    LOOP AT it_dztb_002 INTO wa_dztb_002
       WHERE finished = 'X'.
       IF wa_dztb_002-finished = 'X'.
          l_finished = 'X'.
          EXIT.
       ENDIF.
    ENDLOOP.

* Also check planning if month has been closed
    IF l_finished IS INITIAL.
       SELECT * FROM zdztb_001 INTO TABLE it_dztb_001
          WHERE persno = pi_persno
            AND date LIKE l_month.

       LOOP AT it_dztb_001 INTO wa_dztb_001
          WHERE finished = 'X'.
          IF wa_dztb_002-finished = 'X'.
             l_finished = 'X'.
             EXIT.
          ENDIF.
       ENDLOOP.
    ENDIF.

* No finished entry found
    IF l_finished IS INITIAL.
       CLEAR wa_dztb_002.
       wa_dztb_002-persno = pi_persno.
       wa_dztb_002-date = pi_date.
       wa_dztb_002-activity = pi_activity.
       wa_dztb_002-hrs_compl = pi_hrs.

       CLEAR l_bonus.
       SELECT SINGLE bonus FROM zdztb_004 INTO l_bonus
          WHERE activity = pi_activity.

       IF l_bonus IS NOT INITIAL.
          wa_dztb_002-hrs_bill = pi_hrs.
       ENDIF.

* Insert/change previous entry
```

```
            MODIFY zdztb_002 FROM wa_dztb_002.
            pe_subrc = sy-subrc.
            pe_error_text = 'OK'.

        ELSE.
            pe_subrc = 8.
            pe_error_text = 'Month has already been closed,
                            time recording impossible!'.
        ENDIF.

    ENDFUNCTION.
```

Listing 7.7 Function Module ZDZTB_TR_ADD

Reading out time-recording data

For a personnel number, the time-recording information is read out on a monthly basis. The relevant information for a personnel number and a month is loaded from the time-recording table. After that, the information is returned by the function module.

The function module used to read out time-recording data is called ZDZTB_TR_GET. It is also contained in function group ZDZTB_ACQUISITION. Listing 7.8 shows the source text of the function module.

```
FUNCTION zdztb_tr_get.
*"----------------------------------------------------
*"*"Local interface:
*"  IMPORTING
*"      REFERENCE(PI_PERSNO) TYPE   PERSNO
*"      REFERENCE(PI_MONTH) TYPE   CHAR6
*"  TABLES
*"      PET_TR STRUCTURE   ZDZTB_002
*"----------------------------------------------------

    DATA: l_month TYPE string.

    CONCATENATE pi_month '%' INTO l_month.
    CONDENSE l_month NO-GAPS.

    FREE pet_tr.
    SELECT * FROM zdztb_002 INTO TABLE pet_tr
        WHERE persno = pi_persno
            AND date LIKE l_month.

ENDFUNCTION.
```

Listing 7.8 Function Module ZDZTB_TR_GET

In order to close a month and thus protect it from additional entries, you can use function module ZDZTB_FINISH. This function module selects all data for a given personnel number and a month that has been entered from the planning and time-recording tables, and stores that data in internal tables. Moreover, it sets the FINISHED flag. After that, the database tables are modified using the following statement: MODIFY ... FROM TABLE (see Listing 7.9).

Closing a month

```
FUNCTION zdztb_finish.
*"----------------------------------------------------------
*"*"Local interface:
*"  IMPORTING
*"     REFERENCE(PI_PERSNO) TYPE   PERSNO
*"     REFERENCE(PI_MONTH) TYPE   CHAR6
*"  EXPORTING
*"     REFERENCE(PE_SUBRC) TYPE   SY-SUBRC
*"     REFERENCE(PE_ERROR_TEXT) TYPE   STRING
*"----------------------------------------------------------

  DATA: it_dztb_001  TYPE TABLE OF zdztb_001,
        it_dztb_002  TYPE TABLE OF zdztb_002,

        wa_dztb_001  LIKE LINE OF it_dztb_001,
        wa_dztb_002  LIKE LINE OF it_dztb_002,

        l_month      TYPE string,
        l_error_text TYPE string.

* Select all data corresponding to date of PI_MONTH
* into internal table
  CONCATENATE pi_month '%' INTO l_month.
  CONDENSE l_month NO-GAPS.

  SELECT * FROM zdztb_001 INTO TABLE it_dztb_001
     WHERE persno = pi_persno
       AND date LIKE l_month.

  SELECT * FROM zdztb_002 INTO TABLE it_dztb_002
     WHERE persno = pi_persno
       AND date LIKE l_month.

* Change FINISHED flag for each data record
  LOOP AT it_dztb_001 INTO wa_dztb_001.
     wa_dztb_001-finished = 'X'.
     MODIFY it_dztb_001 FROM wa_dztb_001.
```

```
      ENDLOOP.

      LOOP AT it_dztb_002 INTO wa_dztb_002.
         wa_dztb_002-finished = 'X'.
          MODIFY it_dztb_002 FROM wa_dztb_002.
      ENDLOOP.

  * Modify original table with modified data
      MODIFY zdztb_001 FROM TABLE it_dztb_001.
      MODIFY zdztb_002 FROM TABLE it_dztb_002.
      pe_subrc = sy-subrc.

      IF pe_subrc = 0.
         l_error_text = 'OK'.
      ELSEIF pe_subrc = 4.
         l_error_text = 'No entry found; could not
                     close month!'.
      ELSE.
         l_error_text = 'Unknown error occured!'.
      ENDIF.

  ENDFUNCTION.
```

Listing 7.9 Function Module ZDZTB_FINISH

Reporting Function Modules

Utilization per year   The reporting function modules are used to analyze the recorded
working times. The first function module calculates the capacity utilization of an employee per year, in this case per calendar year. To
identify the report, you must first set the period to Y and the number
of analyzed employees to S (single).

In order to calculate the capacity utilization of the employee, you
need the total amount of recorded hours as well as the billable hours,
which should be a subset of the former. You can easily retrieve these
values by requesting a database total for the entire year.

The capacity utilization of an employee per year is calculated by
function module ZDZTB_TR_OV_01 and is implemented in function
group ZDZTB_REPORTING (see Listing 7.10).

```
FUNCTION zdztb_tr_ov_001.
*"----------------------------------------------------------
*"*"Local interface:
*"  IMPORTING
```

```
*"      REFERENCE(PI_YEAR) TYPE   CHAR4
*"      REFERENCE(PI_PERSNO) TYPE   PERSNO
*"  EXPORTING
*"      REFERENCE(PE_REPORT) TYPE   ZDZTB_REPORT_001_STRU
*"------------------------------------------------------

* Report: Capacity utilization of an employee per year

   DATA: it_dztb_002  TYPE TABLE OF zdztb_002,
         wa_dztb_002  LIKE LINE OF it_dztb_002,
         l_year       TYPE string,
         l_hrs_compl  TYPE int4.

   CLEAR pe_report.

* Annual report (Y) for
* single employee (S = single)
   pe_report-period = 'Y'.
   pe_report-persno_no = 'S'.
   pe_report-persno = pi_persno.
   pe_report-activity = ''.
   pe_report-yearmon = ''.

* Calculate hrs_compl and hrs_bill as a total in the DB
   CONCATENATE pi_year '%' INTO l_year.
   CONDENSE l_year NO-GAPS.

   SELECT SUM( hrs_compl ) FROM zdztb_002
     INTO pe_report-hrs
     WHERE persno = pi_persno
       AND date LIKE l_year.

   SELECT SUM( hrs_bill ) FROM zdztb_002
     INTO pe_report-hrs_bill
     WHERE persno = pi_persno
       AND date LIKE l_year.

ENDFUNCTION.
```

Listing 7.10 Function Module ZDZTB_TR_OV_01

The following function module is used to calculate the capacity utilization of all employees per month. To identify the report, you must first set the period to M (month) and the number of analyzed employees to M (multi).

Utilization per month

In order to calculate the capacity utilization of the employees, you need the total amount of recorded hours as well as the billable hours, which should be a subset of the former. You can easily retrieve these values by requesting a database total for the month that has been entered.

The function module ZDZTB_TR_OV_02 calculates the capacity utilization of the employee per month and is a component of function group ZDZTB_REPORTING. Listing 7.11 shows the source text.

```
FUNCTION zdztb_tr_ov_002.
*"----------------------------------------------------------
*"*"Local interface:
*"  IMPORTING
*"     REFERENCE(PI_MONTH) TYPE  CHAR6
*"  EXPORTING
*"     REFERENCE(PE_REPORT) TYPE  ZDZTB_REPORT_001_STRU
*"----------------------------------------------------------

* Report: Capacity utilization of all employees per month

   DATA: it_dztb_002  TYPE TABLE OF zdztb_002,
         wa_dztb_002  LIKE LINE OF it_dztb_002,
         l_month      TYPE string,
         l_hrs_compl  TYPE int4.

   CLEAR pe_report.

* Monthly report (M) for all employees (M = multi)
   pe_report-period = 'M'.
   pe_report-persno_no = 'M'.
   pe_report-persno = ''.
   pe_report-activity = ''.
   pe_report-yearmon = pi_month.

* Calculate totals of hrs_compl and hrs_bill
   CONCATENATE pi_month '%' INTO l_month.
   CONDENSE l_month NO-GAPS.

   SELECT SUM( hrs_compl ) FROM zdztb_002
     INTO pe_report-hrs
     WHERE date LIKE l_month.

   SELECT SUM( hrs_bill ) FROM zdztb_002
     INTO pe_report-hrs_bill
```

```
      WHERE date LIKE l_month.
```

```
ENDFUNCTION.
```

Listing 7.11 Function Module ZDZTB_TR_OV_02

The following function module is used to calculate the accumulated billable hours for a given year, in this case per calendar year. To identify the report, you must first set the period to M (month) and the number of analyzed employees to M (multi).

Billable hours per year

In order to calculate the billable hours, you need the total amount of recorded hours as well as the billable hours, which should be a subset of the former. You can easily retrieve these values by requesting a database total for the calendar year.

The total amount of billable hours per calendar year is calculated by function module ZDZTB_TR_OV_03 that is contained in function group ZDZTB_REPORTING. Listing 7.12 shows the corresponding source text.

```
FUNCTION zdztb_tr_ov_003.
*"----------------------------------------------------
*"*"Local interface:
*"  IMPORTING
*"     REFERENCE(PI_YEAR) TYPE  CHAR4
*"  EXPORTING
*"     REFERENCE(PE_REPORT) TYPE  ZDZTB_REPORT_001_STRU
*"----------------------------------------------------

  DATA: l_year      TYPE string,
        it_dztb_002 TYPE TABLE OF zdztb_002,
        wa_dztb_002 LIKE LINE OF it_dztb_002.

  pe_report-period = 'Y'.
  pe_report-persno_no = 'M'.
  pe_report-persno = ''.
  pe_report-activity = ''.
  pe_report-yearmon = ''.

* Creat year format
  CLEAR l_year.
  CONCATENATE pi_year '%' INTO l_year.
  CONDENSE l_year NO-GAPS.
```

```
       SELECT SUM( hrs_compl ) FROM zdztb_002
         INTO pe_report-hrs
         WHERE date LIKE l_year.


       SELECT SUM( hrs_bill ) FROM zdztb_002

         INTO pe_report-hrs_bill
         WHERE date LIKE l_year.


    ENDFUNCTION.
```

Listing 7.12 Function Module ZDZTB_TR_OV_03

Month by month distribution

To obtain a graphical analysis of the accumulated working hours per calendar year, with an entry for each individual month, you need another module, one that calculates the capacity utilization of *all* employees for *each* month.

For this purpose, the function module uses the calculation of the monthly utilization of all employees per month (ZDZTB_TR_OV_002), which is carried out for each month. The result is then stored in the output table (see Listing 7.13).

```
FUNCTION zdztb_tr_ov_004.
*"----------------------------------------------------------
*"*"Local interface:
*"  IMPORTING
*"     REFERENCE(PI_YEAR) TYPE  CHAR4
*"  TABLES
*"     PET_REPORT TYPE  ZDZTB_REPORT_001_TAB
*"----------------------------------------------------------

    DATA: l_month     TYPE int4,
          l_month_str TYPE char2,
          l_yearmon   TYPE char6,
          wa_report   LIKE LINE OF pet_report.

  * Each month: Calculate monthly employee utilization
    l_month = 1.

    WHILE l_month <= 12.
       l_month_str = l_month.

       IF l_month < 10.
          CONCATENATE '0' l_month_str INTO l_month_str.
```

```
      CONDENSE l_month_str NO-GAPS.
    ENDIF.

    CONCATENATE pi_year l_month_str INTO l_yearmon.
    CONDENSE l_yearmon NO-GAPS.

    CLEAR wa_report.
    CALL FUNCTION 'ZDZTB_TR_OV_002'
      EXPORTING
        pi_month  = l_yearmon
      IMPORTING
        pe_report = wa_report.

  wa_report-yearmon = l_yearmon.

    APPEND wa_report TO pet_report.
    l_month = l_month + 1.

  ENDWHILE.
ENDFUNCTION.
```

Listing 7.13 Function Module ZDZTB_TR_OV_004

Other Function Modules

Another module we need is a login module, although the name "login" may be a little exaggerated. You can employ a user-management here in order to ensure that only qualified and authorized personnel have access to the tool. For our purposes, however, it is sufficient to check if the entered personnel number is valid. If not, the program cannot be started.

Application login

The login module is called ZDZTB_LOGIN and is a component of function group ZDZTB_OTHER (see Listing 7.14).

```
FUNCTION zdztb_login.
*"----------------------------------------------------
*"*"Local interface:
*"  IMPORTING
*"    REFERENCE(PI_PERSNO) TYPE  PERSNO
*"  EXPORTING
*"    REFERENCE(PE_ERROR_TEXT) TYPE  STRING
*"----------------------------------------------------

  DATA: l_persno TYPE persno.
```

```
CLEAR l_persno.
SELECT SINGLE persno FROM pa0001 INTO l_persno
   WHERE persno = pi_persno.

IF l_persno IS INITIAL.
   pe_error_text = 'Personnel number not found!'.
ELSE.
   pe_error_text = 'OK'.
ENDIF.

ENDFUNCTION.
```

Listing 7.14 Function Module ZDZTB_LOGIN

Figure 7.12 shows all function modules created in the function groups.

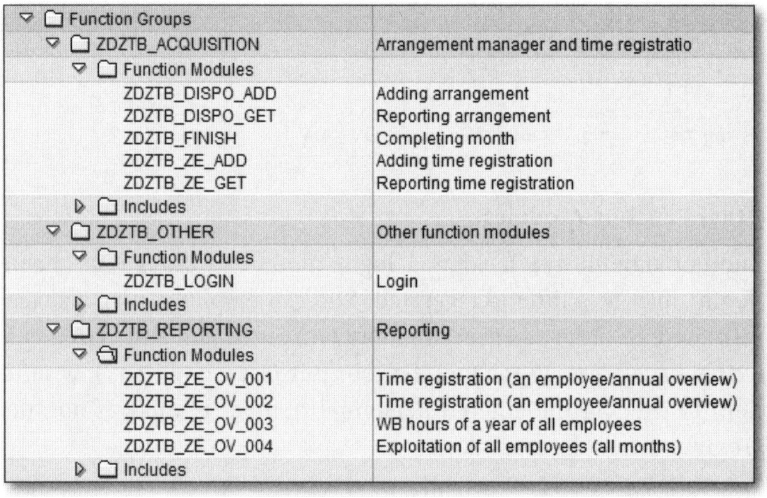

Figure 7.12 Created Function Modules in the Function Groups

7.2.4 BSP Application and XML Files

In the following sections, you'll create the BSP application and the required XML files (pages with flow logic) that can receive and output data.

Extending the application class First you must extend the application class defined in Section 7.2.1 by some attributes that can be referenced within the page fragments (see Figure 7.13).

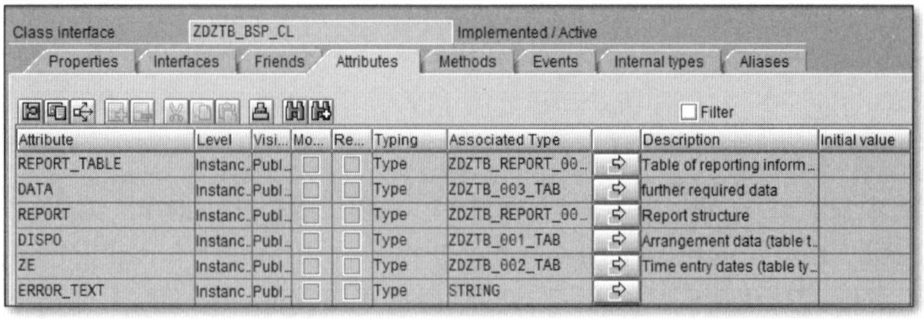

Figure 7.13 Attributes of the Application Class

The REPORT attribute is used to output reporting information and references the structure ZDZTB_REPORT_001_STRU. The planning and time-recording information of a query are stored in the PLAN and TR attributes (as table type of Tables ZDZTB_00*). If an error occurred during the editing process, the error is stored in the ERROR_TEXT attribute. The DATA table can contain additional application-relevant data such as activities, personnel numbers, and so on, according to your requirements, and it has the format of Table ZDZTB_003.

The BSP application is assigned the name ZDZTB_BSP and is generated as a stateful application using the application class ZDZTB_BSP_CL created in Section 7.2.1 (see Figure 7.14).

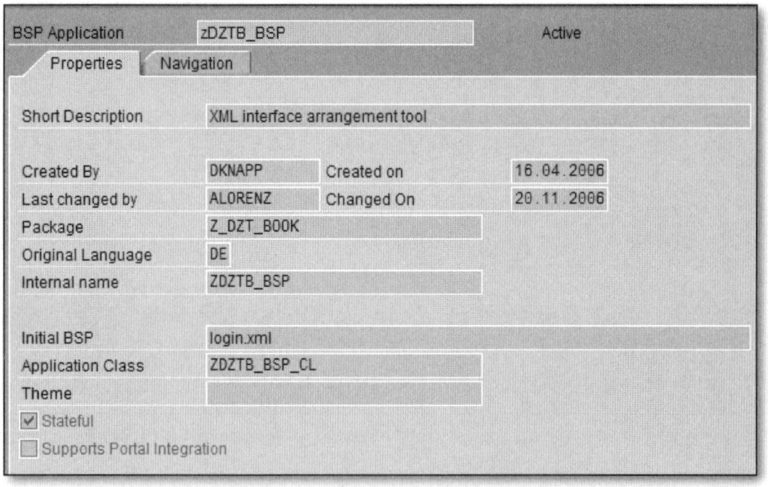

BSP application

Figure 7.14 BSP Application of the Application (XML Interface)

The BSP application is provided with pages that contain a flow logic and in which you can enter input data such as the personnel number, date, and the like. Moreover, these pages can trigger calculations in the back end in order to present the results as an XML file. This way the data can be used in the Flex front end. For this purpose, the XML interface defined in Section 7.1.4 is used.

SICF service

In order to enable the Flex application to cooperate with the BSP application you must assign a background user—even a dialog user, if needed for the sample application—to the SICF service (Internet Communication Framework) that has been assigned to the BSP application. You can do that via Transaction SCIF[3] (see Figure 7.15). Figure 7.15 shows the SICF object that is automatically created during the creation of a BSP application and has the same name as the application. Here you must enter the login data in order to make sure the BSP application can be used by Flex.

Figure 7.15 Storing a Background User for the BSP Application

---

3 This transaction is used to display and define Web services. You can find further information on Web services and Transaction SICF in the SAP Library.

Because modified Web services are stored as inactive, you must reactivate the service.

Adding a Planning Module

In order to add a planning module, you must add the XML file plan_ add.xml as a **Page with Flow Logic** to the BSP application (see Figure 7.16).

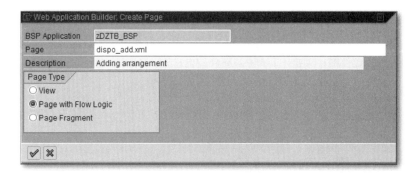

Figure 7.16 Adding Planning Data

The page is supposed to receive the parameters of function module ZDZTB_PLAN_ADD and to return the error message of the module if an error occurred when the planning was added.

To implement this, you must first define the page attributes that are to be transferred later as parameters via the URL (see Figure 7.17). The following attributes were created in the **Page Attributes** tab of the page plan_add.xml: activity, date, and persno.

Page attributes

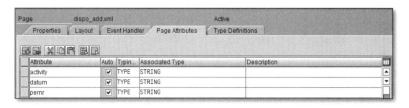

Figure 7.17 Page Attributes plan_add.xml

The data that is entered is analyzed in the OnInitialization event, and the function module is populated with this data. If an error text exists, it is stored in the application class (see Listing 7.15).

```
* OnInitialization
* event handler for data retrieval

DATA: l_subrc       TYPE sy-subrc,
      l_error_text TYPE string,
      l_persno      TYPE persno,
      l_date        TYPE dats,
      l_activity    TYPE zdztb_activity.

l_persno = persno.
l_date = date.
l_activity = activity.
CLEAR application->error_text.

CALL FUNCTION 'ZDZTB_PLAN_ADD'
  EXPORTING
    pi_persno      = l_persno
    pi_date        = l_date
    pi_activity    = l_activity
  IMPORTING
    pe_subrc       = l_subrc
    pe_error_text = l_error_text.

application->error_text = l_error_text.
```

Listing 7.15 OnInitialization Event of File plan_add.xml

The function module ZDZTB_PLAN_ADD has been processed successfully if the error text PE_ERROR_TEXT contains the value **OK**. For this reason, the XML file outputs the error text ERROR_TEXT from the application class in order to indicate whether the operation has been successful (see Listing 7.16).

```
<%@page language="abap"%>
<?xml version="1.0" encoding="iso-8859-1"?>

<error_text><%=application->error_text.%></error_text>
```

Listing 7.16 Layout plan_add.xml

Reading Out Planning

In order to read out planning you must add the XML file plan_get.xml as a **Page with Flow Logic** to the BSP application (see Figure 7.18).

Figure 7.18 Retrieving Planning Data

The page is supposed to receive the parameters of function module ZDZTB_PLAN_GET and to return the error message of the module if an error occurred when the planning data was added. To implement this, you must first define the page attributes that are to be transferred later as parameters via the URL (see Figure 7.19).

Attribute	Auto	Typin...	Associated Type	Description
month	☑	TYPE	STRING	
pernr	☑	TYPE	STRING	
wa_dztb_001	☐	TYPE	ZDZTB_001_STRU	Arrangement data (structure)

Figure 7.19 Page Attributes plan_get.xml

The attribute `month` and `persno` are transferred to the page via the URL. The `wa_dztb_001` parameter is used as a work area for Table `PLAN` of the application class. The information of the work area is output in the layout.

Page attributes

The data that is entered is analyzed in the `OnInitialization` event, and the function module is populated with this data. The planning data of the input month is returned and written to the application class, as shown in Listing 7.17.

```
* OnInitialization
* event handler for data retrieval

  DATA: l_persno TYPE persno,
        l_month TYPE char6.
```

```
l_persno = persno.
l_month = month.

FREE application->plan.

CALL FUNCTION 'ZDZTB_PLAN_GET'
  EXPORTING
    pi_persno  = l_persno
    pi_month   = l_month
  TABLES
    pet_plan = application->plan.
```

Listing 7.17 OnInitialization Event of File plan_get.xml

Output of information in the layout

To output the planning data in the page layout, you must use a `loop` construction. To do that, you must create the XML file in accordance with the interface defined in Section 7.1.4 (see Listing 7.18).

```
<%@page language="abap"%>
<?xml version="1.0" encoding="iso-8859-1"?>

<result>
  <head>
    <persno><%=persno.%></persno>
  </head>
  <pos>
    <% loop at application->plan into wa_dztb_001. %>
    <entry>
      <date><%= wa_dztb_001-date.%></date>
      <activity><%= wa_dztb_001-activity.%></activity>
      <finished><%= wa_dztb_001-finished.%></finished>
    </entry>
    <% endloop. %>
  </pos>
</result>
```

Listing 7.18 Layout of File plan_get.xml

Adding Time Recording

You can add a time-recording function by using the XML file `tr_add.xml`, which you must again add to the BSP application as a **Page with Flow Logic** (see Figure 7.20).

Figure 7.20 Adding Time Recording Data

The page is supposed to receive the parameters of function module ZDZTB_TR_ADD and to return the error message of the module if an error occurred when the time-recording data was added. To implement this, you must first define the page attributes that are to be transferred later as parameters via the URL (see Figure 7.21). In our case, the page tr_add.xml is assigned the following page attributes: activity, date, persno, and hrs.

Defining the page attributes

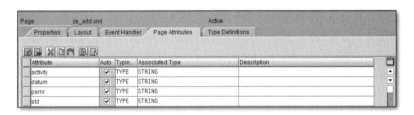

Figure 7.21 Page Attributes tr_add.xml

The data that is entered is analyzed in the OnInitialization event, and the function module is populated with this data. If an error text exists, it is written to the application class. Listing 7.19 shows the source text.

```
* OnInitialization
* event handler for data retrieval

DATA: l_persno     TYPE persno,
      l_date       TYPE dats,
      l_activity   TYPE zdztb_activity,
      l_hrs        TYPE int4,
```

```
    l_subrc        TYPE sy-subrc,
    l_error_text TYPE string.

l_persno = persno.
l_date = date.
l_activity = activity.
l_hrs = hrs.
CLEAR application->error_text.

CALL FUNCTION 'ZDZTB_TR_ADD'
  EXPORTING
    pi_persno      = l_persno
    pi_date        = l_date
    pi_activity    = l_activity
    pi_hrs         = l_hrs
  IMPORTING
    pe_subrc       = l_subrc
    pe_error_text  = l_error_text.

application->error_text = l_error_text.
```

Listing 7.19 OnInitialization Event of File tr_add.xml

The function module ZDZTB_TR_ADD has been processed success-fully if the error text PE_ERROR_TEXT contains the value **OK**. For this reason, the XML file outputs the error text ERROR_TEXT from the application class in order to indicate whether the operation has been successful (see Listing 7.20).

```
<%@page language="abap"%>
<?xml version="1.0" encoding="iso-8859-1"?>

<error_text><%=application->error_text.%></error_text>
```

Listing 7.20 Layout tr_add.xml

Reading Out Recorded Times

In order to read out recorded times, you must add the XML file tr_get.xml as a **Page with Flow Logic** to the BSP application (see Figure 7.22). The page is supposed to receive the parameters of function module ZDZTB_TR_GET and to return the error message of the module if an error occurred when the time-recording data was added.

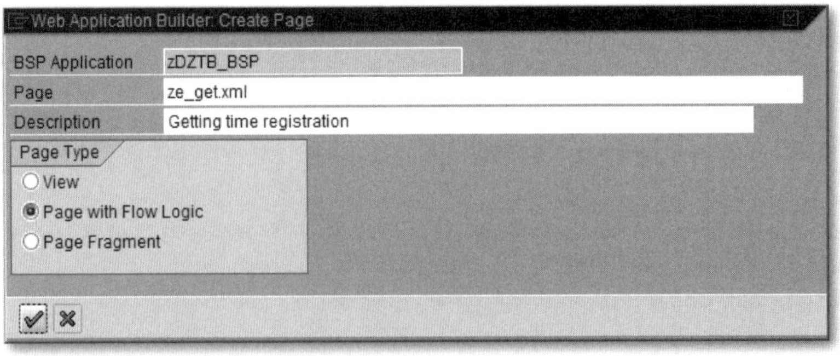

Figure 7.22 Retrieving Time-Recording Data

Figure 7.23 shows the necessary page attributes that are later trans- **Page attributes**
ferred as parameters via the URL.

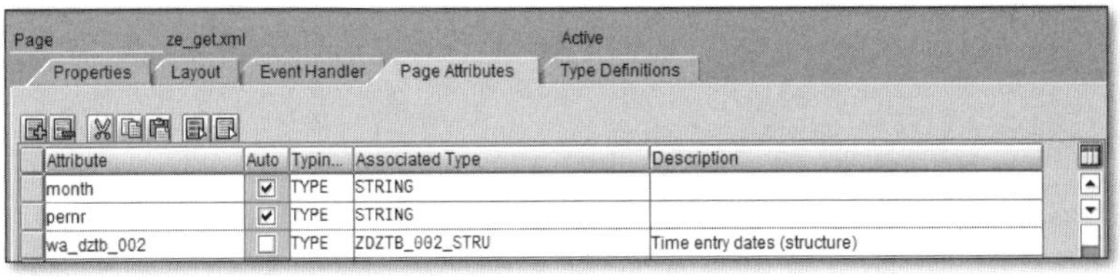

Figure 7.23 Page Attributes tr_get.xml

The attribute `month` and `persno` are transferred to the page via the
URL. The `wa_dztb_002` parameter is used as a work area for Table `TR`
of the application class. The information of the work area is output in
the layout.

The data that is entered is analyzed in the `OnInitialization` event,
and the function module is populated with this data. The time-
recording data of the input month is returned and written to the
application class, as shown in Listing 7.21.

```
* OnInitialization
* event handler for data retrieval

  DATA: l_persno TYPE persno,
        l_month TYPE char6.

  l_persno = persno.
  l_month = month.
```

```
   FREE application->tr.

   CALL FUNCTION 'ZDZTB_TR_GET'
     EXPORTING
       pi_persno = l_persno
       pi_month = l_month
     TABLES
       pet_tr   = application->tr.
```

Listing 7.21 OnInitialization Event of File tr_get.xml

To output the time-recording data in the page layout, you must use a loop construction. To do that, you must create the XML file in accordance with the interface defined in Section 7.1.4 (see Listing 7.22).

```
<%@page language="abap"%>
<?xml version="1.0" encoding="iso-8859-1"?>

<result>
  <head>
    <persno><%=persno.%></persno>
  </head>
  <pos>
    <% loop at application->tr into wa_dztb_002. %>
    <entry>
      <date><%= wa_dztb_002-date.%></date>
      <activity><%= wa_dztb_002-activity.%></activity>
      <hrs_compl><%= wa_dztb_002-hrs_compl.%>
      </hrs_compl>
      <hrs_bill><%=wa_dztb_002-hrs_bill.%></hrs_bill>
      <finished><%= wa_dztb_002-finished.%></finished>
    </entry>
    <% endloop. %>
  </pos>
</result>
```

Listing 7.22 Layout of File tr_get.xml

Closing a Month

To close a month, you must add the XML file finish.xml as a **Page with Flow Logic** to the BSP application, as shown in Figure 7.24.

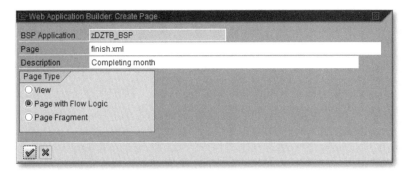

Figure 7.24 Closing a Month

The XML file receives the parameters of function module ZDZTB_ FINISH and returns the error message of the module if such a message exists. For this purpose, the page attributes that are transferred via parameters of the URL are defined, as in the previous cases (see Figure 7.25).

Defining the page attributes

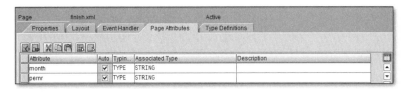

Figure 7.25 Page Attribute finish.xml

The data that is entered is again analyzed in the OnInitialization event, and the function module is populated with this data. If an error text exists, it is written to the application class (see Listing 7.23).

```
* OnInitialization
* event handler for data retrieval

DATA: l_month       TYPE char6,
      l_persno      TYPE persno,
      l_subrc       TYPE sy-subrc,
      l_error_text  TYPE string.

l_month = month.
l_persno = persno.
CLEAR application->error_text.
```

```
CALL FUNCTION 'ZDZTB_FINISH'
  EXPORTING
    pi_persno      = l_persno
    pi_month       = l_month
  IMPORTING
    pe_subrc       = l_subrc
    pe_error_text  = l_error_text.

application->error_text = l_error_text.
```
Listing 7.23 OnInitialization Event of File finish.xml

Error text   Function module ZDZTB_FINISH has been processed successfully if no error text has been written to the output variable PE_ERROR_TEXT. For this reason, the XML file outputs the error text ERROR_TEXT from the application class in order to indicate whether the operation has been successful (see Listing 7.24).

```
<%@page language="abap"%>
<?xml version="1.0" encoding="iso-8859-1"?>

<error_text><%=application->error_text.%></error_text>
```
Listing 7.24 Layout finish.xml

Login

The login process is implemented in XML file finish.xml and added as a **Page with Flow Logic** to the BSP application (see Figure 7.26). The page is supposed to receive the parameters of function module ZDZTB_LOGIN and to return the error message of this module if the process of login to the application contained an error.

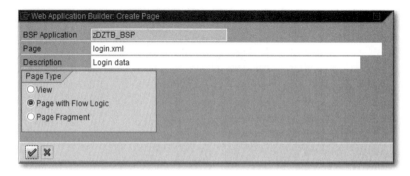

Figure 7.26 Login Data

The page attributes needed for this are shown in Figure 7.27.

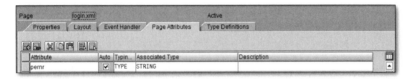

Figure 7.27 Page Attributes login.xml

Similar to the previous files, the input data is analyzed in the `OnIni-`
`tialization` event and then forwarded to the login function module.
If an error occurs during the login process, the error text is written to
the application class. Listing 7.25 contains further information.

```
* OnInitialization
* event handler for data retrieval

DATA: l_persno TYPE persno.

l_persno = persno.
CLEAR application->error_text.

CALL FUNCTION 'ZDZTB_LOGIN'
  EXPORTING
    pi_persno    = l_persno
  IMPORTING
    pe_error_text = application->error_text.
```

Listing 7.25 OnInitialization Event of File finish.xml

Function module ZDZTB_LOGIN has been processed without any   **Error text**
error if no error text has been written to the output variable PE_
ERROR_TEXT. For this reason, the XML file outputs the error text
ERROR_TEXT from the application class in order to indicate whether
the operation has been successful (see Listing 7.26).

```
<%@page language="abap"%>
<?xml version="1.0" encoding="iso-8859-1"?>

<error_text><%=application->error_text.%></error_text>
```

Listing 7.26 Layout login.xml

Output of Reporting Data

Reporting data is output in the XML file report.xml which you must add as a **Page with Flow Logic** to the BSP application (see Figure 7.28).

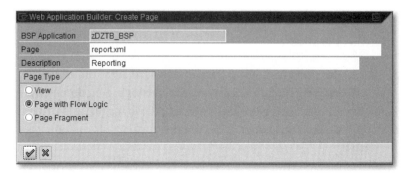

Figure 7.28 Reporting

Based on the input parameters (event) the page decides which type of reporting is to be carried out. The page is supposed to receive the parameters of function module ZDZTB_TR_OV_00* and to return the error message of the module if an error occurred when the data was added.

Page attributes Figure 7.29 shows the page attributes that are later transferred as parameters via the URL. The wa_report_table parameter is required for internal processing, and event is used to transfer the type of reporting; month contains the month, year the year, and persno the personnel number.

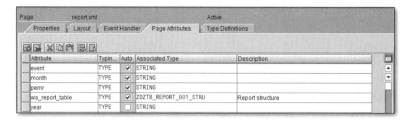

Figure 7.29 Attributes of Page report.xml

The data that is entered is analyzed in the OnInitialization event, and the corresponding function module is populated with this data, as shown in Listing 7.27.

```
* OnInitialization
* event handler for data retrieval

DATA: l_year  TYPE char4,
      l_month TYPE char6,
      l_persno TYPE persno.

IF year IS NOT INITIAL.
  l_year = year.
ENDIF.
IF month IS NOT INITIAL.
  l_month = month.
ENDIF.
IF persno IS NOT INITIAL.
  l_persno = persno.
ENDIF.

FREE application->report.
FREE application->report_table.

IF event = 'OV01'.
  CALL FUNCTION 'ZDZTB_TR_OV_001'
    EXPORTING
      pi_year    = l_year
      pi_persno  = l_persno
    IMPORTING
      pe_report  = application->report.

ELSEIF event = 'OV02'.
  CALL FUNCTION 'ZDZTB_TR_OV_002'
    EXPORTING
      pi_month   = l_month
    IMPORTING
      pe_report  = application->report.

ELSEIF event = 'OV03'.
  CALL FUNCTION 'ZDZTB_TR_OV_003'
    EXPORTING
      pi_year    = l_year
    IMPORTING
      pe_report  = application->report.

ELSEIF event = 'OV04'.
  CALL FUNCTION 'ZDZTB_TR_OV_004'
    EXPORTING
```

```
        pi_year    = l_year
      TABLES
        pet_report = application->report_table.

ENDIF.
```

Listing 7.27 OnInitialization Event of File report.xml

Output of reporting data

The resulting reporting data is output in the file layout. A decision is made as to what type of reporting is used. In the complex case of an analysis of all 12 months, the REPORT_TABLE table is output. In all other cases, the REPORT structure is output. Listing 7.28 shows the source text.

```
<%@page language="abap"%>
<?xml version="1.0" encoding="iso-8859-1"?>

<report>
  <% if event = 'OV04'. %>
    <% loop at application->report_table into
       wa_report_table. %>
    <entry>
      <yearmon>"<%=wa_report_table-yearmon.%>"
        </yearmon>
      <persno><%=wa_report_table-persno.%></persno>
      <activity><%=wa_report_table-ACTIVITY.%>
        </activity>
      <period><%=wa_report_table-PERIOD.%></period>
      <persno_no><%=wa_report_table-PERSNO_NO.%>
        </persno_no>
      <hrs><%=wa_report_table-HRS.%></hrs>
      <hrs_bill><%=wa_report_table-HRS_BILL.%></hrs_bill>
    </entry>
    <% endloop. %>
  <% else. %>
    <entry>
      <persno><%=application->report-PERSNO.%></persno>
      <activity><%=application->report-ACTIVITY.%>
        </activity>
      <period><%=application->report-PERIOD.%></period>
      <persno_no><%=application->report-PERSNO_NO.%>
        </persno_no>
      <hrs><%=application->report-HRS.%></hrs>
      <hrs_bill><%=application->report-
        HRS_BILL.%></hrs_bill>
```

```
      </entry>
    <% endif. %>
  </report>
```
Listing 7.28 Layout report.xml

Other Required Data

For the Flex application, we need more data, such as a list of activities or personnel numbers, at runtime. You can provide this data to the front end by using the file `data.xml` (see Figure 7.30).

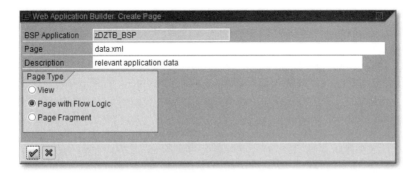

Figure 7.30 Application-Relevant Data

The page attributes of the XML file are limited to the `type` attribute that determines which data is to be retrieved, and to the `wa_data` attribute that is needed for internal processing (see Figure 7.31).

Page attributes

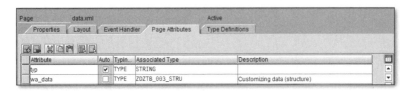

Figure 7.31 Page Attributes data.xml

Based on the input parameter `type` in the URL, a decision is made in the `OnInitialization` event concerning which information is to be transferred to the front end (reading out activities or personnel numbers, as shown in Listing 7.29).

```
* OnInitialization
* event handler for data retrieval
```

```
DATA: l_type TYPE char1,

      it_dztb_004 TYPE TABLE OF zdztb_004,
      it_pa0002   TYPE TABLE OF pa0002,
      it_data     TYPE zdztb_003_stru,

      wa_dztb_004 LIKE LINE OF it_dztb_004,
      wa_pa0002   LIKE LINE OF it_pa0002,
      wa_data     LIKE LINE OF it_data.

l_type = type.
FREE application->data.

* Activity
IF l_type = 'A'.
  SELECT * FROM zdztb_004 INTO TABLE it_dztb_004.

  LOOP AT it_dztb_004 INTO wa_dztb_004.
    CLEAR wa_data.
    wa_data-name = wa_dztb_004-activity.
    wa_data-value = wa_dztb_004-descr.
    APPEND wa_data TO it_data.
  ENDLOOP.

* Personnel number
ELSEIF l_type = 'P'.
  SELECT * FROM pa0002 INTO TABLE it_pa0002.

  SORT it_pa0002 BY persno.
  DELETE ADJACENT DUPLICATES FROM it_pa0002
    COMPARING persno.

  LOOP AT it_pa0002 INTO wa_pa0002.
    CLEAR wa_data.
    wa_data-name = wa_pa0002-persno.
    CONCATENATE wa_pa0002-firstna wa_pa0002-lastna INTO
      wa_data-value SEPARATED BY space.
    APPEND wa_data TO it_data.
  ENDLOOP.

ENDIF.

application->data[] = it_data[].
```

Listing 7.29 OnInitialization Event of File data.xml

The data determined in this way is then transferred to the front end, as shown in Listing 7.30.

```
<%@page language="abap"%>
<?xml version="1.0" encoding="iso-8859-1"?>

<data>
    <type><%=type.%></type>
    <% loop at application->data into wa_data. %>
    <entry>
        <name><%= wa_data-name.%></name>
        <value><%= wa_data-value. %></value>
    </entry>
    <% endloop. %>
</data>
```

Listing 7.30 Layout data.xml

Once you have completed these steps, the BSP ZDZTB_BSP application should contain the elements shown in Figure 7.32.

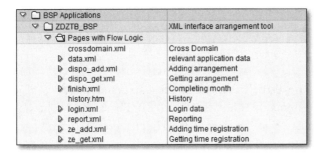

Figure 7.32 Pages with Flow Logic in BSP Application

7.2.5 Final Tests

In order to prove the accuracy of the source text, we'll carry out in this section several tests that receive and output data. Because our application is a sample application, the tests will be kept short.

Testing the pages with flow logic

Adding a Planning Module

A planning is added via the XML file `plan_add.xml` and must contain the parameters for personnel number (`persno`), date (`date`), and activity (`activity`). A URL to add a planning module could be structured as follows.

http://dresden.ixult.net:8001/sap/bc/bsp/sap/zdztb_bsp/plan_add.xml
?persno=00000001&date=20060204&activity=111111111111

Structure of the
XML file

The XML file that is returned has the format shown in Figure 7.33. As is the case in each XML file, the first line consists of the mandatory `xml` tag with the associated encoding; that is, the scripting to be used. The XML file is then output according to the structure defined in the BSP application; that is, the error text surrounded by the `<error_text>` tag.

In order to test the accuracy of the application it is sufficient to enter the URL in the Web browser and then compare the result with the file you expected.

Figure 7.33 Return XML When Adding Planning Data

Table contents in
the SAP system

As you can see, no error occurred in the back end, which is also shown by the contents of Table ZDZTB_001 in Figure 7.34. The figure shows the entry that consists of the client (here: 010), the personnel number (00000001), the date of the planning (02/04/2006), the activity (111111111111), and an indication whether the month has been closed (in this case it has not been closed). You can use Transaction SE16 to display the contents of the table.

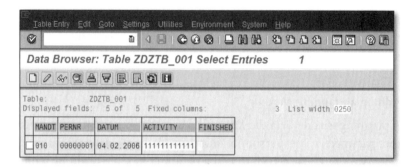

Figure 7.34 Contents of the Planning Table After Testing

If the month has already been closed and you want to post data to a   Closing a month
day in the closed month, an error message displays, as shown in Figure 7.35.

Figure 7.35 Adding Planning Data to a Closed Month

Reading Out Planning Information

In order to read out planning information, you need a personnel
number and the month in the following format: YYYYMM. If you
include this information in the URL, the data from Table ZDZTB_001
is output in the form of the previously defined XML interface, as
shown in Figure 7.36.

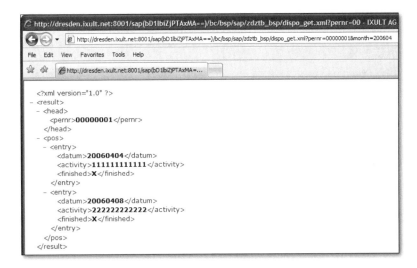

Figure 7.36 Reading Out Planning Information

Adding Time-Recording Data

Similar to creating planning, you can test the adding of time record-ing data. The URL to be used for adding time recording data could be structured as follows.

http://dresden.ixult.net:8001/sap/bc/bsp/sap/zdztb_bsp/tr_add.xml
?persno=00000001&date=20060204&hours=5&activity=222222222222

The XML file that is returned then has the format shown in Figure 7.37.

Figure 7.37 Return XML When Adding Time-Recording Data

As you can see, no error occurred in the back end, which is also shown by the contents of Table ZDZTB_002 in Figure 7.38.

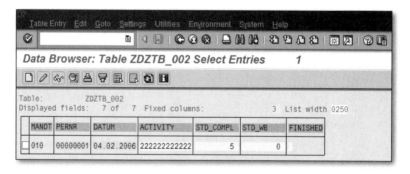

Figure 7.38 Contents of the Time-Recording Table After Testing

Reading Out Time-Recording Data

In order to read out time-recording information you need a person-nel number and the month in the following format: YYYYMM. If you include this information in the URL, the data from Table ZDZTB_002 is output in the form of the previously defined XML interface, as shown in Figure 7.39.

Figure 7.39 Reading Out Time-Recording Information

Closing a Month

The XML file `finish.xml` is responsible for closing a month. This file also needs the personnel number and the month in the format YYYYMM. A URL for closing a month could, for instance, be structured as follows:

finish.xml

*http://dresden.ixult.net:8001/sap/bc/bsp/sap/zdztb_bsp/finish.xml
?persno=00000001&month=200604*

Figure 7.40 shows the result of the test.

Figure 7.40 XML File after Closing the Month 2006/04

Figure 7.41 shows that both the planning and the time-recording table have been correctly updated for the month 2006/04. Note that the figure only shows the time-recording table.

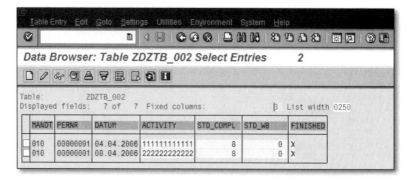

Figure 7.41 Table Contents After Closing the Month

Output of Application-Relevant Data

data.xml   The output of activities and personnel numbers is inevitable for our application. The XML file data.xml specifically created for this purpose outputs the corresponding information depending on the type parameter. You can query the personnel numbers using the following URL:

http://dresden.ixult.net:8001/sap/bc/bsp/sap/zdztb_bsp/data.xml?type=P

The result is shown in Figure 7.42.

Figure 7.42 List of Available Personnel Numbers in the System

The activities contained in Table ZDZTB_004 can be output via the type=A parameter (see Figure 7.43). This parameter must be added as ?type=A to the URL of XML file data.xml. As a result, you'll obtain the XML file containing the data maintained in Table ZDZTB_004. The output of this data in the XML file complies with the interface.

```
http://dresden.ixult.net:8001/sap/(bD1lbiZjPTAxMA==)/bc/bsp/sap/zdztb_bsp/data.xml?typ=A

      http://dresden.ixult.net:8001/sap/(bD1lbiZjPTAxMA==)/bc/bsp/sap/zdztb_bsp/data.xml?typ=A

File   Edit   View   Favorites   Tools   Help

        http://dresden.ixult.net:8001/sap/(bD1lbiZjPTAxMA=...

  <?xml version="1.0" ?>
- <data>
    <type>A</type>
  - <entry>
      <name>000000000001</name>
      <value>IXULT Travelmanagement</value>
    </entry>
  - <entry>
      <name>000000000002</name>
      <value>IXULT HIVE Search Engine</value>
    </entry>
  - <entry>
      <name>000000000003</name>
      <value>SAP Netweaver 2004s Schulung</value>
    </entry>
  </data>
```

Figure 7.43 List of Maintained Activities

Reporting

In order to test the reporting functionality, you must first populate   Test
the tables with plausible data. Then you must carry out the four possible reporting types described in the following bulleted sections, and check their accuracy.

▶ **Utilization per year**
In the following example we'll analyze calendar year 2006 for the employee with personnel number **3**. The following URL is needed for that:

*http://dresden.ixult.net:8001/sap/bc/bsp/sap/zdztb_bsp/report.xml
?event=OV01&year=2006&persno=00000003*

The resulting output is shown in Figure 7.44. As you can see, the output shows the total number of working hours accrued for 2006 divided into total number of hours (hrs) and billable hours (hrs_bill). This enables you to calculate the percentage of capacity utilization.

▶ **Utilization per month**
To analyze, for example, the month of January 2006 for all employees, you need the following URL:

*http://dresden.ixult.net:8001/sap/bc/bsp/sap/zdztb_bsp/report.xml
?event=OV02&month=200601*

Figure 7.44 Capacity Utilization of Individual Employees per Year

The resulting output is shown in Figure 7.45. The output shows the total number of working hours accrued for January 2006, divided into total number of hours (hrs) and billable hours (hrs_bill) for all employees. This enables you to calculate the percentage of capacity utilization.

Figure 7.45 Capacity Utilization of all Employees per Month

▶ **Billable hours per year**

The third option is to analyze calendar year 2006 for all employees. The following URL is needed:

http://dresden.ixult.net:8001/sap/bc/bsp/sap/zdztb_bsp/report.xml? event=OV03&year=2006

The resulting output is shown in Figure 7.46. The output shows the total number of working hours accrued for the calendar year 2006 divided into total number of hours (hrs) and billable hours (hrs_bill) for all employees. This enables you to calculate the percentage of capacity utilization.

Figure 7.46 Billable Hours per Year

▸ **Utilization of all employees**
Finally, you can analyze the calendar year 2006 for all employees. The following URL is needed:

http://dresden.ixult.net:8001/sap/bc/bsp/sap/zdztb_bsp/report.xml ?event=OV04&year=2006

The resulting output is shown in Figure 7.47. The output shows the total number of working hours accrued for the calendar year 2006, divided into total number of hours (hrs) and billable hours (hrs_bill) for all employees, and separated by month. This enables you to calculate the percentage of capacity utilization.

Application Login

The XML file login.xml is used to login to the Flex application. For this purpose, we must transmit a valid personnel number to the back end, as the following sample URL with personnel number 00000001 shows.

http://dresden.ixult.net:8001/sap/bc/bsp/sap/zdztb_bsp/login.xml ?persno=00000001

If the login is successful, an **OK** is returned, as shown in Figure 7.48; in case of an error, the error text is returned (see Figure 7.49).

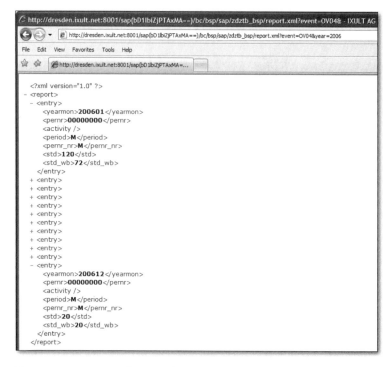

Figure 7.47 Capacity Utilization of all Employees

Figure 7.48 Successful Login

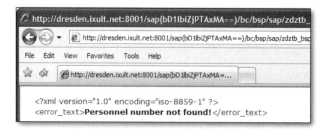

Figure 7.49 Erroneous Login

7.3   Developing Using Adobe Flex

This section describes the necessary developments in the Adobe Flex environment, including the creation of the basic structure (project files and creating components), design of the application, development of the "Planning" and "Time-Recording" components, and the reporting analysis using Flex charts. The section concludes with a final test.

Development in Adobe Flex Builder can be conducted outside of the SAP environment, provided the interface has been defined. This is a decisive advantage over traditional BSP applications that present their data on the basis of HTML.

Advantage

> **Note**
>
> Appendix A contains the complete code listings of the files described in this chapter. You can also download these listings from the web site that accompanies this book on *http://www.sap-press.com*.

7.3.1   Project Structure of the Application Front End

We will develop the front end of the planning and time-recording tool in Adobe Flex Builder 2. Once you have started Flex Builder, you can use a very powerful Eclipse-based development environment.

In the first step, we must define the necessary files for our project. The project contains the Flex project, including the MXML application, the associated MXML components, and the ActionScript files that are to contain the application logic.

Project files

You can start Adobe Flex Builder from the Windows **Start** menu. Usually it is installed in **Start · Programs · Adobe · Adobe Flex Builder**. Once you have successfully started Adobe Flex Builder, you can create a new project via the following menu path: **File · New · Flex Project** (see Figure 7.50).

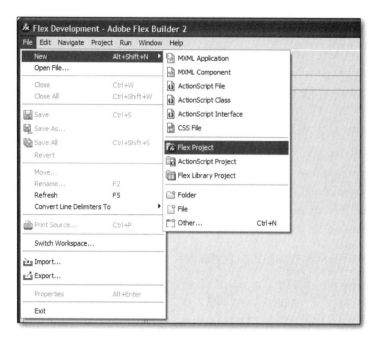

Figure 7.50 Creating the Flex Project

Selecting the
Flex server A dialog opens in which you can make the necessary settings for the project (see Figure 7.51). In the first step, you must select the Flex server on which you want to create the application.

Figure 7.51 Selecting the Flex Server

▶ The **ColdFusion Flash Remoting Service** option is an advanced application that requires the Flex Data Services 2 and ColdFusion MX 7.1. This application is needed in order to combine Flex and ColdFusion applications.

▶ **Flex Data Services** are applications that have been extended by a new architecture (data service architecture) and charting components. They enable you to integrate other technologies with Flex (see Figure 7.52).

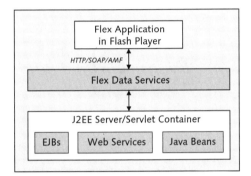

Figure 7.52 Flex Data Services

Because we haven't installed any Flex server for our example, you must choose **None** here and continue. This is the default setting for the creation of Flex projects.

In the next step, you must assign a name to the project. Here you should choose the same name as the one you choose for the package in the ABAP Workbench (Z_DZT_BOOK) in order to attain a unique naming method (see Figure 7.53).

Unique naming conventions

You can keep the **Use default location** setting. This setting specifies the directory in which the files will be stored. Of course, you can also use a different directory for the project.

Once you have defined the name of the project, you can create additional packages and directories that you want to use later on. First you should create a **Source folder** called src that is supposed to contain the MXML files (see Figure 7.54).

Then you can conclude the creation of the Flex project by clicking the **Finish** button.

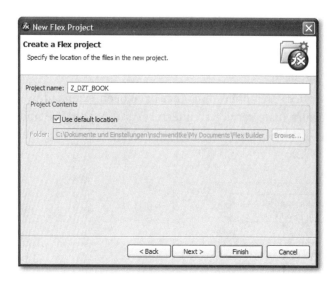

Figure 7.53 Assigning a Project Name

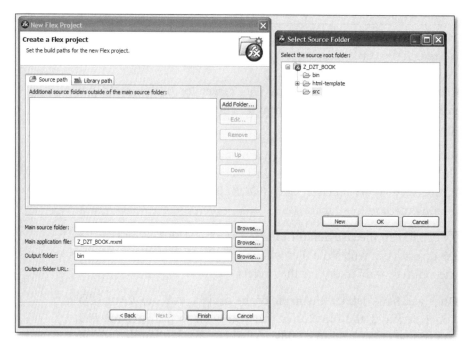

Figure 7.54 Creating Directories

ActionScript folder

Having created the project, you can now begin developing. But first we'll create some more files in order to define the basic structure of the application.

Right-click on the project name and select **New • Folder** from the context menu to create a new folder (see Figure 7.55). We create the folder as for our project. This folder is supposed to contain the ActionScript files.

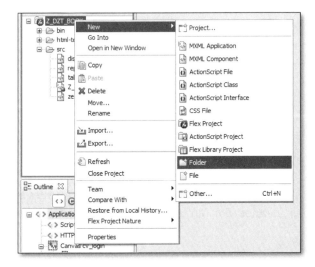

Figure 7.55 Creating a New Folder

The src directory that we defined during creation of the project already contains the file Z_DZT_BOOK.mxml, which is the main page of the application. The main page—and only the main page—contains the <mx:Application> tag including the associated namespace declaration.

Creating the MXML files

Because our application will consist of several sub-sections it makes sense to separate those sub-sections into individual MXML components. We will now create the following files one after the other.

▶ plan.mxml

▶ report.mxml

▶ tabcontrol.mxml

▶ tr.mxml

To do that, you must right-click on the **src** button and select **MXML Component**. The project directory should now look like the one shown in Figure 7.56.

Figure 7.56 Created MXML Files

ActionScript files The as directory in which we want to store the ActionScript files is defined in a similar manner. For our application, you need the following files.

▶ application.as

▶ plan.as

▶ global.as

▶ report.as

▶ tr.as

The final project directory has the structure shown in Figure 7.57.

Figure 7.57 Project Directory After Creating the Files

7.3.2 Basic Structure of the Frontend

We want to implement the functionality of the sample application using tabstrips. That is to say, we will display the **Planning**, **Time Recording**, and **Reporting** functions in separate tabs. Tabstrips provide a very useful technique for displaying many pieces of information clearly on one page.

Tabstrips

The main page is divided into the login section and the tabstrips that are stored in the file tabcontrol.mxml. Figure 7.58 shows the logical structure of the file.

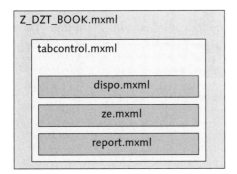

Figure 7.58 Logical Structure of Files

You can implement this rough structure in MXML, as shown in Listing 7.31. To include this source text in the application, change from the **Design** view into the **Source** view.

```
<mx:Application
    xmlns:mx="http://www.adobe.com/2006/mxml" xmlns="*"
    layout="absolute" xmlns:comp="*"
    width="900" height="700">

    <mx:Canvas id="cv_login">
        <mx:VBox>
            <!-- Login section -->
        </mx:VBox>

    </mx:Canvas>
    <mx:Canvas id="cv_tabs">

        <mx:VBox>
            <comp:tabcontrol/>
        </mx:VBox>
```

```
        </mx:Canvas>
</mx:Application>
```
Listing 7.31 Application File Z_DZT_BOOK.mxml

Creating the namespace

The namespace comp must be created in order to access components. Although it is not necessary to reserve a specific namespace for this purpose, doing so reduces the degree of complexity of the source text considerably. The application is divided into two <mx:Canvas> areas that contain the login section and the Tabstrip component. The size of the application is defined centrally in the <mx:Application> tag and is specified with 900 by 700 pixels here.

The tabcontrol.mxml component contains the **Planning**, **Time Recording**, and **Reporting** tabstrips. Excerpts from these are shown in Listing 7.32.

```
<mx:Canvas xmlns:mx="http://www.adobe.com/2006/mxml"
    xmlns="*" xmlns:comp="*">


    <mx:VBox>
        <mx:Label text="Planning Manager"
            fontFamily="Arial" fontSize="20"
            fontWeight="bold"/>

        <mx:TabNavigator height="650" width="850">
            <comp:report label="Reporting"/>
            <comp:plan label="Planning"/>
            <comp:tr label="Time Recording"/>
        </mx:TabNavigator>
    </mx:VBox>


</mx:Canvas>
```
Listing 7.32 Excerpts from MXML Component tabcontrol.mxml

Tab labels

As you can see, no <mx:Application> tag is included here because we are dealing only with a component instead of the main file. The label tag of the individual components in the <mx:TabNavigator> tag is used to define the labels of the tabs, while the superordinate <mx:Label> tag specifies the label.

The application defined in this way can already be displayed in the design mode of Flex Builder. Note, however, that the components do not yet contain any data. Figure 7.59 shows the labels of the tabs as well as the label defined in the `tabcontrol.mxml` file (**Planning Man-ager**).

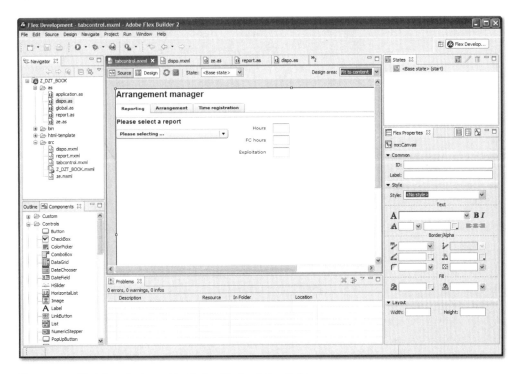

Figure 7.59 File tabcontrol.mxml in Design Mode of Flex Builder

Listing 7.33 shows the complete file `tabcontrol.mxml`. The file con-tains a short script section that can receive data from the main appli-cation and distribute this data across the components. We'll describe this process in more detail later in this chapter.

```
<?xml version="1.0" encoding="iso-8859-1"?>
<mx:Canvas xmlns:mx="http://www.adobe.com/2006/mxml"
    xmlns="*" xmlns:comp="*">

  <mx:Script>
    <![CDATA[
      [Bindable]
      public var tab_persno:String;

      [Bindable]
      public var tab_url_plan:String;
```

```
          [Bindable]
          public var tab_url_tr:String;
        ]]>
      </mx:Script>
      <mx:VBox>
        <mx:Label text="Planning Manager"
            fontFamily="Arial" fontSize="20"
            fontWeight="bold"/>

        <!-- Tab display and integration of the
            components -->
        <mx:TabNavigator height="650" width="850">
          <comp:report label="Reporting"
                l_persno="{tab_persno}"/>
          <comp:plan  label="Planning"
                l_persno="{tab_persno}"
                l_url="{tab_url_plan}"/>
          <comp:tr label="Time Recording"
                l_persno="{tab_persno}"
                l_url="{tab_url_tr}"/>
        </mx:TabNavigator>
      </mx:VBox>
    </mx:Canvas>
```

Listing 7.33 File tabcontrol.mxml

Now that you have defined the basic structure of the application, you can use it for your further development work.

7.3.3 Developing the Planning Component

Both the planning and time-recording components are referred to as *recording components*. This section describes step by step how you can present the planning component and integrate it with the back end, while Section 7.3.4 describes the same procedure for the time-recording component.

Structure of the planning component We want to structure the planning component in such a way that you can enter planning data on the left-hand side and display the data on the right-hand side. Our goal is to design the layout of the planning component so that it looks like the one shown in Figure 7.60.

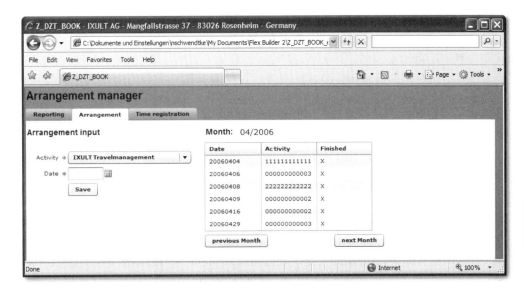

Figure 7.60 Layout of the Planning Component

As a rule, Flex positions individual components below each other when they are integrated into the layout. To avoid this, you must encapsulate components in layout areas: `<mx:HBox>` and `<mx:VBox>`. The HBox component groups elements at the horizontal level, while the VBox component groups them at a vertical level.

Layout components

As you can see in Figure 7.60, the planning component is divided into two areas: the area on the left is used to enter data, while the area on the right outputs data. Both areas are separated by a `<mx:HBox>` tag.

```
<mx:HBox>
    <!-- Left-hand side -->
    <!-- Right-hand side -->
</mx:HBox>
```

The necessary fields for data entry are the **Planning Entries** label, the input fields, and the **Submit** button, all of which must be displayed one above the other. For this purpose, the elements on the left must be subdivided in a `<mx:VBox>` tag. The same holds true for the right-hand side that consists of the month, a table, and two buttons. Listing 7.34 shows the structure with these layout elements.

```
<mx:HBox>
   <!-- Left-hand side: Planning Entries -->
   <mx:VBox>
      <!-- Input elements -->
   </mx:VBox>

   <!-- Right-hand side: Display of plannings -->
   <mx:VBox>
      <!-- Display elements -->
   </mx:VBox>
</mx:HBox>
```

Listing 7.34 Layout Elements of File plan.mxml

Left-Hand Side of the Planning Component

You can now add functional elements to the two sides. Once you have defined the function module for adding planning data (see Section 7.2.3), the personnel number, date, and activity are required. The personnel number is defined during the login process so that the user only needs to select a date and an activity.

`<mx:Form>` For this purpose, Flex provides a simple technique to integrate the so-called *form elements*: the `<mx:Form>` tag. The `<mx:Form>` tag is subdivided into separate `<mx:FormItem>` tags that contain the actual elements. This enables a structured distribution of the components.

The following are required for the planning component.

▶ The `<mx:ComboBox>` component is used to list the activities as a drop-down list.

▶ The `<mx:DateField>` component provides a convenient way to integrate a date.

▶ The `<mx:Button>` component will present the **Submit** of the planning component.

Listing 7.35 shows the `<mx:Form>` tag of the planning component.

```
<mx:Form id="form_plan">
   <mx:FormItem label="Activity" required="true">
      <mx:ComboBox id="form_activity"
            dataProvider="" labelField="value"/>
   </mx:FormItem>
   <mx:FormItem label="Date" required="true">
```

```
      <mx:DateField id="form_date"
          labelFunction="df_convert"/>
    </mx:FormItem>
    <mx:FormItem>
      <mx:Button id="form_submit" label="Submit"
          click="add_planning()"/>
    </mx:FormItem>
</mx:Form>
```

Listing 7.35 Form Elements of the Planning Component

The first `FormItem` element is used to display the activity and con- **FormItem Activity**
tains the corresponding label. The `required` property indicates
whether the item is a mandatory field.

> **Note**
>
> The `required` property is merely a display variant and displays a red
> asterisk (*) next to the field. It does not check whether the field was actu-
> ally filled with data.

The `FormItem` element itself contains the `ComboBox` that is supposed
to display the activities. The activities originate in the back end and
are transferred to the front end using the `data.xml` file. The `dataPro-`
`vider` property is responsible for filling the `ComboBox` with data. This
property will be described in greater detail later on in this chapter.

It is important that you set the `labelField` property in order to indicate which element of the XML structure you want to display.

The second `FormItem` element displays the date and is also assigned **FormItem Date**
the `required` property. The `FormItem` is also assigned the `<mx:Date-`
`Field>` tag as a child, and this in turn is assigned an ID and a `label-`
`Function`. `labelFunction` enables you to format a date according to
your requirements prior to displaying it. The `df_convert()` function
is implemented later in the `global.as` file.

The `DateField` is a component that consists of an input field and a
button that resembles a small calendar. If you click on this button, a
calendar opens that facilitates the entry of the date (see Figure 7.61).

Figure 7.61 Easy Input in the DateField

FormItem Button To transfer the user entries to the back end, you need a button. This button is integrated using the third `FormItem` element, and it contains the `<mx:Button>` tag. You can assign to this tag an event—in this case it is the system event `click`—that anticipates a function being processed. The `add_planning()` function that this event receives will become part of the file `plan.as`.

The planning code defined in this way has the layout shown in Figure 7.62.

Figure 7.62 Layout of the Form Tag

Right-Hand Side of the Planning Component

Integrating tables The right-hand side of the planning component is used to display the user entries in a table that covers one month. In Flex, you can integrate tables using the `<mx:DataGrid>` tag. Usually, the tables are automatically assigned the table headers.

Two buttons are created that enable forward and backward navigation between the individual months, as shown in Figure 7.63.

As mentioned earlier in this chapter, the elements are encapsulated in a `<mx:VBox>` tag in order to position them one above the other. However, the `VBox` element contains other `HBox` elements for a horizontal display of the month and the two buttons.

Figure 7.63 Right-Hand Side of the Planning Component

To display the month, you need two labels within a `<mx:HBox>` construction. The first one is a static text containing the text "Month:" whereas the second label is assigned its text dynamically, which is carried out by means of a data binding to an ActionScript variable.

Displaying the month

```
<mx:HBox>
    <mx:Label text="Month:" fontFamily="Arial"
        fontSize="14" fontWeight="bold"/>
    <mx:Label text="{l_month_displ}" fontSize="14"/>
</mx:HBox>
```

In addition to defining the text, you must assign both labels the font, size, and display type (e.g., bold). The `l_month_displ` variable is used for the data-binding process. You can use curly brackets (`{}`) to integrate this variable.

As mentioned above, you must use the `<mx:DataGrid>` tag to integrate tables. When doing so, you must specify a `dataProvider` that contains the data to be displayed. In our example, that's the content of XML file `plan_get.xml` from the SAP server.

Integrating the DataGrid

Because the columns in the `DataGrid` are assigned the names of the XML tags[4] it makes sense to correct the names manually:

```
<mx:DataGrid sortableColumns="true" id="dg"
    dataProvider="">
    <mx:columns>
        <mx:DataGridColumn headerText="Date"
            dataField="date"/>
```

---

4 The `<persno>` tag would cause the column name **persno** to be created in the `DataGrid`.

```
        <mx:DataGridColumn headerText="Activity"
            dataField="activity"/>
        <mx:DataGridColumn headerText="Closed"
            dataField="finished"/>
    </mx:columns>
</mx:DataGrid>
```

You can correct the column names using the <mx:columns> tag that contains the child elements <mx:DataGridColumn>. The tags are assigned the properties headerText (column name) and dataField (displayed element). The column names are defined as follows: **Date**, **Activity**, and **Closed**.

Forward/Back-ward buttons
The two buttons that are supposed to enable the navigation between the months are encapsulated in a <mx:HBox> element that is assigned the attribute horizontalGap, which indicates the spacing between the individual elements of the HBox.

```
<mx:HBox horizontalGap="120">
    <mx:Button label="Previous month"
        click="button_click('back',1_month)"/>
    <mx:Button label="Next month"
        click="button_click('fwd',1_month)"/>
</mx:HBox>
```

Both buttons are assigned the click event, including a corresponding function. The button_click function receives the month that is currently being processed as well as the direction in which the user wants to navigate.

Implementing the Logic

Now that you have implemented the layout elements of the application, you can assign logic to them. To enable the adding, reading out, and display of planning data and activities, you must fill the data-Provider of each corresponding component with data. You can do that using ActionScript functions (implemented in global.as and plan.as) and the <mx:HTTPService> element.

Integrating XML files
To integrate an XML file that is located on the server, you need the <mx:HTTPService> tag. Because three different XML files must be processed in the planning component, you must integrate three <mx:HTTPService> tags correspondingly:

228

```
<!-- HTTPServices -->
<mx:HTTPService url="{l_url}" useProxy="false"
    id="plan_data"/>
<mx:HTTPService url="{l_url_activity}" useProxy="false"
    id="activity_data"/>
<mx:HTTPService url="{l_url_send}" useProxy="false"
    id="plan_add"
    result="analyze_text(event.target.result.error_text)"/>
```

An HTTPService always requires a URL in order to locate the file that is to be transferred. The URL is set and updated dynamically via a data-binding process (to be identified by the curly brackets). The result of an HTTPService is always stored in the <id_of_ser-vice>.result variable. Then you can access the individual elements of the XML file via tag.tag.tag.

Data binding

Note
During a data-binding process, the attribute value changes as soon as you change the variable that's contained in the data binding. This means that no event must be triggered in order to assign the new value to the attribute.

So that it can be retrieved later, the data of the HTTPService is assigned an ID. Moreover, the result attribute can be used to edit the result before it is output. For this purpose, a function must be stored that receives the content of the resulting XML file. In our example, that's the analyze_text function that's implemented in the file global.as.

The retrieved ActionScript files are integrated into the component including the source attribute via the <mx:Script> tag:

<mx:Script>

```
<mx:Script source="../as/global.as"/>
<mx:Script source="../as/plan.as"/>
```

Because the MXML files are located in the src directory, the as files are located in the relative path ../as/. Listing 7.36 shows the complete source text of file plan.mxml.

```
<?xml version="1.0" encoding="iso-8859-1"?>
<mx:Canvas xmlns:mx=http://www.adobe.com/2006/mxml
    xmlns="*" creationComplete="fire()" xmlns:comp="*">
```

```
<mx:Script source="../as/global.as"/>
<mx:Script source="../as/plan.as"/>

<mx:DateFormatter id="df_date"
    formatString="YYYYMMDD"/>

<!-- HTTP services -->
<mx:HTTPService url="{l_url}" useProxy="false"
    id="plan_data"/>
<mx:HTTPService url="{l_url_activity}"
    useProxy="false" id="activity_data"/>
<mx:HTTPService url="{l_url_send}" useProxy="false"
    id="plan_add"
    result=
        "analyze_text(event.target.result.error_text)"/>

<mx:HBox>
    <!-- Left-hand side: Planning Entries -->
    <mx:VBox>
        <mx:Label text="Planning Entries"
            fontSize="14" fontWeight="bold"
            fontFamily="Arial"/>
        <mx:Form id="form_plan">
            <mx:FormItem label="Activity"
                required="true">
                <mx:ComboBox id="form_activity"
                    dataProvider=
                    "{activity_data.result.data.entry}"
                    labelField="value"/>
            </mx:FormItem>
            <mx:FormItem label="Date" required="true">
                <mx:DateField id="form_date"
                    labelFunction="df_convert"/>
            </mx:FormItem>
            <mx:FormItem>
                <mx:Button id="form_submit"
                    label="Submit"
                    click="add_planning()"/>
            </mx:FormItem>
        </mx:Form>
    </mx:VBox>

    <!-- Right-hand side: Display of Planning Data -->
    <mx:VBox>
        <mx:HBox>
```

```
                <mx:Label text="Month:" fontFamily="Arial"
                    fontSize="14" fontWeight="bold"/>
                <mx:Label text="{l_month_displ}"
                    fontSize="14"/>
            </mx:HBox>

            <mx:DataGrid sortableColumns="true" id="dg"
                dataProvider=
                "{plan_data.result.result.pos.entry}">
                <mx:columns>
                    <mx:DataGridColumn headerText="Date"
                        dataField="date"/>
                    <mx:DataGridColumn
                        headerText="Activity"
                        dataField="activity"/>
                    <mx:DataGridColumn
                        headerText="Closed"
                        dataField="finished"/>
                </mx:columns>
            </mx:DataGrid>

            <mx:HBox horizontalGap="120">
                <mx:Button label="Previous month"
                    click="button_click('back',l_month)"/>
                <mx:Button label="Next month"
                    click="button_click('fwd',l_month)"/>
            </mx:HBox>
        </mx:VBox>
    </mx:HBox>
</mx:Canvas>
```
Listing 7.36 Source Text of File plan.mxml

Creating a dataProvider

The dataProviders of the DataGrid or ComboBox must now be filled with data using ActionScript. For this purpose, you must define the URLs of the <mx:HTTPService> tags so that the data can be retrieved from the back end.

We want the application to first retrieve the data from the server that pertains to the current month. To do that, you must define the current date in the first section of the plan.as file.

Setting the month

```
// Current date (required for start view)
private var l_month_current:Date = new Date();
```

231

The date is formatted in such a way that it corresponds to the variable of XML file `plan_get.xml` so that it can be received. For example, if the current date is "06/12/2006," it must be converted into "200606":

```
// Current month
[Bindable]
public var l_month:String =
    (++l_month_current.month < 10) ?
    l_month_current.fullYear.toString() + "0" +
    l_month_current.month.toString() :
    l_month_current.fullYear.toString() +
    l_month_current.month.toString();
```

This statement is a construction of the following type:

```
(A < B) ? X=10 : X=11;
```

This means: "If A is smaller than B, set X to 10; otherwise set X to 11." This construction is necessary for the date because the Flex date does generally not display months as two-digit numbers; e. g., January is identified as 1 instead of 01. Thus, if the current month is smaller than 10, a 0 is added in front of the month; if not, the existing number can be adopted. The `fullYear` and `month` properties enable you to access the year or month respectively.

Displaying the month

To display the month on the right-hand side of the planning component, we want the format to be as follows: MM/YYYY. You can easily attain this conversion by using simple string concatenations:

```
// Current month in format that can be displayed
[Bindable]
public var l_month_displ:String = l_month.substr(4,2) +
    "/" + l_month.substr(0,4);
```

Displaying the URL

The URL must contain all parameters needed in order to correctly execute the file `plan_get.xml`. For this purpose, the following values must be transferred:

▶ Personnel number (persno)

▶ Month (month)

You can create the URL string l_url as follows:

```
// Basic URL and URL settings
public var l_base_url:String =
    "http://server:port/sap/bc/bsp/sap/zdztb_bsp/";
    public var l_dataget:String = "data.xml";

// URL to be finally called
[Bindable]
public var l_url:String;

// URL of the activity
[Bindable]
public var l_url_activity:String = l_base_url +
    l_dataget + "?typ=A";

// Sending URL
[Bindable]
public var l_url_send:String;
```

The final URL is defined using auxiliary variables before it is concatenated. If you don't know the URL of the system, you can use Transaction SE80 in the BSP application in order to read it out (see Figure 7.64). To do this, open Transaction SE80 and select the BSP application ZDZTB_BSP as well as the file plan_add.xml in the pages that contain flow logic. The URL of the page is contained in the bottom line of the file properties.

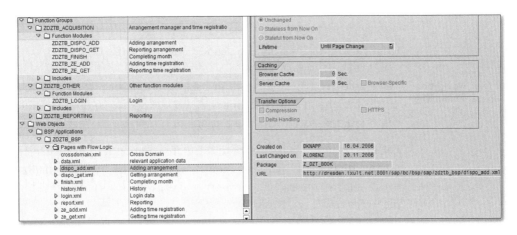

Figure 7.64 Reading Out the URL Parameter

fire()   You must define a `fire()` function in the `CreationComplete` event of the `<mx:Canvas>` tag in file `plan.mxml`. The event is triggered once the component has been loaded and is supposed to trigger the retrieval of the XML files. Because setting the URL in the `<mx:HTTPService>` tag is not sufficient for retrieving the data, you must find a way to solve this problem, such as using ActionScript[5]. The `fire()` function carries out this activity.

```
// Retrieve all relevant data
public function fire():void {
        plan_data.send();
        activity_data.send();
}
```

The data-retrieval process is triggered using `<id_of_http_service>.send()` and is carried out in the `fire()` function for both the `ComboBox` (activities) and the `DataGrid` (planning data). This means that both the `DataGrid` and the `ComboBox` can use the data for display purposes, as shown in Figure 7.65.

Figure 7.65 Activities and Planning Data Retrieved from the Server

Navigation between months   To be able to navigate forward or backward to a specific month, you must implement the function `button_click(direction,current_month)` that is stored with the buttons in file `plan.mxml`.

For this reason, it is necessary to calculate the month to be displayed on the basis of the current month. This is done by the function `month_action(direction,current_month)`, which is implemented in file `global.as` (see Listing 7.37).

---

5   You can compare this process to the `onLoad` attribute of a `<body>` HTML tag.

```
// Navigate one month forward or back
public function month_action(direction:String,
      current_month:String):String {

   var l_month:Number;
   var l_month_str:String;
   var l_year:Number;
   var l_year_str:String;
   var l_yearmon:String;

// Get year and month
   l_year_str = current_month.substr(0,4);
   l_year = Number(l_year_str);

   l_moth_str = current_month.substr(4,2);
   l_month = Number(l_month_str);

// Determine new month based on direction
   if (direction == "fwd") {

      if (l_month == 12) {
         l_month = 1;
         l_year++;
      }
      else
         l_month++;
   }
   else {

      if (l_month == 1) {
         l_month = 12;
         l_year--;
      }
      else
         l_month--;
   }

// Extend string to two characters
   if (l_month < 10)
      l_month_str = "0" + l_month.toString();
   else
      l_month_str = l_month.toString();

   l_year_str = l_year.toString();
```

```
        l_yearmon = l_year_str + l_month_str;

    return l_yearmon;
    }
```

Listing 7.37 Function month_action(direction,current_month)

Calculating the month Depending on the direction and the current month, the function calculates the month that is to be displayed next. For this purpose, the month must usually be extended by 1 (forward navigation) or reduced by 1 (backward navigation). The two special cases of December (forward) and January (backward) are treated separately because they require the year to be adjusted as well.

Then you must extend the month values to two characters again in order to display the string as a CHAR6 value. This function enables you to implement the function button_click(direction,current_month) (see Listing 7.38).

```
// Reaction to forward or back button (planning)
public function button_click(direction:String,
                curent_month:String):void {

    var l_yearmon:String;

// Get new month
    l_yearmon = month_action(direction,current_month);

// Calculate new URL
    l_url = l_base_url + "plan_get.xml?persno=" +
            l_persno + "&month=" + l_yearmon;
    l_month = l_yearmon;
    l_month_displ = l_month.substr(4,2) + "/" +
                l_month.substr(0,4);

// Initialize previous view in order to avoid displaying old
// data if no data exists
    dg.dataProvider = "";

// Send HTTP request
    plan_data.send();
}
```

Listing 7.38 Function button_click(direction,current_month) for the Planning Component

The function uses the `month_action` function that has just been defined in order to retrieve the month to be displayed. The new URL then is defined (because of the data binding, the URL is automatically set anew in the `HTTPService`). The previous view is initialized via `dg.dataProvider` in order to avoid displaying the old data if no new data is available. After that, an HTTP request can be sent using the `send()` function.

The user now can navigate between months. In order not to exceed the scope of a sample application, we won't implement an error-checking process for the data entry at this point.

You can add planning data using the XML file `plan_add.xml`, to which you must add the personnel number, date, and activity. The function `add_planning()` reads this data from the `Form` fields on the left-hand side of the planning component in order to create the sending URL `l_url_send` (see Listing 7.39).

Adding planning data

```
// Add planning
public function add_planning():void {

    var l_date:String = form_date.text;
    var l_activity:String =
        form_activity.selectedItem.name.toString();

// Determine sending URL
    l_url_send = l_base_url + "plan_add.xml?persno=" +
        l_persno + "&date=" + l_date + "&activity=" +
        l_activity;

// Send requests (PLAN_ADD with
// subsequent PLAN_GET)
        plan_add.send();
        plan_data.send();
}
```

Listing 7.39 Function add_planning()

The function determines the entered texts from the two `Form` fields, `form_activity` and `form_date`, and uses these texts to create the sending URL. After that, the HTTP requests are sent using the `send()` command. This process involves sending the data and retrieving the modified data afterwards.

Error output
If errors occurred when the planning data was added, these errors are automatically output through an alert window. To implement this, you must store the function `analyze_text(error_text)` in the `<mx:HTTPService>` tag of the sending URL in the `result` attribute. The function checks whether the result contains errors. If it doesn't, the function returns the value **OK**; otherwise it returns an error text:

```
// Output error messages
public function analyze_text(error:String):void {
    if (error != "OK")
        Alert.show(error,"Warning!");
}
```

This function is also contained in the `global.as` file.

DateFormatter
As mentioned earlier in this chapter, you can use a `labelFunction` to format a date (or other elements) according to your requirements before it is displayed. In our example, we need the date in the SAP format of the `DATS` data type (`YYYYMMDD`), which means that we first have to transform the date created by the `DateField` component (automatically) into the following required format.

```
// Date formatter
public function df_convert(date:Date):String {
    return df_date.format(date);
}

<mx:DateFormatter id="df_date"
    formatString="YYYYMMDD"/>

<mx:DateField id="form_date"
    labelFunction="df_convert"/>
```

The specification of `df_convert(date)` makes sure that this function is used to modify the date format before the date is output. The function calls the `DateFormatter` via `df_date`. The `DateFormatter` contains the new string to be displayed (`formatString`). The conversion process itself is carried out by Flex.

The function `df_convert(date)` is contained in the ActionScript file `global.as`, while the `DateFormatter` and `DateField` come from `plan.mxml`.

7.3.4   Time-recording Component

We want to structure the time-recording component in such a way that you can enter time-recording data on the left-hand side and display the data on the right. Our goal is to design the layout of the time-recording component so that it looks like the one shown in Figure 7.66.

Structure of time recording

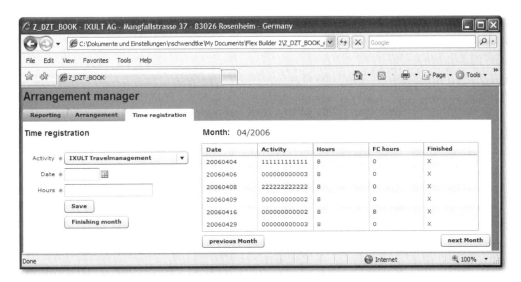

Figure 7.66 Display of the Time-Recording Tab

As you can see in Figure 7.66, the time-recording component is also divided into two sections: the left-hand part is used to enter data, while the right-hand area is responsible for displaying this data. Both areas must therefore be separated by a `<mx:HBox>` tag.

```
<mx:HBox>
    <!-- Left-hand side -->
    <!-- Right-hand side -->
</mx:HBox>
```

The necessary fields for data entry are the **Time Recording Entries** label as well as the input fields and the **Submit** and **Close month** buttons, all of which must be displayed one above the other. For this purpose, the elements on the left must be subdivided in a `<mx:VBox>` tag. The same holds true for the right-hand side that consists of the month, a table, and two buttons. Listing 7.40 shows the structure with these layout elements.

Required fields

```
<mx:HBox>
  <!-- Left-hand side: Time recording entries -->
  <mx:VBox>
     <!-- Input elements -->
  </mx:VBox>

  <!-- Right-hand side: Display of time recording data -->
  <mx:VBox>
     <!-- Display elements -->
  </mx:VBox>
</mx:HBox>
```

Listing 7.40 Layout Elements of File plan.mxml

Left-Hand Side of the Time-recording Component

<mx:Form> You can now add functional elements to the two sides. Once you have defined the function module for adding time-recording data (see Section 7.2.3), the personnel number, date, and activity are required. The personnel number is defined during the login process so that the user only needs to select a date, the number of working hours, and an activity. As is the case with the planning component, you must use the <mx:Form> tag here.

▶ The first FormItem element is used to display the activity and contains the corresponding label. The required property indicates whether the item is a mandatory field.

▶ The FormItem element itself contains the ComboBox that is supposed to display the activities. The activities originate from the front end and are transferred to the front end using the data.xml file. The dataProvider property is responsible for filling the ComboBox with data. This property will be described in greater detail later in this chapter.

It is important that you set the labelField property in order to indicate which element of the XML structure you want to display.

▶ The next FormItem is used to record the working hours. For this purpose, you must use the <mx:TextInput> tag. You can compare the TextInput field to the HTML tag <input>, as it has the same properties.

▶ The second FormItem element represents the date. You must add the required property to this element as well. The FormItem contains the <mx:DateField> tag as a child, which is assigned the ID

and the labelFunction (in the same way as the planning component). The labelFunction, in turn, contains the function df_con-
vert(date).

▸ To transfer the user entries to the back end, you need a button.
This button is integrated using the fourth FormItem element and it
contains the <mx:Button> tag. Again, you must assign the system
event click to this tag. The system event contains the function
add_tr().

▸ In addition to the function for transferring time-recording data,
you also need a function for closing a month so that no more data
can be recorded for this period. For this purpose, you must once
again define a <mx:Button> tag, including the default event click
that is procesed by the month_complete() function.

Listing 7.41 shows the <mx:Form> tag of the time-recording component.

```
<mx:Form id="form_tr">
   <mx:FormItem label="Activity" required="true">
      <mx:ComboBox id="form_activity"
           dataProvider="" labelField="value"/>
   </mx:FormItem>
   <mx:FormItem label="Date" required="true">
      <mx:DateField id="form_date"
           labelFunction="df_convert"/>
   </mx:FormItem>
   <mx:FormItem label="Hours" required="true">
      <mx:TextInput id="form_hrs"/>
   </mx:FormItem>
   <mx:FormItem>
      <mx:Button id="form_submit" label="Save"
           click="add_tr()"/>
   </mx:FormItem>
   <mx:FormItem>
      <mx:Button id="form_complete" label="Finishing
           month" click="month_complete()"/>
   </mx:FormItem>
</mx:Form>
```

Listing 7.41 Form Elements of the Time-recording Component

The layout displayed in Figure 7.67 is the result of Listing 7.41.

Figure 7.67 Layout of the Form Tag

Right-Hand Side of the Time-Recording Component

The right-hand side of the time-recording component is similar to that of the planning component. For this reason, we won't go into much detail here, as you can use the information provided for the right-hand side of the planning component.

Integrating XML files

The relevant XML files are again implemented using the `<mx:HTTP-Service>` tag. Because we must handle three different XML files in the time-recording component you have to integrate three tags:

```
<mx:HTTPService url="{l_url}" useProxy="false"
    id="tr_data"/>
<mx:HTTPService url="{l_url_activity}" useProxy="false"
    id="activity_data"/>
<mx:HTTPService url="{l_url_send}" useProxy="false"
    id="tr_add"
    result="analyze_text(event.target.result.error_text)"/>
```

To be able to retrieve the data of the `HTTPService` at a later stage, the data is assigned an ID. Moreover, the `result` attribute can be used to edit the result before it is output. For this purpose, a function must be stored that receives the content of the resulting XML file. In our example, that's the `analyze_text` function implemented in the file `global.as`.

`<mx:Script>`

The retrieved ActionScript files are integrated into the component including the `source` attribute via the `<mx:Script>` tag:

```
<mx:Script source="../as/global.as"/>
<mx:Script source="../as/tr.as"/>
```

Because the MXML files are located in the `src` directory, the as files are located in the relative path `../as/`. Listing 7.42 shows the complete source text of file `tr.mxml`.

```
<?xml version="1.0" encoding="iso-8859-1"?>
<mx:Canvas xmlns:mx="http://www.adobe.com/2006/mxml"
    xmlns="*" creationComplete="fire()">

   <mx:Script source="../as/global.as"/>
   <mx:Script source="../as/tr.as"/>

   <mx:DateFormatter id="df_date" formatString="YYYYMMDD"/>

   <!-- HTTPServices -->
   <mx:HTTPService url="{l_url}" useProxy="false"
       id="tr_data"/>
   <mx:HTTPService url="{l_url_activity}" useProxy="false"
       id="activity_data"/>
   <mx:HTTPService url="{l_url_send}" useProxy="false"
       id="tr_add"
     result="analyze_text(event.target.result.error_text)"/>

   <mx:HBox>
      <!-- Left-hand side: Time Recording Entries -->
      <mx:VBox>
         <mx:Label text="Time Recording Entries"
             fontSize="14" fontWeight="bold"
             fontFamily="Arial"/>

         <mx:Form id="form_tr">
            <mx:FormItem label="Activity" required="true">
              <mx:ComboBox id="form_activity"
            dataProvider="{activity_data.result.data.entry}"
                labelField="value"/>
            </mx:FormItem>
            <mx:FormItem label="Date" required="true">
              <mx:DateField id="form_date"
                 labelFunction="df_convert"/>
            </mx:FormItem>
            <mx:FormItem label="Hours" required="true">
              <mx:TextInput id="form_hrs"/>
            </mx:FormItem>
            <mx:FormItem>
              <mx:Button id="form_submit" label="Save"
                 click="add_tr()"/>
            </mx:FormItem>
            <mx:FormItem>
              <mx:Button id="form_complete" label="Finishing
                 month" click="month_complete()"/>
```

```
                    </mx:FormItem>
                </mx:Form>
            </mx:VBox>

            <!-- Right-hand side: Display of time recording
             data -->
            <mx:VBox>
                <mx:HBox>
                    <mx:Label text="Month:" fontFamily="Arial"
                        fontSize="14" fontWeight="bold"/>
                    <mx:Label text="{l_month_displ}" fontSize="14"/>
                </mx:HBox>

                <mx:DataGrid sortableColumns="true" id="dg2"
                  dataProvider="{tr_data.result.result.pos.entry}">
                    <mx:columns>
                        <mx:DataGridColumn headerText="Date"
                            dataField="date"/>
                        <mx:DataGridColumn headerText="Activity"
                            dataField="activity"/>
                        <mx:DataGridColumn headerText="Hours"
                            dataField="hrs_compl"/>
                        <mx:DataGridColumn headerText=
                            "Billable Hours"
                            dataField="hrs_bill"/>
                        <mx:DataGridColumn headerText="Finished"
                            dataField="finished"/>
                    </mx:columns>
                </mx:DataGrid>

                <mx:HBox horizontalGap="320">
                    <mx:Button label="Previous month"
                        click="button_click('back',l_month)"/>
                    <mx:Button label="Next month"
                        click="button_click('fwd',l_month)"/>
                </mx:HBox>
            </mx:VBox>
        </mx:HBox>
    </mx:Canvas>
```

Listing 7.42 Source Text of File tr.mxml

The `dataProviders` of the `DataGrid` or `ComboBox` must now be filled
with data using ActionScript. For this purpose, you must define the
URLs of the `<mx:HTTPService>` tags so that the data can be retrieved
from the back-end server.

Except for a few names, the functions for displaying the month and URL for the time-recording component are identical to those for the planning component and therefore don't need further explanation.

To be able to navigate forward or backward to a specific month, you must implement the function `button_click(direction,current_month)` that is stored with the buttons in file `tr.mxml`. This function is also identical to the function `button_click(direction,current_month)` used in the planning component and is therefore not described again at this point.

Navigation
between months

In order not to exceed the scope of a sample application, we won't implement an error-checking process for the data entry at this point.

Adding time-
recording data

The actual adding of time-recording data is implemented by the XML file `tr_add.xml` to which you must assign the personnel number, the date, the number of recorded working hours, and the activity. The function `add_tr()` reads this data from the `Form` fields on the left-hand side of the time-recording component in order to create the sending URL `l_url_send` (see Listing 7.43).

```
// Add time recording (no error check)
public function add_tr():void {

    var l_date:String = form_date.text;
    var l_activity:String =
        form_activity.selectedItem.name.toString();
    var l_hrs:String = form_hrs.text;

    if (l_hrs == "")
        analyze_text("Please enter a value for the number of
                     hours!");
    else {
        l_url_send = l_base_url + "tr_add.xml?persno=" +
        l_persno + "&date=" + l_date + "&activity=" +
        l_activity + "&hrs=" + l_hrs;

        tr_add.send();
        tr_data.send();
    }
}
```

Listing 7.43 Function add_tr()

The function determines the entered texts from the three Form fields, form_activity, form_hrs, and form_date, and uses these texts to create the sending URL. After that, the HTTP requests are sent using the send() command. This process involves sending the data and retrieving the modified data afterwards.

Error output If errors occurred when the time-recording data was added, these errors are automatically output through an alert window. To implement this, you must store the function analyze_text(error_text) in the <mx:HTTPService> tag of the sending URL in the result attribute. The function checks whether the result contains errors. If it doesn't, the function returns the value **OK**; otherwise it returns an error text.

Closing a month To close a month, the same flow is used as when you add time-recording data, the only difference being the URL:

```
// Closing a month
public function month_complete():void {

    l_url_send = l_base_url + "finish.xml?persno=" +
    l_persno + "&month=" + l_month;

    tr_add.send();
    tr_data.send();
}
```

The personnel number and month are transferred to the URL, and the XML file finish.xml is called on the back end to close the month on the server as well. The modified data is then retrieved from the server[6].

7.3.5 Developing the Reporting Component

Capacity utilization of an employee in a givenperiod The reporting component is supposed to represent the function modules from the back end and to display the capacity utilization of employees for a specific period of time. To display the utilization of all employees for an entire year, the data should be presented in a chart.

---

6 To keep the application simple, the date is only retrieved once. You could optimize by changing the data on the client side in order to keep the volume of data to be transferred between the front end and the back end as small as possible.

Once again, we only want to describe the basic functions here in order not to exceed the scope of the application. Thus, it won't be possible to select a specific calendar year as we'll focus on the current year only. However, you can easily change this by using the methods described here.

Because the reporting functions have returned only one work area, a graphical analysis doesn't make much sense in the following three cases:

▶ Capacity utilization of an employee per month

▶ Capacity utilization of an employee per year

▶ Billable hours of all employees per year

Thus, it is useful to use input fields for the display. A bar chart can be used for presenting the capacity utilization of all employees per month. In addition, the reporting component contains a drop-down box for selecting the type of report (see Figure 7.68).

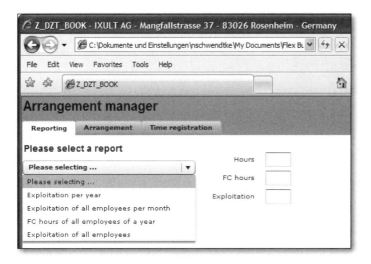

Figure 7.68 Drop-down Box for Reporting

Depending on the selected item, the application must determine what type of reporting is to be performed. For the first three items, the **Hours**, **FC Hours**, and **Exploitation** on the right are filled with data, while the fourth item should be displayed as a graphic.

The reporting component is divided into two sections: the left-hand side enables you to select the type of reporting, while the right-hand

Reporting layout

side displays the results. Consequently, you must subdivide the reporting component into a `<mx:HBox>`:

```
<mx:HBox>
    <!-- Left-hand side -->
    <!-- Right-hand side -->
</mx:HBox>
```

The left-hand side consists of a `Label` and a `ComboBox`, which, in turn, must be encapsulated in a `<mx:VBox>`:

```
<!-- Left-hand side -->
<mx:VBox>
    <mx:Label/>
    <mx:ComboBox/>
</mx:VBox>
```

The upper part of the right-hand side for displaying the results is contained in a `<mx:VBox>` consisting of `TextInput` fields, while the lower part consists of a graphic (not yet displayed). The graphic is supposed to consist of a bar chart (`<mx:ColumnChart>`) and a legend (`<mx:Legend>`):

```
<!-- Right-hand side -->
<mx:VBox>
    <mx:Form>
        <!-- Text elements of reporting -->
    </mx:Form>
    <mx:ColumnChart/>
    <mx:Legend/>
</mx:VBox>
```

Left-Hand Side of the Reporting Component

Static Because the selection of the reporting item does not necessarily have to be dynamic; you can implement it statically. To do that, you must assign an array containing the data to the `<mx:ComboBox>` tag (see Listing 7.44).

```
<mx:ComboBox id="cb_type" labelField="value"
    change="get_report()">

    <mx:Array>
```

248

```
      <mx:Object name="OV00"
          value="Please select..."/>
      <mx:Object name="OV01"
          value="Capacity utilization per year"/>
      <mx:Object name="OV02" value="Capacity
        utilization of all employees per month"/>
      <mx:Object name="OV03" value="Billable hours of
        all employees for a year"/>
      <mx:Object name="OV04" value="Capacity
        utilization of all employees"/>
   </mx:Array>
</mx:ComboBox>
```

Listing 7.44 Static ComboBox for the Reporting Component

You can integrate the data using a `<mx:Array>` element that you must create as a child of the `<mx:ComboBox>` tag. The array contains `<mx:Object>` tags that consist of the name (not displayed) and the value (displayed as the content of the `ComboBox`). The first entry, `OV00`, is only needed for selection purposes and has no direct effect on the reporting process.

Integrating the data

You can use the `name` values from the `<mx:Object>` tag to select the correct function module for the `report.xml` file at a later stage. The internal `change` event of the `<mx:ComboBox>` event triggers the retrieval of new values from the back end. This event is triggered whenever the value in the drop-down box changes.

Right-Hand Side of the Reporting Component

Similar to the planning and time-recording components, you need `TextInput` fields that can take up the values in order to display the reporting results on the right-hand side (see Listing 7.45).

```
<mx:Form>
   <mx:FormItem label="Hours">
      <mx:TextInput editable="false" text=""
          id="ti_hrs" width="40"/>
   </mx:FormItem>
   <mx:FormItem label="FC Hours">
      <mx:TextInput editable="false" text=""
          id="ti_hrs_bill" width="40"/>
   </mx:FormItem>
   <mx:FormItem label="Exploitation">
```

```
        <mx:TextInput editable="false" text=""
            id="ti_util" width="40"/>
    </mx:FormItem>
</mx:Form>
```

Listing 7.45 Form Elements of the Reporting Component

For each TextInput field, you need an ID in order to reference the fields via ActionScript later on. Keep setting the editable field to false so that the values cannot be edited manually. However, you can still select the values, for example in order to copy them into another program.

Graphical output We want to output the results of the fourth reporting type in a bar chart that we'll implement using a <mx:ColumnChart> element (see Listing 7.46).

```
<mx:ColumnChart id="bar_report" paddingLeft="5"
    height="300" width="500" paddingRight="5"
    dataProvider="{array_report}"
    showDataTips="true" visible="false">

    <mx:horizontalAxis>
        <mx:CategoryAxis dataProvider="{array_report}"
            categoryField="yearmon"/>
    </mx:horizontalAxis>
    <mx:series>
        <mx:Array>
            <mx:ColumnSeries xField="yearmon" yField="hrs"
                displayName="Hours"/>
            <mx:ColumnSeries xField="yearmon"
                yField="hrs_bill" displayName="FC Hours"/>
        </mx:Array>
    </mx:series>
</mx:ColumnChart>
<mx:Legend dataProvider="{bar_report}" visible="false"
    id="bar_report_legend"/>
```

Listing 7.46 ColumnChart Object

As is the case with many other components, you must assign a dataProvider to the bar chart. In our example, the dataProvider is the result of the XML file of the back end, which is stored in a global array: array_report. The additional showDataTips attribute ensures that when you move the mouse cursor over a bar in the chart, the corresponding value is presented as a *tooltip*.

In order to correctly label the horizontal x-axis, you must insert a `<mx:horizontalAxis>` tag that contains the field to be displayed. Unfortunately, the `DataProvider` defined in the `<mx:ColumnChart>` tag is not inherited by the `<mx:horizontalAxis>` element, which is why you must define the tag once again at this point. The field that is responsible for labeling the axis in our application is called `yearmon` (`categoryField="yearmon"`).

Labeling the x-axis

The actual data is then stored in the `<mx:series>` tag. You must define an array that is supposed to contain the elements to be displayed (`<mx:ColumnSeries>`). In our case this means the data that is to be displayed for each month. Because the return XML file contains more data than is actually needed, we only output the fields `hrs` (Hours) and `hrs_bill` (Billable Hours) per month.

The `<mx:ColumnSeries>` tag requires the following information:

Labeling the y-axis

► `xField`, which specifies which field on the x-axis is addressed

► `yField`, which specifies the name of the field in the XML file that is to be displayed on the y-axis

► The name to be displayed in the legend (`displayName`)

The `<mx:Legend>` element that contains the information on the graphic as a `dataProvider` automatically places the legend underneath the graphic. Figure 7.69 shows the final result.

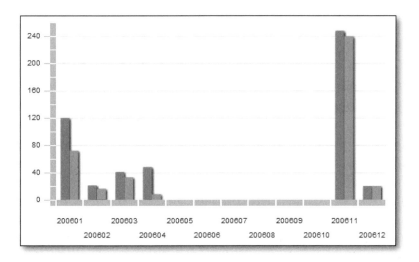

Figure 7.69 Completed Reporting with Bar Chart Display

Complex setting
options

Remarks
The setting options for charts are very complex. For this reason we refer you to the *LiveDocs* that can be found at Adobe Labs (see Section 7.5). Here you can find more detailed information on the properties and functions of charts.

Listing 7.47 shows the complete source text of file `report.mxml`.

```
<?xml version="1.0" encoding="iso-8859-1"?>
<mx:Canvas xmlns:mx="http://www.adobe.com/2006/mxml"
    xmlns="*">

  <mx:Script source="../as/report.as"/>

  <!-- HTTPService -->
    <mx:HTTPService url="{l_url}" id="reporting_data"
        useProxy="false"
        result="compute_utilization()"/>

  <mx:HBox>
    <!-- Select reporting -->
    <mx:VBox>
      <mx:Label text="Please select a reporting
                      type"
        fontFamily="Arial" fontSize="14"
        fontWeight="bold"/>
      <mx:ComboBox id="cb_type" labelField="value"
        change="get_report()">

        <mx:Array>
          <mx:Object name="OV00" value="Please
              select..."/>
          <mx:Object name="OV01" value="Capacity
            utilization per year"/>
          <mx:Object name="OV02" value="Capacity
            utilization of all employees per
            month"/>
          <mx:Object name="OV03" value="Billable
            hours of all employees for a year"/>
          <mx:Object name="OV04" value="Capacity
            utilization of all employees"/>
        </mx:Array>
      </mx:ComboBox>
    </mx:VBox>
```

```
<!-- Display reporting -->
<mx:VBox>
   <mx:Form>
      <mx:FormItem label="Hours">
         <mx:TextInput editable="false" text=""
            id="ti_hrs" width="40"/>
      </mx:FormItem>
      <mx:FormItem label="FC Hours">
         <mx:TextInput editable="false" text=""
            id="ti_hrs_bill" width="40"/>
      </mx:FormItem>
      <mx:FormItem label="Exploitation">
         <mx:TextInput editable="false" text=""
            id="ti_ausl" width="40"/>
      </mx:FormItem>
   </mx:Form>

   <!-- Graphic for last report -->
   <mx:ColumnChart id="bar_report"
      paddingLeft="5" height="300"
      width="500" paddingRight="5"
      dataProvider="{array_report}"
      showDataTips="true" visible="false">

      <mx:horizontalAxis>
         <mx:CategoryAxis
            dataProvider="{array_report}"
            categoryField="yearmon"/>
      </mx:horizontalAxis>
      <mx:series>
         <mx:Array>
            <mx:ColumnSeries xField="yearmon"
               yField="hrs"
               displayName="Hours"/>
            <mx:ColumnSeries xField="yearmon"
               yField="hrs_bill"
               displayName="FC hours"/>
         </mx:Array>
      </mx:series>
   </mx:ColumnChart>
   <mx:Legend dataProvider="{bar_report}"
      visible="false" id="bar_report_legend"/>
</mx:VBox>
   </mx:HBox>
</mx:Canvas>
```

Listing 7.47 File report.mxml

253

To change the URL that contains the reporting XML file, you must again proceed as you did with the planning and time-recording components. We won't describe this process further here.

The `get_report()` function that is located in the change event of the ComboBox is important: You must define which report (hence which URL) is called when the status of the ComboBox changes (see Listing 7.48).

```
// Get reporting data
public function get_report():void {

    bar_report.visible = false;
    bar_report_legend.visible = false;

// Which report was called?
    if (cb_type.selectedIndex == 1) {
        var l_year:String = l_month.substr(0,4);
        l_url = l_base_url + l_report + "OV01&year=" +
                l_year + "&persno=" + l_persno;
    }
    else if (cb_type.selectedIndex == 2) {
        l_url = l_base_url + l_report + "OV02&month=" +
                l_month;
    }
    else if (cb_type.selectedIndex == 3) {
        var l_year:String = l_month.substr(0,4);
        l_url = l_base_url + l_report + "OV03&year=" +
                l_year;
    }
    else if (cb_type.selectedIndex == 4) {
        var l_year:String = l_month.substr(0,4);
        l_url = l_base_url + l_report + "OV04&year=" +
                l_year;
    }

// Send HTTP request
    reporting_data.send();
}
```

Listing 7.48 Function get_report()

In the first step, the `get_report()` function hides the graphic and the legend so that it doesn't have to perform this step in each `if` statement. Then a decision is made via the `selectedIndex` of the ComboBox as to which report has been clicked on. Counting begins with 0, which means that only those URLs can be called that begin at `selectedIndex` 1; 0 represents the value, **Please select...**

The corresponding parameters for the URLs are then compiled in each `if` statement, and the URL is set. The data binding of the URL to the `HTTPService` also makes sure that the attribute of the `<mx:HTTP-Service>` tag is set correctly.

Prior to calling the `send()` method, the `dataProvider` of the chart mode is initialized in order to avoid multiple displays.

Because the back end only provides the values for the total number of hours and billable hours, we still need to calculate the capacity utilization; i. e., the percentage of billable hours in relation to the total number of hours. The function `compute_utilization()` is responsible for this.

Calculating the capacity utilization

In addition, the function for calculating the capacity utilization places the values of the XML return file into the corresponding input fields and is stored as a `result` function of the `<mx:HTTPService>` tag (see Listing 7.49).

```
// Calculate capacity utilization
public function compute_utilization():void {

   if (cb_type.selectedIndex != 4) {
      ti_hrs.text =
          reporting_data.result.report.entry.hrs;
      ti_hrs_bill.text =
          reporting_data.result.report.entry.hrs_bill;
      var l_utilization:Number =
   (Number(reporting_data.result.report.entry.hrs_bill) /
   Number(reporting_data.result.report.entry..hrs))*100;
      ti_util.text = l_utilization.toString();

   } else {
      array_report = new Array();
      array_report =
          reporting_data.result.report.entry;
      bar_report.visible = true;
      bar_report_legend.visible = true;
      ti_hrs.text = "";
      ti_hrs_bill.text = "";
```

```
                ti_util.text = "";
            }
        }
    }
```

Listing 7.49 Function compute_utilization(values)

Calculating the capacity utilization

The first step within the function decides which reporting has been called, given that the structure of the XML file can depend on which of the four types of reporting is in use. In types 1 through 3 it is a structure, whereas in type 4 it is a table. In the first case, the hrs and hrs_bill values are placed into the TextInput fields ti_hrs and ti_hrs_bill. The capacity utilization is then calculated in the subsequent step (percentage of billable hours in relation to the total number of hours multiplied by 100).

In the case of capacity utilization reporting for all employees per month, the TextInput fields are deleted and the graphic is set to the value visible.

7.3.6   Login Area

Up to now, we haven't handled the main file. As mentioned earlier, the main file is subdivided into the tabstrip area and the login area. Before anyone can use the application, they must log in to it, which can be done in the login screen shown in Figure 7.70.

Figure 7.70 Login Area of the Application

Layout of the login area

The layout of the login area is made up of a title—**Planning Manager**—and the <mx:Form> tag that has been supplemented with a heading for this particular case:

```
<mx:VBox>
   <mx:Label text="Planning Manager"
       fontFamily="Arial" fontSize="20"
       fontWeight="bold"/>
   <mx:Form>
      <mx:FormHeading label="Please login"/>
      <mx:FormItem label="Please enter your
          personnel number:">
         <mx:TextInput id="ti_persno" text=""/>
      </mx:FormItem>
      <mx:FormItem>
         <mx:Button id="bt" click="makeEvent()"
             label="Login"/>
      </mx:FormItem>
   </mx:Form>
</mx:VBox>
```

You can insert the heading for the `Form` tag using `<mx:FormHeading>` and the `label` attribute; it is displayed in alignment with the `FormItems`.

The login area is responsible for a central function of the application, as it provides the tabs with the personnel number and the first URL to be presented. To make this possible, the personnel number that was entered must be transferred to the other components.

Functionality

If the personnel number gets changed in the login area, it is transferred via the `makeEvent()` function to a global variable, `g_persno`, that has been defined in `application.as`. After that, the login file, `login.xml`, is retrieved from the back end and checked for errors (`result` function of the `<mx:HTTPService>` tag). If no error has occurred, the first URLs to be displayed are built for the tabs. The `makeEvent()` is defined as follows:

```
public function makeEvent():void {
   g_persno = ti_persno.text;
   g_url = g_base_url + "login.xml?persno=" + g_persno;

   login_data.send();
}
```

The personnel number, `g_persno`, is set to the value of the `TextInput` field, `ti_persno.text`, and this data is then forwarded to the back end (`<mx:HTTPService>` tag with `login_data` ID). The `check_ login(error)` function checks the result on the server for errors (see Listing 7.50).

```
public function check_login(error:String):void {
    if (error == "OK") {
        cv_login.visible = false;
        cv_tabs.visible = true;
        g_url_plan = g_base_url + "plan_get.xml?persno="
                     + g_persno + "&month=" + l_month;
        g_url_tr = g_base_url + "tr_get.xml?persno=" +
                   g_persno + "&month=" + l_month;
    }
    else
        Alert.show(error,"Error");
}
```

Listing 7.50 Function check_login

Transferring the URLs If no errors have occurred (`error == "OK"`), the login area gets hidden, while the tabstrips appear. In addition, the URLs to be displayed by the tabs are created. To transfer the newly created URLs to the components, you should use the following technique:

```
<comp:tabcontrol id="tc_tabs" tab_persno="{g_persno}"
        tab_url_plan="{g_url_plan}"
        tab_url_tr="{g_url_tr}"/>
```

The globally defined variables, `tab_persno`, `tab_url_plan`, and `tab_ url_tr` (defined as `[Bindable]` and `public`), can be referenced directly when integrating the component. To transfer data changes to the `tabcontrol` component, the contents of the variable are defined as data binding. This means that if the URL in file Z_DZT_ BOOK.mxml changes, those changes will also be displayed in `tabcontrol`.mxml.

The URLs transferred in this way are also distributed to the components within the `tabcontrol`.mxml file; the variables that receive the personnel number and the URL are `l_persno` and `l_url`:

```
<comp:report label="Reporting" l_persno="{tab_persno}"/>
<comp:plan   label="Planning" l_persno="{tab_persno}"
        l_url="{tab_url_plan}"/>
```

```
<comp:tr label="Time Recording" l_persno="{tab_persno}"
    l_url="{tab_url_tr}"/>
```

Listing 7.51 shows the complete `Z_DZT_BOOK`.mxml file of the application. The file `application.as` included in `Z_DZT_BOOK`.mxml is listed in Appendix A.

```
<?xml version="1.0" encoding="iso-8859-1"?>
<mx:Application
    xmlns:mx="http://www.adobe.com/2006/mxml" xmlns="*"
    layout="absolute" xmlns:comp="*"
    width="900" height="700">

    <mx:Script source="../as/application.as"/>

    <mx:HTTPService url="{g_url}" id="login_data"
        useProxy="false"
        result=
        "check_login(event.target.result.error_text)"/>

    <!-- Login area -->
    <mx:Canvas id="cv_login">
        <mx:VBox>
            <mx:Label text="Planning Manager"
                fontFamily="Arial" fontSize="20"
                fontWeight="bold"/>
            <mx:Form>
                <mx:FormHeading label="Please login"/>
                <mx:FormItem label="Pleas enter your
                    personnel number:">
                    <mx:TextInput id="ti_persno" text=""/>
                </mx:FormItem>
                <mx:FormItem>
                    <mx:Button id="bt" click="makeEvent()"
                        label="Login"/>
                </mx:FormItem>
            </mx:Form>
        </mx:VBox>
    </mx:Canvas>

    <!-- Tabstrip area -->
    <mx:Canvas id="cv_tabs" visible="false">
        <comp:tabcontrol id="tc_tabs"
            tab_persno="{g_persno}"
```

```
                    tab_url_plan="{g_url_plan}"
                    tab_url_tr="{g_url_tr}"/>
        </mx:Canvas>
    </mx:Application>
```

Listing 7.51 File Z_DZT_BOOK.mxml

7.4 Integration into SAP NetWeaver Portal

Because we developed our application using Flex Builder, it can be easily integrated into SAP NetWeaver Portal. For this purpose, we must first compile the Flex application Planning Manager, then add an HTML file to it, and finally include both files in the BSP application we created earlier so that they can be implemented in a plain iView.

Three steps   The following sections briefly describe the necessary steps involved. This example represents the easiest way to integrate Flex content into SAP NetWeaver Portal.[7]

1. **Compiling the Flex application**
   If the **Build Automatically** flag is set in the **Project** menu item, the Flex application is compiled automatically as soon as you save the project using the key combination, **Ctrl+S**. Alternatively, you can trigger this process via **Project · Build Project**.

2. **Creating the additional HTML page**
   The additional HTML file is needed to embed the compiled Flash file (*.swf*). Ths file must later be integrated in the BSP application. The file is created automatically during the compilation of the Flex application. Its name is <PROJECTNAME>.html, and it is stored in the bin directory of the project.

3. **Integrating the files in the BSP application**
   Finally, you must add the HTML file to the BSP application. To do this, you must copy the contents of the file, which is then integrated into a new **Page with Flow Logic** of the BSP application (see Figure 7.71).

---

7 With the introduction of the new version of SAP NetWeaver Visual Composer in SAP NetWeaver 2004s, the integration of a Flex application into SAP NetWeaver Portal will become easier. Please refer to the SAP Library and the SAP Developer Network (*http://sdn.sap.com*) for further information on this subject.

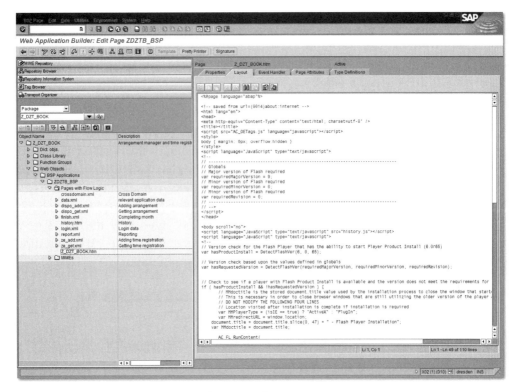

Figure 7.71 Integrating the HTML File in the BSP Application

You then can activate the HTML page. Furthermore, you must integrate the automatically created SWF file of the Flex application as a MIME object into the BSP application. To do that, select **Create • Mime Object • Import**, as shown in Figure 7.72.

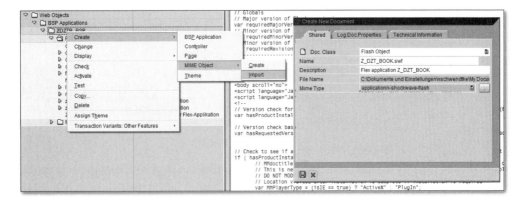

Figure 7.72 Integrating the SWF File in the BSP Application

Error caused by <noscript>

If you call the HTML page from SAP GUI using the **Execute** command and the page does not display correctly, the problem is the `<noscript>` tag that's contained in the HTML page. In this case, you should remove this tag as well as the corresponding closing tag from the page.

▶ **Creating a new iView**

In SAP NetWeaver Portal, you can create an iView in Content Administration. Make sure that you have the required authorization to create a new iView via **Content Administration • Portal Content**. Right-click on **Portal Content,** and select **New • iView** (see Figure 7.73). Then select **iView SAP BSP** from the list that opens. The BSP page that you then select is actually the file Z_DZT_BOOK.html that has just been integrated into the BSP application and that contains the compiled Flex application.

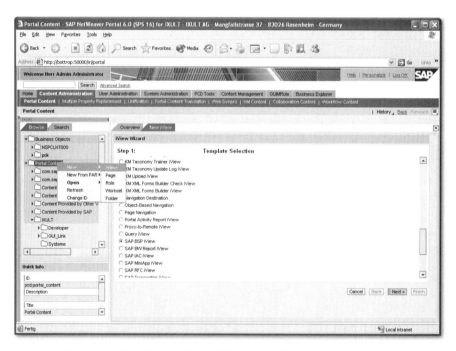

Figure 7.73 New iView in SAP NetWeaver Portal

▶ **Setting iView parameters**

In the next step, you must maintain the general parameters of the iView. You can freely select a name here (see Figure 7.74). Then click on **Next,** and select the BSP definition typs **BSP** in order to establish a direct link to our BSP application.

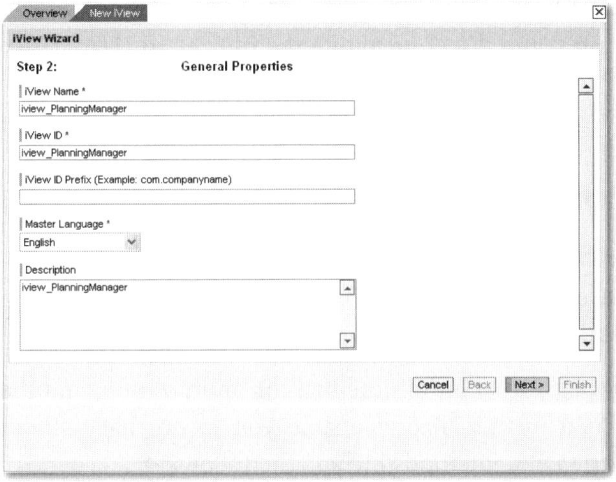

Figure 7.74 General Properties of the iView

▶ **Defining BSP parameters**

In the final step, you must define the exact BSP parameters that enable SAP NetWeaver Portal to access the application. For this purpose, you must select the system to be called (i.e., the SAP Web Application Server to be called) from a drop-down list. This drop-down list contains all business systems maintained in the *System Landscape Directory* (SLD). Then you must enter the path for the BSP application. In our case, that's `/sap/bc/bsp/sap/zdztb_bsp` (see Figure 7.75).

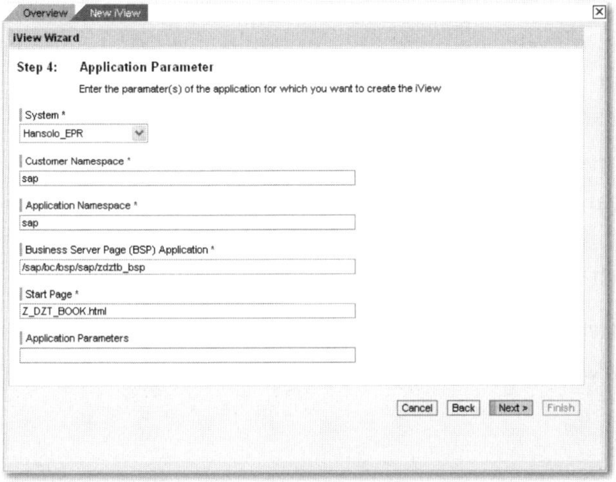

Figure 7.75 Setting the Application Parameters of the iView

▶ **Testing the iView**
You then can test the iView including the integrated HTML page from the BSP application.

7.5   Final Remarks

At this point, we'd like to stress that the application is a sample application that we use to describe basic functions. It is not a final product that can be used in a live system, and you should not try to do that.

Potential for optimizing the application   The application provides a lot of potential for optimization, and the methods described in this chapter enable you to do that without much extra effort. These methods include the following.

▶ Integration of improved user-management functions, including password entry (modification of the `login.xml` interface, maintenance of users and passwords on the server)

▶ Integration of an additional tab that allows the maintenance of activities (adding and changing, assigning activities to users)

▶ Integration of presence and absence types as additional activities

▶ Modernization of the layout using your own styles

▶ Formatting the display date in the table (which also can be done via a `labelFunction`) in order to avoid the SAP DATS format

▶ Checking the plausibility of times that are entered (for example, a week must consist of at least 40 hours)

▶ Supporting multiple languages; for example, by using another XML file that contains the texts to be displayed in the login language, the texts can be retrieved from the Online Text Repository

▶ Other reporting features; these include querying other users, already prepared for via `data.xml`, which is able to return personnel numbers. You also can display additional graphics, such as pie charts, line charts, and so on.

Additional information   The following two Web sites provide additional detailed information on MXML and ActionScript as well as a language reference and many examples.

▶ Adobe Labs
  (*http://labs.macromedia.com*)

▶ Macromedia LiveDocs
  (*http://livedocs.macromedia.com/labs/1/ flex20beta2*)

Compared to pure HTML applications, Flex applications are striking because of their functional versatility. This chapter will give you ideas for business applications that previously appeared technically impossible. We will also describe the future development possibilities in the SAP environment.

8 Enhancements and Outlook

The examples used in this book theoretically could also have been achieved using conventional means. While the work involved, readability, maintenance, and costs would have borne no relation to the methods described here, they would have been possible from a technical point of view.

The following sections provide an insight into the technical barriers you will be able to overcome in the future with Flex applications, thus implementing greater benefits for your applications, even if not in the same depth as in the sample application.

8.1 Offline Applications

Previously, Web applications only worked online. This is mainly because Web applications that are developed with HTML involve thin clients: Each piece of information displayed to the user must be transferred from a server. This is why, already, an offline application is impossible from a technical point of view, because there is no connection to a server.

Correct solution strategy for known requirements

Flex applications, being Rich Internet Applications (RIAs), are characterized by the fact that they no longer work with a thin client, but rather with a rich client; that is, parts of the application are situated locally on the user's server.

Think back to the sample application from Chapter 7 and to the hourly recording function. If one imagines field sales and service staff, or a consultant who travels a lot, the possibility of offline hourly recording would be very desirable. This activity could be performed quite comfortably while traveling. Flex gives you the possibility of building an application that stores information offline. The application has to be designed so that it can store online and offline data; in the latter case, the data could be stored locally and uploaded to the server the next time the computing device is online.

This gives rise to a number of requirements that need to be taken into consideration in the design:

▶ **Defining the interface**
The application's data transfer structure must remain the same, as far as possible; that is, no changes should be performed. This is because conflicts could occur if field staff only establishes a connection to the server every two weeks, but the data interface has already changed several times within that period.

▶ **Defining the required offline data**
One must consider the distribution of the application. What information does an offline application require while it is not connected to the server (e. g. cost centers, PSP elements, etc.)?

▶ **Defining an online check**
Another function that needs to be considered is a check to see if an online connection can be established. Ideally, one should be able to determine this in the application by a symbol indicating whether there is a link to the desired system, or whether one could be established. In the case of the sample application from Chapter 7, this would be the case if the application could transfer the working times in SAP HR. This can be achieved by first testing to see if the server can be reached (e. g., using a separate Web service).

▶ **Defining the security settings**
Flex applications must access the local system if they are to work offline. Flex's security design is very restrictive; that is, Flex applications only have one file available into which they can write data. Flex applications therefore cannot access the entire system and execute any operating system operations. This restricts the functionality of the client, because it cannot access any local data.

▶ **Defining the offline data volume**
Even if the central file that the Flex application accesses can contain any data, you should not confuse this file with a database and

assume limitless size and speed. The data is stored in an object-oriented way, so that no select statements can be transmitted, as is possible in an SQL database. This also means that one must expect restricted system performance with large volumes of data.

▶ **Shared objects**
The data is stored locally as a shared object. This class completely looks after the storing and reading of the corresponding data. Nevertheless, you must ensure that each SWF file has its own shared object. This means that even two different SWF files from the same domain cannot mutually exchange any data.

The shared object reaches a maximum size of 100KB as standard. Settings on the local machine allow you to set the size of these shared objects.

▶ **Defining the access rights**
There are other ways to regulate the data access to the system. Two main methods are relevant for this:

- ▶ Macromedia Security Configuration (*mms.cfg*)
- ▶ Global trust directory

When the Flash Player is started, the settings of the security files are read and applied according to the settings. The *mms.cfg* file contains the following elements:

- ▶ Data loading
- ▶ Privacy controls
- ▶ Flash Player updates
- ▶ Legacy file support
- ▶ Local file security

There are many setting possibilities for the Flash Player, and the configuration possibilities for administrators are also very diverse. In the Adobe documentation, you will find further information on how these files must be maintained to achieve the desired effects.

8.2 Push Data Services

With Web applications it is usually necessary for a request command to be sent before a response delivers the data for display. In this context, you are no doubt familiar with the **Refresh** button in the Web-

or SAP GUI applications, with which you can update the display. When web applications do not require this intermediate step, either a Rich Internet Application is in use or the request command is triggered automatically; e.g., by JavaScript.

In the latter case, the application attempts to achieve more user-friendliness, and pays for this through a high system load, both on the server side and in terms of the network bandwidth. Flex applications can now be written so that the data will always be sent to a client if the data basis for the display has changed.

Data is sent independently

We will look at the following practical example. A call-center manager wants to see the incoming orders in his user specific cockpit with a Flex application. Before he had the Flex application, he had to update the data himself (refresh). If at that stage the incorrect cache settings were still activated in the Web browser, so that he would still receive the old data even after repeatedly executing a refresh.

Socket connection

With a Flex application, this is no longer the case. The Flex application is opened, and a socket connection is established to the server. When changes are made, the data is then continually transferred to the desired client and the changes are immediately displayed to the user. A similar procedure is applied to the display of real-time share prices, for example.

We distinguish between two types of socket connection:

▶ XML Socket Connection

▶ Binary Socket Connection

Unlike the XML Socket Connection, the Binary Socket Connection enables you not only to transfer XML data, but the widest possible variety of data. It is thus possible, for instance, to use the logs POP3, SMTP, IMAP, and NNTP, as well as to put in place a comprehensive email integration system.

This also works when you have many clients. Similar to an SAP system, the hardware and software instances do need to be adjusted. However, this should prevent performance problems. There are many different Internet applications that use this technology to serve several thousand users around the world at the same time.

8.3   Dynamization of Screens

The dynamic properties of graphical user interfaces can be quite extensive. Often it may not be easy to know whether the benefits to be gained justify the work involved. When the project begins, one usually begins with a relatively simple dynamization for cost reasons.

Increasing the usability

To obtain an appreciation of what makes sense, the easiest thing is to take the SAP GUI as an example. After all, the Flex applications exist also to access the functions of the SAP system and enhance them with useful Flex functions. Here we must consider not only the technical possibilities of the GUI, but also the much deeper data structures.

▶ **Multilingual support**
In the SAP system, most texts that will be displayed in the application in different languages (e.g. material texts, error messages, etc.) are translated. The multilingual capability of the client thus already represents a certain dynamization.

Even if this is the simplest form that one could imagine for complex applications, how would this multilingual support be achieved in a Flex application? There are two variants for this:

▷ Using the language references from the SAP Online Text Repository (OTR)

▷ Providing separate language files (e.g., in the form of XML files)

Which path is correct will depend on the source of the original data and the proximity and reusability of the data. If the required information is already stored in the SAP OTR in the SAP systems, these should also be used. If this is not the case, the processing of XML documents can simplify a translation process. If one assumes that translations are carried out by persons who do not work with the SAP OTR, then these XML files will be easier to exchange and adjust. If the information involves SAP-typical data (e.g., error messages, material short texts, long texts) and if these are still required language-dependently in other applications, the information should also be stored in SAP OTR. If the data is more "remote" from SAP and if it affects the Flex application itself (e.g.

names of buttons, menu items, etc.), then the route via the XML files should be taken.

At the time this book was written, some fonts could not yet be displayed within the Flash plug-in. You should therefore refer to the documentation under *http://livedocs.macromedia.com/labs/1/flex/langref/charset-codes.html* for the relevant languages that are currently supported.

► **Customizing**
If one draws again on the SAP interfaces as a reference, some SAP transactions will allow you to control the sequence of the screens using Customizing settings. Of course, this is also possible in any conceivable level of detail with Flex applications. You can use the Customizing to control screens, sub-areas of the interfaces, individual fields, and even field content. Nevertheless, you should note that the Customizing of a Flex application has already been taken into account during design and development.

Bear in mind that you can organize the Customizing settings in two different ways. You can do this in the SAP system, in which case you will need to copy the settings each time from the system to the applications. The second option is to store the settings in the form of XML files.

If a Flex application is developed that is to handle different user rights, it is often possible that the screen information will also be displayed accordingly. For example, some users may only display the information with read authorization, while others may also be able to change the data. When the screen is now displayed ready for input, it can either be firmly stored in the application, or you can use a Customizing setting that is linked to the SAP authorization system. The latter option increases the dynamization of the application, reduces maintenance, and conforms to SAP's existing procedures.

8.4   Integrating Multiple Back-end Systems

Up to now, we have only shown the development and communication with an SAP system. However, in most companies the system landscape consists not only of an SAP system but may include several SAP and third-party systems.

With conventional Web applications, the system would only give you an answer that has been specifically requested. If you now wanted to display or edit bundled information from several systems, the central Web server would have to take over this service and connect through all information to the individual systems. This not only lengthens the Web application's response time, but also significantly increases the implementation work involved.

Thanks to the rich client approach, Flex applications can query several systems in parallel or at different times and display the results after receiving them. You can thus query and display customer information from a mySAP CRM system, payment movements from an R/3 system, and tracking information from a shipment service provider, among other actions.

The easiest way to establish communication with the individual systems is by using the known functions, the MXML Web service, or the HTTP service. If the information is to be sent in a push process, you can apply the socket connection described further above.

8.5 Integrated Deployment Options in SAP NetWeaver

Flex allows you to create appealingly designed interactive Web applications. The interactivity of such Web applications is usually created on the client-side and thus avoids server calls. Especially when analyzing business data in the SAP Business Information Warehouse, this enables data to be analyzed in a hands-on manner. Future developments in the Flex architecture will allow, among other things, the graphic composition of such applications.

As well as the possibilities that you have been shown so far in this book, SAP supports the requirement for Flex technology in different ways "innately." This occurs, first, by the integration of the Flex Builder into the development environment of SAP NetWeaver, and, second, by enhancing SAP NetWeaver Business Intelligence with SAP Analytics to provide Flex-based Web applications.

8.5.1   SAP NetWeaver Visual Composer

The integration of Adobe Flex into SAP NetWeaver through the SAP NetWeaver Visual Composer allows SAP-based RIAs to be developed. Here, the SAP NetWeaver Visual Composer supports the model-driven approach for the code-free creation of content, which can be displayed as a Web application encapsulated in iViews in the SAP NetWeaver Portal.

SAP NetWeaver Visual Composer

Visual Composer is certain to become more important in the future. In the medium to long term, not only will all key business intelligence applications be created with the Visual Composer, but conventional business applications will also be planned and implemented using this tool. The main emphasis here will be on user friendliness and on a minimal amount of programming work being involved. The Visual Composer is an effective tool for creating applications that support decision-making processes. No programming knowledge is required for this, because the application is wholly developed graphically. It is therefore possible that experienced subject-area users will also be able to design the application as it appears necessary for their daily work.

Currently there are many different technologies available for the creation of reports and business intelligence applications. This will continue to be the case in the future, in order to meet the different technological requirements. These technologies will also continue to be employed, depending on the existing expertise within a company. Applications and reports in the SAP GUI will continue to be just as necessary as those that are HTML-based. However, with Flex technology, SAP is taking a further step forward to offer the user a simple interface on which future business applications can be built.

Business intelligence patterns

In the course of following the planned roadmap, it will be possible to store *business intelligence patterns* in the Visual Composer. All of the functions of the Business Explorer (BEx) are integrated into the Visual Composer. The Business Intelligence Kit allows the user to create both assistant-based and free Flex-based applications. Ultimately, you will be able to find all reporting-related functions in the Visual Composer. However, the system will continue to support all other tools such as the Business Explorer.

As you can see in Figure 8.1, the SAP roadmap for business intelligence, assigns SAP NetWeaver Visual Composer a key role in the creation of development environments for SAP applications.

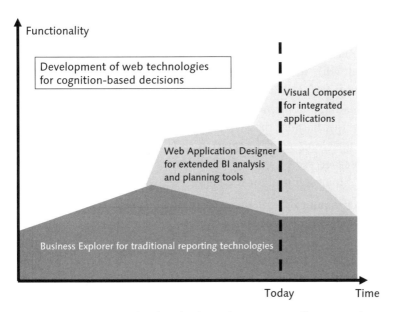

Figure 8.1 Development of Web Technologies for Business Intelligence Applications in the SAP Environment

When an application is being created in the Visual Composer, the developer is supported by different views of the application. The **Design View** shows the data flow, visualization, and events. The **Layout View** allows a detailed results summary of the application. The **Simulator View** allows a view of the graphic interface prior to the deployment of the application into the SAP NetWeaver Portal and thereby gives the developer direct feedback for his or her work. The **Source View** allows you to look at the code. The code is created in the background while the application is created and can be displayed for checking purposes.

An application created in the Visual Composer becomes language-independent through the model-based approach. The specific user-interface technology is chosen during deployment; here you can select Flex, DHTML, and Web Dynpro. Flex is implemented by the Flex Framework in this context. With this operation, the model created by the Visual Composer is converted into executable code according to the interface technology selected.

Flex is thus a key component of the Visual Composer. Flex as a future platform for business applications is characterized in particular by the following attributes.

▶ **Robust server technology**
The Flex server, which can be used to provide SWF files created dynamically (and thus at runtime) for the client, will become integrated with SAP NetWeaver in the long term. The interplay between SAP NetWeaver and the Flex server facilitates both the installation and maintenance and administration of an RIA server landscape. Because the Flex server is based on existing J2EE servers, the long-term integration into the Java Stack of SAP NetWeaver seems inevitable. However, for better scalability, a stand-alone solution for the Flex server is also a good alternative.

▶ **Future viability**
Flex applications that are not hosted on a Flex server, but rather provided statically, can be ported to a Flex server without further ado. MXML and ActionScript allow applications to be easily maintained and used again. It does not matter here how the Flex server is integrated into the system landscape. Unlike Flash files created in the FLA format, which can only be edited graphically, the source texts of MXML can be quickly extended and changed. This makes Flex's architecture a development tool that is to be taken seriously, because RIAs can now undergo source-text based versioning and be maintained by different processors.

▶ **Strong development environments**
Porting the Flex Builder into an up-to-date Eclipse format allows experienced developers to create and compile extensive Flex applications. The Flex Builder therefore represents a future viable and ideal development environment for complex Flash applications, while the Visual Composer within the SAP Analytics framework supports development of knowledge-based business intelligence applications.

8.5.2 SAP Analytics

Business decisions need to be taken quickly and without long error-prone searches in different databases and tables. A decision depends, in particular, on an understanding of the composition of a key figure.

There can be many specific questions here that must be answered by applications that can be intuitively used.

This problem is solved by analytical applications that are built with SAP Analytics. SAP Analytics applications use the SAP NetWeaver Visual Composer and Adobe Flex for the implementation. Using Flex applications based on SAP Analytics allows users to evaluate data interactively through a dynamic Web application, without having extensive programming knowledge. Users can thus do the following.

▶ Create a new model for the application in SAP Analytics

▶ Select data services using the BI Content Wizard

▶ Add and configure elements such as tables and diagrams to display the imported data

▶ Generate the analytical applications; i. e., compile the created MXML file into an SWF file, which is subsequently stored in the SAP NetWeaver Portal

For a Flex project, you can therefore choose between the two tools described. If you need a more complex reporting, the Visual Composer is the right choice. With the Visual Composer as a part of SAP Analytics you can meet the complex requirements of future business-intelligence projects. If a Flex application is required that corresponds to a classical business application or an employee self-service application, for example, you should choose the Flex Builder.

The right tool for every project

8.6   Summary and Perspective

The progressive development of the Flash Player allows you to create more and more complex RIAs. With this potential and the continually improving performance on the client side, future applications will be increasingly better designed and offer ever-broader interaction possibilities.

In the future, Adobe Flex will prevail over conventional Web applications because of the better design and functionality of its user interface. In the longer-term, RIAs will enable networked business applications. In the same way that ABAP and Java have complemented each other within the SAP system landscape in recent years, future RIAs will benefit from the interplay between the two development strands of Flash and Java.

Mobile terminals

Expansion to other application areas, such as mobile communications, has already begun. Many kinds of cell phones already support the new Flash standard for mobile devices in addition to the Java 2 Micro Edition, and thereby open a new dimension of application dissemination. Some new developments are based on these very possibilities. This technology could spread in mobile computing in particular, because a special value is placed here on the design of an application. Heavy requirements for the user interface require a high degree of user-friendliness and intuitive icons.

Flex, in conjunction with mobile client market players and the associated devices, has the potential to support the expected breakthrough of mobile business scenarios. Whereas applications for mobile devices have had to be installed locally, the easily distributed application basis of Flex will bring out the true added value of mini- and micro devices. As a result, one can imagine not only mobile business applications with conventional PDAs, but also mobile Flex applications that embrace new user groups, given that the cell phone affords an acceptable device.

In conjunction with business applications, you can therefore secure existing investments without new purchases on the user side. It is the possibility of using Flex applications to make content available without being requested, using Push technologies, that makes mobile Flex, in conjunction with SAP business applications, an important module for events-based control and recommendations.

A look ahead

Because of their simple graphic display of complex content, RIAs could also expand into other, predominantly technical areas for controlling and regulating control systems. With Flex, actors can more quickly identify the possible effects on their activities and so react accordingly, particularly with mobile devices.

Initially, though, the main application area will be the Web applications that are relevant for corporate management for monitoring and controlling business processes. SAP has taken a step in this direction with SAP Analytics. A new, dynamic type of RIA will allow relationships to be more quickly understood, and their causes to be established.

With its SAP NetWeaver Visual Composer as a tool for model-based development, SAP is picking up on a trend mandated by the ever-shortening technology cycles. Because of this shift in approach, and the advantage that technological specifics do not have to be learned in the process, Flex will become quickly established in the SAP environment.

A ActionScript Files of the Sample Application

This appendix contains the complete ActionScript files of the sample application, Z_DZT_BOOK. Chapter 7 already outlined parts of the source text, but you need the entire source text in order to implement the application.

The ActionScript files can be divided as follows:

▶ application.as
  Main file of the application (see Section A.1)

▶ plan.as
  Planning functions of the application (see Section A.2)

▶ global.as
  Globally required functions for simplification purposes (see Section A.3)

▶ report.as
  Reporting functions of the application (see Section A.4)

▶ tr.as
  Time-recording functions of the application (see Section A.5)

A.1 application.as

```
// ActionScript file
import mx.controls.Alert;

private var g_base_url:String =
    "http://server:port/sap/bc/bsp/sap/zdztb_bsp/";

// Current date (required for initial view)
private var l_month_current:Date = new Date();

// Current month
[Bindable]
public var l_month:String = (++l_month_current.month <
    10) ? l_month_current.fullYear.toString() + "0" +
    l_month_current.month.toString() :
    l_month_current.fullYear.toString() +
```

```
        l_month_current.month.toString();

[Bindable]
public var g_persno:String;

[Bindable]
public var g_url:String;

[Bindable]
public var g_url_plan:String;

[Bindable]
public var g_url_tr:String;

public function makeEvent():void {
    g_persno = ti_persno.text;
    g_url = g_base_url + "login.xml?persno=" + g_persno;
    login_data.send();
}

public function check_login(error:String):void {
    if (error == "OK") {
        cv_login.visible = false;
        cv_tabs.visible = true;
        g_url_plan = g_base_url + "plan_get.xml?persno="
                        + g_persno + "&month=" + l_month;
        g_url_tr = g_base_url + "tr_get.xml?persno=" +
                    g_persno + "&month=" + l_month;
    }
    else
        Alert.show(error,"Error");
}
```

Listing A.1 File application.as

A.2   plan.as

```
// ActionScript file
// Alert window
import mx.controls.Alert;

// Current date (required for initial view)
private var l_month_current:Date = new Date();

// Personnel number logged in
```

```
[Bindable]
public var l_persno:String;

// Current month
[Bindable]
public var l_month:String = (++l_month_current.month <
    10) ? l_month_current.fullYear.toString() + "0" +
    l_month_current.month.toString() :
    l_month_current.fullYear.toString() +
    l_month_current.month.toString();

// Current month in format that can be displayed
[Bindable]
public var l_month_displ:String = l_month.substr(4,2) +
    "/" + l_month.substr(0,4);

// Basic URL and URL settings
public var l_base_url:String =
    "http://server:port/sap/bc/bsp/sap/zdztb_bsp/";
public var l_dataget:String = "data.xml";

// URL to be finally called
[Bindable]
public var l_url:String;

// URL of activity
[Bindable]
public var l_url_activity:String = l_base_url +
    l_dataget + "?typ=A";

// Sending URL
[Bindable]
public var l_url_send:String;

// Retrieve all relevant data
public function fire():void {
   plan_data.send();
   activity_data.send();
}

// Reaction to foward or back button (planning)
public function button_click(direction:String,
                 current_month:String):void {

   var l_yearmon:String;
```

```
// Get new month
   l_yearmon = monat_action(direction,current_month);

// Calculate new URL
   l_url = l_base_url + "plan_get.xml?persno=" +
   l_persno + "&month=" +
           l_yearmon;
   l_month = l_yearmon;
   l_month_displ = l_month.substr(4,2) + "/" +
                   l_month.substr(0,4);

// Initialize previous view in order to avoid displaying old
// data if no data exists
   dg.dataProvider = "";

// Send HTTP request
   plan_data.send();
}

// Add planning (no
// error check)
public function add_planning():void {
   var l_date:String = form_date.text;
   var l_activity:String =
       form_activity.selectedItem.name.toString();

// Determine sending URL
   l_url_send = l_base_url + "plan_add.xml?persno=" +
                l_persno + "&date=" + l_date +
                "&activity=" + l_activity;

// Send requests (PLAN_ADD with
// subsequent PLAN_GET)
       plan_add.send();
       plan_data.send();
}
```

Listing A.2 Source Text plan.as

A.3   global.as

```
// ActionScript file
// Date formatter
public function df_convert(date:Date):String {
```

```
   return df_date.format(date);
}


// Output error messages
public function analyze_text(error:String):void {
   if (error != "OK")
      Alert.show(error,"Warning!");
}


// Navigate one month forward or back
public function month_action(direction:String,
                current_month:String):String {

   var l_month:Number;
   var l_month_str:String;
   var l_year:Number;
   var l_year_str:String;
   var l_yearmon:String;

// Get year and month
   l_year_str = current_month.substr(0,4);
   l_year = Number(l_year_str);

   l_month_str = current_month.substr(4,2);
   l_month = Number(l_month_str);

// Determine new month based on direction
   if (direction == "fwd") {

      if (l_month == 12) {
         l_month = 1;
         l_year++;
      }
      else
         l_month++;
   }
   else {
      if (l_month == 1) {
         l_month = 12;
         l_year--;
      }
      else
         l_month--;
   }
```

```
// Extend string to two characters
   if (l_month < 10)
      l_month_str = "0" + l_month.toString();
   else
      l_month_str = l_month.toString();

   l_year_str = l_year.toString();

   l_yearmon = l_year_str + l_month_str;

   return l_yearmon;
}
```

Listing A.3 Source Text global.as

A.4   report.as

```
// ActionScript file
// Current date (required for initial view)
private var l_month_current:Date = new Date();

// Current month
[Bindable]
public var l_month:String = (l_month_current.month < 10)
     ? l_month_current.fullYear.toString() + "0" +
     l_month_current.month.toString() :
     l_month_current.fullYear.toString() +
     l_month_current.month.toString();

// Personnel number logged in
[Bindable]
public var l_persno:String;

// Basic URL and URL settings
public var l_base_url:String =
     "http://server:port/sap/bc/bsp/sap/zdztb_bsp/";
public var l_report:String = "report.xml?event=";

// URL to be finally called
[Bindable]
public var l_url:String = l_base_url + l_report;

// Array to contain the reporting data
[Bindable]
public var array_report:Array;
```

```
// Get reporting data
public function get_report():void {

   bar_report.visible = false;
   bar_report_legend.visible = false;

// Which report was called?
   if (cb_type.selectedIndex == 1) {
      var l_year:String = l_month.substr(0,4);
      l_url = l_base_url + l_report + "OV01&year=" +
               l_year + "&persno=" + l_persno;
   }
   else if (cb_type.selectedIndex == 2) {
      l_url = l_base_url + l_report + "OV02&month=" +
               l_month;
   }
   else if (cb_type.selectedIndex == 3) {
      var l_year:String = l_month.substr(0,4);
      l_url = l_base_url + l_report + "OV03&year=" +
               l_year;
   }
   else if (cb_type.selectedIndex == 4) {
      var l_year:String = l_month.substr(0,4);
      l_url = l_base_url + l_report + "OV04&year=" +
               l_year;
   }

// Send HTTP request
   reporting_data.send();
}

// Calculate capacity utilization
public function compute_utilization():void {

   if (cb_type.selectedIndex != 4) {
      ti_hrs.text =
           reporting_data.result.report.entry.hrs;
      ti_hrs_bill.text =
           reporting_data.result.report.entry.hrs_bill;
      var l_utilization:Number =
   (Number(reporting_data.result.report.entry.hrs_bill) /
  Number(reporting_data.result.report.entry..hrs))*100;
      ti_util.text = l_utilization.toString();
```

```
  } else {
     array_report = new Array();
     array_report =
         reporting_data.result.report.entry;
     bar_report.visible = true;
     bar_report_legend.visible = true;
     ti_hrs.text = "";
     ti_hrs_bill.text = "";
     ti_util.text = "";
  }
}
```

Listing A.4 Source Text report.as

A.5   tr.as

```
// ActionScript file
// Alert window
import mx.controls.Alert;

// Current date (required for initial view)
private var l_month_current:Date = new Date();

// Personnel number logged in
[Bindable]
public var l_persno:String;

// Current month
[Bindable]
public var l_month:String = (++l_month_current.month <
    10) ? l_month_current.fullYear.toString() + "0" +
    l_month_current.month.toString() :
    l_month_current.fullYear.toString() +
    l_month_current.month.toString();

// Current month in format that can be displayed
[Bindable]
public var l_month_displ:String = l_month.substr(4,2) +
    "/" + l_month.substr(0,4);

// Basic URL and URL settings
public var l_base_url:String =
    "http://server:port/sap/bc/bsp/sap/zdztb_bsp/";
public var l_dataget:String = "data.xml";
```

```
// URL to be finally called
[Bindable]
public var l_url:String = l_base_url +
    "tr_get.xml?persno=" + l_persno +
    "&month=" + l_month;

// URL of activity
[Bindable]
public var l_url_activity:String = l_base_url +
    l_dataget + "?typ=A";

// Sending URL
[Bindable]
public var l_url_send:String;

// Get all relevant data
public function fire():void {
        tr_data.send();
        activity_data.send();
}

// Reaction to forward or back button (time recording)
public function button_click(drection:String,
                current_month:String):void {

    var l_yearmon:String;

// Get new month
    l_yearmon = month_action(direction,current_month);

// Calculate new URL
    l_url = l_base_url + "tr_get.xml?persno=" +
     l_persno + "&month=" + l_yearmon;
    l_month = l_yearmon;
    l_month_displ = l_month.substr(4,2) + "/" +
                    l_month.substr(0,4);

// Initialize previous view in order to avoid displaying old
// data if no data exists
    dg2.dataProvider = "";

// Send HTTP request
    tr_data.send();
}
```

```
// Add time recording (no
// error check)
public function add_tr():void {
    var l_date:String = form_date.text;
    var l_activity:String =
        form_activity.selectedItem.name.toString();
    var l_std:String = form_std.text;
    if (l_std == "") {
        analyze_
text("Please enter a value for the number of hours!");
    }
    else {
        l_url_send = l_base_url + "tr_add.xml?persno=" +
                     l_persno + "&date=" + l_date +
                     "&activity=" + l_activity + "&hour(s)="
                     + l_std;
        tr_add.send();
        tr_data.send();
    }
}


// Closing a month
public function month_complete():void {
    l_url_send = l_base_url + "finish.xml?persno=" +
                 l_persno + "&month=" + l_month;

    tr_add.send();
    tr_data.send();
}
```

Listing A.5 Source Text tr.as

The Authors

Armin Lorenz first worked as a controller in the media industry during and after his studies until he joined a leading and globally operating home-shopping TV company, where he worked as an SAP consultant. There, he was responsible for the interfaces and the development of cross-application programs between distributed SAP and non-SAP systems. As a co-founder and member of the executive board at IXULT AG, Armin Lorenz is responsible for the areas of CRM, usability, and enterprise search (HIVE). Recent customer requirements caused the implementation of numerous Flex projects in which he participated as a project manager and head of the development team.

Dr. Gunther Schöppe has studied physics with a focus on simulation physics. He received his doctorate at the Institute for Theoretical Physics at the University of Heidelberg, Germany. After that he joined a major consulting firm, where he worked as an SAP consultant in the area of Web development. During this time, he implemented comprehensive customer-specific Web applications on the basis of SAP Web Application Server until he became a member of the executive board at IXULT AG. In this position, he currently heads up the project-based business in the area of Web applications.

Felix Consbruch holds a degree in engineering in the area of media technology and is responsible for systems integration at IXULT AG. Since 2004, he has managed projects that focused on integrating SAP and non-SAP systems. His primary area of responsibility as a project manager consists of the design and implementation of interfaces for user interfaces and back-end services. Furthermore, Felix is responsible for finding solutions for integrating the Adobe Flex Framework with application development.

Daniel Knapp joined IXULT AG in 2004 as an SAP Technology Consultant. Since the introduction of Rich Internet Applications, he has been working as a developer in the Flash and Flex environments. After earning a degree in information technology, he gathered much experience in numerous projects. He has a profound knowledge of SAP systems.

Frank Sonnenberg holds a degree in engineering in Computer Science. He joined IXULT AG in 2005 as an SAP Technology Consultant. His work as a developer in numerous projects focuses on optimizing business processes and the integration of new technologies, such as Adobe Flex. The work on these projects has helped him to acquire deep knowledge regarding SAP systems.

Index

Index

Undefined 93, 102
Usability 156, 271
UserDefinedNamespace 124

V

Variable names
  Dynamic 105
Variable types 105
Variables 103
  Global 106
  Local 105
VBox 59, 223, 226, 239
VDividedBox 59
Vector Markup Language 24
Video 128, 132
  Methods 134
  Properties 133
Video files 132
VideoStream 136
View 19
ViewStack 62, 63

W

Web Dynpro 15, 17, 37, 275
Web service 54
While loop 119
WYSIWYG 37, 40

X

XML 52, 65
XML documents 271
XML files 184
  Structure 204
XML interface 160

Z

ZDZTB_001 159
ZDZTB_002 159
ZDZTB_003 159
ZDZTB_004 159

298

Detailed comparison of ABAP and JAVA/J2EE concepts

Comprehensive introduction to the SAP NetWeaver Developer Studio

Tutorials on the Java Dictionary, Web Dynpro, Session Beans, Message Driven Beans and much more

495 pp., 2005, 69,95 Euro / US$ 69,95
ISBN 978-1-59229-027-7

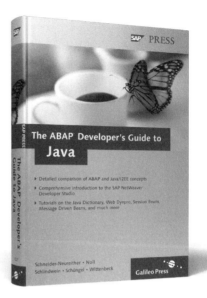

The ABAP Developer's Guide to Java

www.sap-press.com

A. Schneider-Neureither (Ed.)

The ABAP Developer's Guide to Java

Leverage your ABAP skills to climb up the Java learning curve

This all-new reference book is an indispensable guide for ABAP developers who need a smooth transition to Java. The authors highlight each fundamental aspect pertaining to the development of business applications in both languages, and the differences as well as similarities are analyzed in detail. This book helps any developer learn techniques to master development tools and objects, application design, application layers and much more. Learn about Beans, OpenSQL for Java, JDBC, Security, and more.

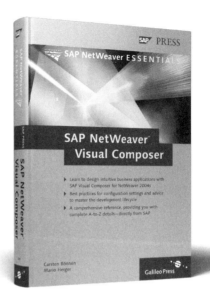

Learn to design intuitive business applications with SAP Visual Composer for NetWeaver 2004s

Best practices for configuration settings and advice to master the development lifecycle

524 pp., 2007, 69,95 Euro / US$ 69,95
ISBN 978-1-59229-099-4

SAP NetWeaver
Visual Composer
www.sap-press.com

C. Bönnen, M. Herger

SAP NetWeaver Visual Composer

Instead of conventional programming and implementation, SAP NetWeaver Visual Composer (VC) enables you to model your processes graphically via drag & drop—potentially without ever having to write a single line of code. This book not only shows you how, but also serves as a comprehensive reference, providing you with complete details on all aspects of VC. You learn the ins and outs of the VC architecture—including details on all components and concepts, as well as essential information on model-based development and on the preparation of different types of applications. Readers quickly broaden their knowledge by tapping into practical expert advice on the various aspects of the Development Lifecycle as well as on selected applications, which have been modeled with the VC and are currently delivered by SAP as standard applications.

Insights on the architecture and tools of SAP Web AS Java 6.40

Sample application for Web Dynpro and SAP NetWeaver Development Infrastructure

Includes 180-day trial version of SAP Web AS Java 6.40 on DVD

514 pp., 2005, with DVD, 69,95 Euro / US$ 69,95
ISBN 978-1-59229-020-8

Java Programming with the SAP Web Application Server

www.sap-press.com

K. Kessler, P. Tillert, P. Dobrikov

Java Programming with the SAP Web Application Server

Without proper guidance, the development of business oriented Java applications can be challenging. This book introduces you systematically to highly detailed concepts, architecture, and to all components of the SAP Web Application Server Java (Release 6.40), while and equipping you with all that's needed to ensure superior programming. First, benefit from an SAP NetWeaver overview, followed by the authors' guided tour through the SAP NetWeaver Developer Studio. After an excursion into the world of Web services, you then learn about the different facets of Web Dynpro technology, with in-depth details on user interfaces. This information is further bolstered with insights on the SAP NetWeaver Java Development Infrastructure and the architecture of SAP Web AS Java.

Third, completely new edition
of the benchmark ABAP
compendium

All-new chapters on Web
Dynpro, Shared Objects, ABAP
& XML, Regular Expressions,
Dynamic Programming, and
more!

approx. 1050 pp., 3. edition, with DVD 5, 79,95 Euro .
US$ 79,95
ISBN 978-1-59229-079-6, March 2007

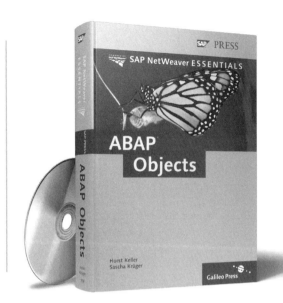

ABAP Objects

www.sap-press.com

H. Keller, S. Krüger

ABAP Objects

ABAP Programming in SAP NetWeaver

This completely new third edition of our best-
selling ABAP book provides detailed coverage
of ABAP programming with SAP NetWeaver.
This outstanding compendium treats all
concepts of modern ABAP up to release 7.0.
New topics include ABAP and Unicode, Shared
Objects, exception handling, Web Dynpro for
ABAP, Object Services, and of course ABAP and
XML. Bonus: All readers will receive the SAP
NetWeaver 2004s ABAP Trial Version ("Mini-
SAP") on DVD.

Improve your Design Process with "Contextual Design"

182 pp., 2006, 49,95 Euro / US$ 49,95
ISBN 978-1-59229-065-9

Designing
Composite Applications

www.sap-press.com

Jörg Beringer, Karen Holtzblatt

Designing Composite Applications

Driving user productivity and business innovation for next generation business applications

This book helps any serious developer hit the ground running by providing a highly detailed and comprehensive introduction to modern application design, using the SAP Enterprise Services Architecture (ESA) toolset and the methodology of "Contextual Design". Readers will benefit immediately from exclusive insights on design processes based on SAPs Business Process Platform and learn valuable tricks and techniques that can drastically improve user productivity. Anybody involved in the process of enterprise application design and usability/quality management stands to benefit from this book.

Examples of dynamic programming, componentization, integration of applications, navigation, and much more

Essential and practical knowledge about installation, configuration, and administration of the Web Dynpro runtime

497 pp., 2006, 69,95 Euro / US$
ISBN 978-1-59229-077-2

Maximizing
Web Dynpro for Java
www.sap-press.com

B. Ganz, J. Gürtler, T. Lakner

Maximizing Web Dynpro for Java

Standard examples of Web Dynpro applications can leave SAP developers with many questions and severe limitations. This book takes you to the next level with detailed examples that show you exactly what you need to know in order to leverage Web Dynpro applications. From the interaction with the Java Developer Infrastructure (JDI), to the use of Web Dynpro components, to the integration into the portal and the use of its services—this unique book delivers it all. In addition, readers get dozens of tips and tricks on fine-tuning Web Dynpro applications in terms of response time, security, and structure. Expert insights on the configuration and administration of the Web Dynpro runtime environment serve to round out this comprehensive book.

Basic principles, architecture, and configuration

Development of dynamic, reusable UI components

Volumes of sample code and screen captures for help you maximize key tools

360 pp., 2006, 69,95 Euro / US$
ISBN 978-1-59229-078-9

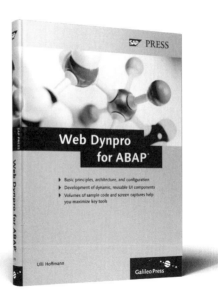

Web Dynpro for ABAP

www.sap-press.com

U. Hoffmann

Web Dynpro for ABAP

Serious developers must stay ahead of the curve by ensuring that they are up-to-date with all of the latest standards. This book illustrates the many benefits that can be realized with component-based UI development using Web Dynpro for ABAP. On the basis of specifically developed sample components, readers are introduced to the architecture of the runtime and development environment and receive highly-detailed descriptions of the different functions and tools that enable you to efficiently implement Web Dynpro technology on the basis of SAP NetWeaver 2004s. Numerous code listings, screen captures, and little-known tricks make this book your indispensable companion for the practical design of modern user interfaces.